FAMOUS PEOPLE ON FILM

by

CAROL A. EMMENS

/ ' /

The Scarecrow Press, Inc.
Metuchen, N.J.   1977

Library of Congress Cataloging in Publication Data

Emmens, Carol A
  Famous people on film.

  Includes indexes.
  1. Biography--Film catalogs. I. Title.
CT86.Z9E45   016.92'002   77-3449
ISBN 0-8108-1051-4

To
my husband Chris, who ate sandwiches,
and
my son Scott, who will soon understand

CONTENTS

v

ACKNOWLEDGMENTS

My special thanks to Harry Maglione, Media Specialist for the Manasquan School District (N.J.), for the many hours of help and especially for preparing the index.

My thanks to the Educational Film Library Association, 43 West 61st Street, New York, N.Y. for use of their resources, which were vital to the completion of this book.

My thanks to the many distributors who cooperated by providing information and stills.

And my thanks to my husband and mother, who babysat.

vi

INTRODUCTION

Biographies are an integral part of school and college/university curricula because they cut across every discipline. Biographies are also an integral and very popular genre in library collections. An abundance of print and non-print biographical materials exists, yet no other current bibliography contains a comprehensive list of 16mm films about famous people.

The aim of this guide is to list all the non-theatrical films on famous people available in the United States by major distributors; thus eliminating the time-consuming and tedious searches previously necessary in order to locate films on a specific person. Famous People on Film is a comprehensive guide, which includes personalities as diverse as Leo Tolstoy and Billie Jean King. The famous, the infamous, and the near-famous of all races, religions, and nationalities, from all walks of life, from all countries and from all time periods are indexed. Films for all age levels are included, though the titles for junior high and above predominate.

All biographical films located are listed. But often a person is defined by his work--an artist whose paintings reflect his inner thoughts or his lifestyle, for example. Therefore, some titles devoted to works of art are found here, especially if no biographical film could be found. Others, such as psychologists or philosophers, are noteworthy because their theories or ideas are popular or revolutionary; thus, 'interview' films of them are often noted.

People such as Vince Lombardi sometimes appear in motivational sales films or in films supporting a cause, e.g., preservation of the environment. These films were omitted because they are found in subject bibliographies. Also omitted were films which deal with a panorama of a historical period; for example, films on the Revolutionary War which briefly mention Washington and others but whose main purpose is to present the ideas, doctrines, battles, etc.

To facilitate easy use this guide is arranged alphabetically by the last name of each personality. If more than one film was located on a particular person, the titles are then arranged alphabetically below the name. Every effort has been made to provide complete bibliographical information for each entry. Entries are arranged as follows:

EDISON, THOMAS ALVA

Title⟶ The Wizard Who Spat on the Floor: Thomas
Running   Alva Edison.   Production
time⟶ 60 min.   color   1974   SCA ⟵   or release
Producer &⟶Prod: BBC-TV.   Dist: Time-Life (avail-   date
distributor   able on video or in a 41-minute ver-   Grade
                      sion)   levels
                           An interview with his only living
                  daughter and actual footage of famous mo-
                  ments in his life are included in this study.
Annotation⟶ The drama and philosophy of his inventions,
                  such as the stock-ticker and the light bulb,
                  come to life.

GRADE LEVELS

P   Primary grades, K-3

I   Intermediate, 4-6

J   Junior High, 7-9

S   Senior High, 10-12

C   College

A   Adult

The grade levels are those recommended by the distributors
or the secondary sources, primarily rental catalogs.

The entries were culled primarily from the 1975-76 catalogs
of the major distributors, though other sources such as reviews or
publicity releases were also used.   A listing does not imply recom-
mendation.   The descriptions are taken from materials provided by
the distributors or rental sources.   Where information is omitted it
is because no source could provide it before going to press.   As
someone told me, some of the titles date back to a time when record
keeping was "more casual."   The bibliographic information in distributors' catalogs varies greatly; some give complete information,
others little more than the title; few name the directors of the films;
often dates and grade levels are omitted; some distributors provide
production dates, others release dates.   Because these discrepancies
exist, verification of information is difficult.

Though most distributors sell and rent their films (exceptions
are noted), additional rental sources are also indicated, for several
reasons.   First, some films are officially withdrawn by the distributor and are, therefore, available only through the rental sources.
Withdrawal of a title does not necessarily reflect poor quality or
limited usefulness.   Second, the rental fees charged by the univer-

sities are generally lower than those charged by commercial distributors. Third, all of the prints of a title held by a particular distributor may be booked for the date desired.

Large rental collections from each geographical area of the United States were indexed: Syracuse University from the Northeast; the University of South Florida from the South; Indiana University, Universities of Michigan and Minnesota from the Mid-West; and the Universities of Southern California and California from the West.

Many other universities and colleges also rent films, but time and space necessitated indexing only selected collections.

Omission of a distributor for an entry indicates that the information about the title was taken from a rental catalog. In some cases it impossible to track down the original source of a film because the educational film market is so fluid--scores of companies come and go yearly.

FEATURES

Hollywood usually adds a generous fillip of drama and romance to the real life stories portrayed on the screen; therefore, the feature films are listed in a separate appendix. The list is selective and the descriptions are very brief because information on features is easily accessible. For a more complete guide see James Limbacher's Feature Films on 8mm and 16mm.

INDEXES

The subject index is arranged primarily by occupations because the work of a person is, in a sense, the person. A figure who is a sculptor and a painter or a novelist and a poet, is listed under both headings.

Non-theatrical and theatrical film titles are listed alphabetically in one index. If distributors include the series name as part of the title such as Poetry: William Carlos Williams, there is also an entry for the sub-title, "William Carlos Williams."

The distributor/rental source directory is arranged alphabetically. Codes are frustrating and difficult to use; therefore, I have used the names of companies in the main body of the book, but often in an abbreviated form. For example, BFA Educational Media is listed as BFA. The universities are listed as Syracuse or California instead of Syracuse University or University of California. Note, however, that the directory is arranged by the complete name, e.g., University of California.

Famous People on Film was designed for use by schools, colleges, universities, libraries and community groups ranging from the Little League to the League of Women Voters. As such it has been made as ·complete and easy to use as possible.

Please send any suggestions for future editions to me in care of Scarecrow Press.

Carol A. Emmens
Nutley, N. J.

September 22, 1976

FAMOUS PEOPLE ON FILM

ABDUL-JABBAR, KAREEM

Nobody Roots for Goliath--Kareem Abdul-Jabbar (The Winners Series)
48 min.   color   1976   SCA
Prod: Laurel.   Dist: Counselor
   A sports-file of the Most Valuable Player of the N. B. A. for
the 1973-74 season.

ADAMS, ANSEL

Ansel Adams--Photographer
20 min.   b&w   1958   SCA
Prod: Larry Dawson.   Dist: International Film Bureau.   Rental:
   Michigan, Minnesota
   Focuses on his photography, his home and his hobbies.
Shows some of the scenes he's shooting and the results.

Photography as an Art (Photography: Incisive Art Series)
29 min.   b&w   1960
Prod: KQED.   Dist:
Rental: California, Minnesota
   Adams as he photographs Yosemite National Park and as he
explains the "art" of photography.

ADAMS, JOHN

John Adams (Profiles in Courage Series)
50 min.   b&w   1964   IJSA
Prod: Robert Saudek Associates.   Dist: IQ Films.   Rental: Michigan, Minnesota, Syracuse
   As a young lawyer he risked his career to defend British
soldiers.

John Yankee: John Adams and the Boston Massacre
21 min.   b&w   1953
Prod: Teaching Film Custodians.   Dist: Indiana (lease).   Rental:
   Minnesota
   A dramatization of his defense of eight British soldiers ac-
cused of murder during the Boston Massacre.   An excerpt from the
Cavalcade of America Motion picture for television.

1

The Right of Dissent: John Adams vs. Matthew Lyon--1798 (History
  Alive! Series)
20 min.   1970   JSC
Prod: Turnley Walker.   Dist: Walt Disney (long term license)
    A dramatization of the conflict between Adams and Lyon, who
outspokenly criticized the President.

ADAMS, JOHN QUINCY

John Quincy Adams
18 min.   b&w   1951   IJSCA
Prod: Encyclopaedia Britannica.   Dist: Withdrawn by EB.   Rental:
  Minnesota, Nebraska, Southern California
    Key events of his life with emphasis on his diplomatic skills
as an American representative in Europe and as Secretary of State.

John Quincy Adams (Profiles in Courage Series)
50 min.   b&w   1965   SA
Prod: Robert Saudek Associates.   Dist: IQ Films.   Rental: Michigan, Minnesota, Syracuse
    How and why he risked his political career to fight for the
Bill of Rights.

The Right of Petition: John Quincy Adams vs. Thomas Marshall--
  1842 (History Alive! Series)
13 min.   1970   JSC
Prod: Turnley Walker.   Dist: Walt Disney (long term license)
    A dispute over the "gag rule," which the Southern states
used to prevent anti-slavery petitions from being introduced in Congress, is dramatized.

ADENAUER, KONRAD

Kokoschka Paints Adenauer
13 min.   color
Prod: Dist: Association-Sterling (free loan)
    The famous expressionist painter catches him on canvas as
the camera catches their evolving friendship.

Konrad Adenauer
10 1/2 min.   b&w   1974
Prod: Hearst Corp.   Dist: Withdrawn by E. M. Hale.   Rental:
  Syracuse
    How he helped rebuild Germany beginning in 1945.

ALCINDOR, LOU See ABDUL-JABBAR, KAREEM

ALCOTT, LOUISA MAY

Louisa May Alcott

18 min.   b&w   1950   JS
Prod. and dist: Encyclopaedia Britannica (available on video by special order).   Rental: Indiana, Michigan, Minnesota, Southern California, Syracuse
    Through dramatization the film shows how her novels Little
Women, Little Men and Jo's Boys were based largely on her life.

From the Encyclopaedia Britannica film, Louisa May Alcott

ALENÇON, DUKE OF   See   ELIZABETH I (Elizabeth R.)

ALEXANDER III OF MACEDON (THE GREAT)
    See also Alexander the Great (feature)

Alexander the Great and the Hellenistic Age
13 min.   b&w or color   1970   IJS
Prod. and dist: Coronet.   Rental: Indiana, Syracuse
    Photographed on sites on which he fought, the film follows
his tremendous military campaigns and analyzes the spread of Greek
culture.

The Triumph of Alexander the Great (You Are There Series)
27 min.   b&w   1955   JSCA
Prod: CBS.   Dist: McGraw-Hill.   Rental: Indiana, Minnesota,
   Syracuse
   Suppression of a mutiny by his men.

ALEXANDER, PETER

Peter Alexander (Artists in America Series)
30 min.   color   1971   SCA
Prod: NET.   Dist: Indiana.   Rental: California
His philosophy of art and his plastic sculptures.

ALFRED THE GREAT   See   Alfred the Great (feature)

ALI   See   MUHAMMAD ALI

ALLENDE, SALVADOR

Interview with President Salvador Allende
31 min.   color   1972   SCA
Dir: Saul Landau.   Dist: Impact, New Yorker
   An interview several months before his murder.   In Spanish
with English sub-titles.

ALTGELD, JOHN PETER

John Peter Altgeld (Profiles in Courage Series)
50 min.   b&w   1965   IJSA
Prod: Robert Saudek Associates.   Dist: IQ Films.   Rental:
   Syracuse
   He risked his career to grant a full pardon to anarchists,
whom he believed were illegally convicted.

AMIN, IDI (GENERAL)

General Idi Amin Dada
90 min.   color   1976   SCA
Prod: Jean Pierre Rassam and Charles-Henri Favrod.   Dist:
   Tinc Productions
   A close-up documentary of the leader of Uganda, which reveals his sometimes extraordinary views on his country, his cabinet, the military, women, and Jews.

AMOS   See   JOB (Prophetic Voices of the Bible)

AMUNDSEN, ROALD
See also BYRD, RICHARD EVELYN (Byrd vs. Amundsen)

Roald Amundsen (Age of Exploration Series)
52 min.   color   1976   SCA
Prod: BBC-TV. Dist: Time-Life (available on video)
    A dramatization of the race to reach the South Pole. He
beat Robert Falcon Scott by 34 days.

ANDERSEN, HANS CHRISTIAN
See also Hans Christian Andersen (feature)

Hans Christian Andersen: At the Photographers
13 min.   color
Dist: Royal Danish Consulate General (free loan)
    International photographs, paintings, and drawings of him.

The Story of My Life: Hans Christian Andersen
27 min.   b&w   1955   PI
Dir: Jorgen Roos. Prod: Danish Culture. Dist: Macmillan.
    Rental: Syracuse
    Uses his diary to tell the story of his life and the tempo of
his times.

ANDERSON, MARIAN

The Lady in the Lincoln Memorial
18 min.   color   1971   JSCA
Prod. and dist: Rediscovery Productions
    How she overcame racial inequality.

Marian Anderson (Concerts on Film Series)
27 min.   b&w   1953   JSCA
Prod: World Artists. Rental: Indiana
    A program of songs including "He's Got the Whole World in
His Hand," "Comin' thro' the Rye," and a sketch of her life, her
friends and her Connecticut farm.

ANDRETTI, MARIO

Andretti
28 min.   color   1967   CA
Dist: McDonnell Douglas Corp., Santa Monica Library (free loan
    for college and adult groups only)
    A year of competition.

Driver: Mario Andretti (The Winners Series)
48 min.   color   1976   SCA
Prod: Laurel. Dist: Counselor
    Three days with him at his hideaway.

ANGELICO, FRA

The Adoration of the Magi
7 min.   color   1973   SCA
Prod. and dist: National Gallery of Art (free loan)
    A study of the paintings by him and Fra Filippo Lippi with
medieval music as the background.

Fra Angelico
30 min.   color   1975   SCA
Prod: Scala Art Films by Dedo Weigert.   Dist: Macmillan.
His paintings within the historical context.

Fra Angelico
30 min.
Rental: Southern Baptist Radio-TV Commission
    His philosophy and life, the patronage of Cosimo di Medici,
and his works of art.

ANKA, PAUL
Lonely Boy
27 min.   b&w   1962
Prod: National Film Board of Canada.   Dist: McGraw-Hill.
Rental: California
    A cinéma vérité portrait of him in front of and behind the
footlights.

ANNE OF CLEAVES See HENRY VIII (The Six Wives of Henry
    VIII); Henry VIII and His Six Wives (feature)

ANTHONY, SUSAN B.

Susan B. Anthony
19 min.   b&w   1951   JS
Prod: Encyclopaedia Britannica.   Dist: WD by EB.   Rental: In-
    diana, Michigan, Minnesota, Nebraska, Southern California,
    Syracuse
    Highlights her efforts on behalf of women's suffrage and re-
enacts the trial in which she states her case.

The Trial of Susan B. Anthony (You Are There Series)
22 min.   color   1972   JSA
Prod: CBS.   Dist: BFA.   Rental: Syracuse
    A dramatization of the trial in which she was charged with
voting illegally.

APGAR, VIRGINIA See GIOVANNI, NIKKI (Accomplished Women)

APPEL, KAREL

The Reality of Karel Appel
13 min.   color   1964   C
Dir: Jan Vrijman.   Dist: Withdrawn by McGraw-Hill.   Rental:
    Southern California
    At work in his Paris studio.

ARISTOTLE

Aristotle and the Scientific Method (Men of Science Series)
13 1/2 min.   color   1959   JSC
Prod. and dist: Coronet (sale only).   Rental: Indiana, Michigan,
    Syracuse
    Stresses his contributions to scientific thinking.

ARMITAGE, KENNETH

Five British Sculptors Work and Talk
28 min.   color   1964   C
Dir: Warren Forma.   Dist: Withdrawn by McGraw-Hill.   Rental:
    Michigan, Southern California
    Barbara Hepworth, Reg Butler, Armitage, Lynn Chadwick,
and Henry Moore at home, talking about themselves and their work.

ARMSTRONG, LOUIS

Louis Armstrong
13 min.   color   1973   JSCA
Prod: Hearst Metrotone News.   Dist: Counselor Films.   Rental:
    Southern California, Syracuse
    Moves back and forth between scenes of his funeral and
scenes of him in past performances.

ARNOLD, BENEDICT

Benedict Arnold's Plot Against West Point (You Are There Series)
26 min.   b&w   1956   JSCA
Prod. and dist: CBS.   Rental: Indiana, Minnesota, Syracuse
    An "on the scene" interview combined with "reporting" to
cover the betrayal of West Point from the time he conferred with
the British agent until his capture and exile.

Betrayal: Benedict Arnold
20 min.   b&w   1953   JS
Prod: Teaching Film Custodians.   Dist: Indiana
    A dramatization of his brilliant Army career and the events
leading to his treason.   An excerpt from the television series,
"Cavalcade of America. "

The Treason of Benedict Arnold (You Are There Series)
22 min.   color   1972   LJS
Prod: CBS.   Dist: BFA.   Rental: Syracuse
    Why he committed treason and the effect on the war.

ATATURK, KEMAL

Ataturk, Father of Modern Turkey
26 min.   b&w   1960   SA
Prod: CBS.   Dist: .Withdrawn.   Rental: Minnesota, South Florida,
    Southern California, Syracuse
    At the close of World War I he controlled Turkey and led
it out of the Middle Ages and into the 20th century.

Ataturk--Of Man and Nation
30 min.   color
Rental: Minnesota
    The transformation of Turkey from the days of the Ottoman
Empire to the nation of today under his leadership.

ATGET, EUGENE

Atget (Creative Person Series)
30 min.   b&w   1967   JSCA
Prod: NET.   Dist: Indiana.   Rental: California
    Representative photographs with a commentary by Bernice
Abbott, a former protégée.

Eugene Atget
10 min.   b&w   1969   SCA
Prod: Harold Becker.   Dist: Withdrawn by McGraw-Hill
    Paris as seen in his rare photographs.

AUDUBON, JOHN JAMES

Audubon
58 min.   color   1969   SCA
Prod: NET.   Dist: Indiana University
    Traces his travels throughout Europe and North America.
Shows scenes from his famous book, The Birds of America.

Audubon and The Birds of America
15 min.   color   1958   IJSA
Prod. and dist: Coronet (sale only).   Rental: Indiana, Michigan,
    Minnesota, South Florida, Syracuse
    His youth, his business failures, his marriage, and his
eventual interest in wildlife are recreated.   Illustrates his engrav-
ing methods for The Birds of America.

John James Audubon
4 min.   color   1963   SCA
Prod: Westinghouse Broadcasting Corp.   Dist: Films Inc.
   Rental: South Florida
      His paintings for The Birds of America.

AUERBACH, ARNOLD JACOB (RED)

Red Auerbach (Sports Legends Series)
20 min.   color   1975   IJSC
Prod. and dist: Sports Legends Inc.   Rental: Southern California
      The coach of the Boston Celtics talks candidly about him-
self, his players, and his sports philosophy.

AUGUSTINE, SAINT

Saint Augustine (A Third Testament Series)
55 min.   color   1976   SCA
Prod: BBC-TV.   Dist: Time-Life (available on video)
      Malcolm Muggeridge compares the declining world in which
St. Augustine lived with today's society.   His book City of God reveals his philosophy.

BACH, JOHANN SEBASTIAN

Johann Sebastian Bach (Great Composers Series)
26 1/2 min.   color   1974   JSCA
Prod: Seabourne Enterprises.   Dist: International Film Bureau.
   Rental: Syracuse
      An introduction to his life and music with emphasis on the
latter, including musical excerpts from "French Suite" and "Bran-
denburg Concerto."

Music Experiences--Bach Is Beautiful
15 min.   color   1971   IJSA
Prod: J. P. Stevens & Co.   Dist: Aims
      Using animation and live action, the film presents Bach and
an elementary introduction to music.

BACON, FRANCIS (Painter)

Francis Bacon
31 min.   b&w   1969   SCA
Prod: BBC-TV.   Dist: Time-Life (available for special order
   purchase only.   No previews or rentals)
      He talks about himself and his art.

Francis Bacon--Paintings 1944-1962
11 min.   color   1971   SCA

Prod: Arts Council of Great Britain. Dist: Films Inc.
Interpretation of his works.

BALBOA, VASCO NUÑEZ DE

Age of Discovery: Spanish and Portuguese Explorations
11 min.   color or b&w   1950   I
Prod. and dist: Coronet (sale only). Rental: Indiana, Michigan,
Nebraska, South Florida, Syracuse
    Story and routes of early North and South American explorers.

Balboa of Darien
11 min.   color   1962   IJ
Prod: Cardan Prod.   Dist: Classroom Film Distributors. Rental:
Michigan
    Begins with his boyhood in Spain and proceeds through his
discovery of the Pacific Ocean.

BALDWIN, JAMES (ARTHUR)

James Baldwin from Another Place
11 1/2 min.   b&w   1975 (rel.)   SCA
Dir. and prod: Sedat Pakay. Dist: Film Images
    A return in 1970 to Istanbul, where he talks about his
American past, his poetry, his personal life, and self-exile.

Meeting the Man
27 min.   color   1971   SCA
Dir: Terence Dixon. Dist: Impact
    A provocative self-portrait revealed by his writings.

My Childhood: James Baldwin's Harlem (Part II)
51 min. (both parts)   b&w   1968   JSCA
Prod: Metromedia TV. Dist: Benchmark. Rental: Indiana,
Michigan, Southern California, Syracuse, Viewfinders
    He recalls the grinding poverty, hopelessness, and hatred
of the ghetto. Part I of this set focuses on the childhood of Hubert Humphrey.

BALZAC, HONORE DE

Balzac à Paris
20 min.   b&w   1964   SC
Prod: Associated Television Ltd. (France). Dist: Withdrawn.
Rental: Indiana, Southern California
    A visit to the home in which he lived, now a museum.
Presents the places in Paris about which he wrote and includes
dramatizations from his works Le Colonel Chabert and Père Goriot.
Advanced French narration.

Honoré de Balzac
24 min.   SC   1951
Dir: Jean Vidal.   Prod: Films du Compas.   Rental: FACSEA
    In French dialogue only.   Photographs, etchings, and illus-
trations of his books help tell the story of his life.

BANNEKER, BENJAMIN

Benjamin Banneker: Man of Science
9 min.   color   1972   IJS
Prod. and dist: Encyclopaedia Britannica (available on video by
    special order).   Rental: Syracuse
    How this free black man eventually won acclaim for his
scientific almanac during colonial times.

BANNISTER, ROGER GILBERT

The Impact of Roger Bannister
26 min.   b&w and color   1973   SCA
Prod: Koplin and Grinker.   Dist: Pictura
    The transition from runner to neurologist is told by Bannis-
ter himself in London.

BARRAUD, HENRI

Rhapsodies
50 min.   SC
Dir: Denise Billon.   Prod: ORTF.   Rental: FACSEA
    French dialogue only.   An interview of him by Bernard
Gavoty and an analysis of his works with musical excerpts.

BARRYMORE, JOHN B.

John Barrymore (Biography Series)
27 min.   b&w   1965   SC
Prod: Metromedia Productions.   Dist: Sterling (sale only; avail-
    able on 8mm).   Rental: Syracuse
    A character study revealing his successes and failures, his
joys and sorrows.   Utilizes footage from his motion pictures.
Narrated by Mike Wallace.

BARTON, CLARA H.

Angel of Mercy: Clara Barton
10 min.   b&w   1940
Prod: Teaching Film Custodians.   Rental: Syracuse
    Begins with her attempts to organize women to work in the
field hospitals during the Civil War and the founding of the Red Cross.

Heroism of Clara Barton (You Are There Series)
30 min.   b&w   1956
Prod. and dist: CBS.   Rental: Minnesota
    A dramatization of a news broadcast of her administering
first aid to the wounded at the Antietam Creek battlefield.

BARUCH, BERNARD MANNES

The Trouble Shooter
15 min.   b&w   1952-53   JSCA
Prod: Mike Sklar.   Dist: Star Film
    Compiled from the Fox Movietone News Library, reveals
his accomplishments as an advisor to presidents.

BATISTA Y ZALDIVAR, FULGENCIO

Castro vs. Batista
30 min.   b&w   1965   JSCA
Prod: United Artists.   Dist: Films Inc.   Rental: Michigan,
    Minnesota
    Batista's rule of Cuba until Castro overthrew him.

BAUDELAIRE, CHARLES PIERRE   See   DELACROIX, EUGENE
    (Le Peintre et le Poète)

BAYLOR, ELGIN

Elgin Baylor (Sports Legends Series)
20 min.   color   1975   IJ
Prod. and dist: Sports Legends Inc.   Rental: Southern Cali-
    fornia
    Highlights from his basketball career, including footage
from the game in which he scored 71 points.

BAZAINE, JEAN

Bazaine
15 min.   color   SC
Dir: Jacques Simonnet.   Prod: Sorafilms.   Rental: FACSEA
    (available in French dialogue)
    At work he talks about what inspires him.

BAZILLE, FREDERIC

Bazille, the First Impressionist
15 min.   color   1971   SCA
Dir. and prod: Roger Leenhardt.   Dist: Film Images

Traces his life from Montpellier to Paris, where he was a friend of Monet and Renoir. Compares his work with that of his contemporaries.

BEALE, EDITH BOUVIER

Grey Gardens
94 min.   color   1975   SCA
Prod. and dist: Maysles
A cinéma vérité look at Edith Beale and her mother, cousins of Jacqueline Kennedy Onassis.

BEATLES

Braverman's Condensed Cream of Beatles
15 min.   color   1973   JSCA
Dir: Charles Braverman. Dist: Pyramid. Rental: Images, Michigan, Southern California, Viewfinders
A kinestatic collage of the '60s and the Beatles.

What's Happening? The Beatles in the U.S.
55 min.   b&w   1966   CH
Prod. and dist: Maysles
On tour.

BECKET, THOMAS A
See also Becket (feature); Murder in the Cathedral (feature)

Becket
32 min.   color   1964   JSCA
Prod: Teaching Film Custodians. Dist: Indiana. Rental: California
An excerpt from the Paramount motion picture of the same name, it shows his devotion to the church and the conflict between him and Henry II.

BEETHOVEN, LUDWIG VAN
See also The Magnificent Rebel (feature)

Beethoven (Great Composers Series)
27 min.   color   1975   JSA
Prod: Seabourne Enterprises. Dist: International Film Bureau. Rental: Syracuse
An introduction to his life and music.

Beethoven and His Music
12 1/2 min.   color   1954   IJSCA

Prod. and dist: Coronet (sale only).   Rental: Indiana, Michigan,
Minnesota, Nebraska, Syracuse
    How his environment and the social conditions of the late
18th century, i.e., the French Revolution, affected his music, together with a brief biographical sketch. A portion of "Pastoral
Symphony" is played.

Beethoven: Ordeal and Triumph (Saga of Western Man Series)
52 min.   color   1967   SCA
Prod: ABC.   Dist: McGraw-Hill.   Rental: Michigan, Minnesota,
Southern California, Syracuse
    His ordeal when he learned he was becoming deaf.

Bernstein on Beethoven--A Tribute
14 min.   color   JSCA
Prod: CBS.   Dist: BFA.   Rental: Southern California
    Bernstein traces his life and also plays selections from
"Piano Concerto #1" in C major.

Ludwig Van Beethoven--Who Rise Above Their Fellow Man (Touch
of Fame Series)
29 min.   b&w   1962   SCA
Prod: KNXT.   Dist: Southern California
    Dr. Herman Harvey, a psychology professor, analyzes
Beethoven's motivations for greatness and explains his style of
composition. A kinescope.

The Torment of Beethoven (You Are There Series)
30 min.   b&w   1955   JSCA
Prod. and dist: CBS.   Rental: Minnesota
    Walter Cronkite in a dramatization announces his plans to
interview Beethoven and talks about his deafness.

BEHAN, BRENDAN

Brendan Behan: The Man Behind the Myth
52 min.   color   1974   SCA
Prod: BBC-TV.   Dist: Time-Life (available on video)
    Interviews with his friends and relatives, an appearance of
Behan, a dramatized sequence from Borstal Boy, his IRA activities and imprisonment, his sudden success and later decay are all
explored in this in-depth portrait.

Brendan Behan's Dublin
29 min.   color   1968   SCA
Prod: Norcon Film.   Dist: International Film Bureau.   Rental:
California, Syracuse
    The views of him held by his father, mother, wife and
daughter and, especially, himself. His home, his city and his
friends are also presented.

BELL, ALEXANDER GRAHAM

For You, Mr. Bell
16 min.   color   1973   IJSCA
Dir: William Canning.   Prod: National Film Board of Canada.
    Dist: Learning.   Rental: Michigan, Southern California, Syra-
    cuse
        A warm portrait of him, his many inventions, his interest
in the deaf, and his founding of the National Geographic Society.
Intercut with scenes of today.

BELLOW, SAUL

Novel: Saul Bellow--The Work of the Dangling Man
29 min.   b&w   1966   JSCA
Prod: NET.   Dist: Indiana.   Rental: California
        A commentary on his novels: The Dangling Man, The Vic-
tim, The Adventures of Augie March, Seize the Day, Henderson
the Rain King and Herzog.

BEN-GURION, DAVID

Ben Gurion
26 min.   b&w   1963   JSA
Rental: Minnesota, Southern California, Syracuse
        Traces his life and service to Israel as Prime Minister
and later as War Minister.

BENTLEY, ERIC

Eric Bentley
29 min.
Dir: Stefan Sharff.   Prod: Erik Barnouw and Sumner Glimcher.
    Dist: Center for Mass Communication (sale only).   Rental:
    California, Minnesota
        Shown as a writer, musician, critic, translator, playwright
and poet, as well as a force in the American theater.

BENTON, THOMAS HART

Thomas Hart Benton (Profiles in Courage Series)
50 min.   b&w   1964   IJSA
Prod: Robert Saudek Associates.   Dist: IQ Films.   Rental:
    Michigan, Minnesota, Syracuse
        Upholds his interpretation of the Constitution, though his
supporters give him different instructions.

BERG, PAT

Fairway to Fame
15 min.   b&w   1952-53   JSCA
Prod: Mike Sklar. Dist: Star Film
        Her career as a golfer.   Compiled from the Fox Movietone
News Library footage.

BERGMAN, (ERNST) INGMAR

Ingmar Bergman
50 min.   color   1973   SC
Prod: Swedish Film Institute. Dist: Films Inc. Rental: Michi-
    gan, Viewfinders
        Seen on location. Clips from his films "Persona" and "The
Touch" are interspersed with interviews with him, Bibi Andersson,
Max von Sydow, Liv Ullman.

BERGMAN, INGRID

Conversation with Ingrid Bergman
59 min.   b&w   1967   JSCA
Prod: NET. Dist: Indiana
        An interview with Los Angeles Times drama critic Cecil
Smith in which she describes her first movie role.

BERNHARDT, SARAH

Final Performance of Sarah Bernhardt (You Are There Series)
28 min.   b&w   1955   SCA
Prod. and dist: CBS (sale only; no previews). Rental: Michigan,
    Minnesota
        A news report dramatization of her retirement and good-bye
to her public.

BETHUNE, NORMAN

Bethune
60 min.   b&w   1972   SCA
Prod: National Film Board of Canada. Dist: Withdrawn by
    McGraw-Hill. Rental: Indiana
        The remarkable career of the Canadian doctor who fought
with the Spanish during the Civil War and with the North Chinese
Army during the Sino-Japanese War. He introduced the first mo-
bile blood transfusion service.

BISMARCK, PRINCE OTTO VON

Bismarck: Germany from Blood and Iron

30 min.   color   1976   JSCA
Dir: John Irvin.   Prod. and dist: Learning Corp.
    His manipulation of King Wilhelm of Prussia and the eventu-
al unification of Germany are re-enacted.

BISMILLAH KHAN

Bismillah Khan
29 min.   b&w   1967   SCA
Prod: NET. Dist: Indiana. Rental: California
    A typical day for one of India's leading musicians and ex-
ponent of the shenai, a reed instrument.

BISSIERE, ROGER

Bissière
15 min.   color
Dir: Jacques Simonnet and Guy Suzuki.   Prod: Sorafilms.
   Rental: FACSEA
        French dialogue only. A commentary on his life and works.

BIZET, GEORGES (ALEXANDRE CESAR)

Immortal Bizet
26 min.   b&w   1952   JSCA
Dist: Withdrawn. Rental: Michigan
        His life told against the background settings of Paris and
Italy. Includes selections from his musical compositions.

BLACK, HUGO

Justice Black and the Bill of Rights
32 min.   color   1969   JSCA
Prod: CBS News. Dist: BFA. Rental: Indiana, Minnesota,
   Syracuse
        An interview conducted by Eric Sevareid on issues such as
freedom of speech.

BLAKE, WILLIAM

Essay on William Blake
52 min.   color   1969   SCA
Prod: NET. Dist: Indiana. Rental: California
        A drama of the poet and painter considered a heretic, re-
ligious poet, idealist and madman--while alive. Many of his
poems are read.

A Portrait of William Blake, Parts I and II

30 min.   each   b&w   1972
Prod: ABC.   Rental: National Council of Churches of Christ
    Innocence and Experience (Part I) is devoted to his early
years.   The Prophet (Part II) is devoted to his later, troubled
years and the themes which recur in his works.

The Vision of William Blake
27 min.   color   1970   SA
Prod: Blake Film Trust.   Dist: Withdrawn by McGraw-Hill.
    Rental: Southern California
    His own books and pictures are used to tell about his inner
struggles.

William Blake (Romantic Versus Classic Art Series)
26 min.   color   1974   JSCA
Prod: Reader's Digest.   Dist: Pyramid.   Rental: Southern Cali-
    fornia (listed in the catalog under the series title)
    A study of the artist and his work, narrated by Kenneth
Clark.

William Blake (Third Testament Series)
55 min.   color   1976   SCA
Prod: BBC-TV.   Dist: Time-Life (available on video)
    His poetry and paintings are used to reflect his bizarre life
and belief in the Heavenly City.

BLEIER, ROCKY

I'm Back: The Rocky Bleier Story
48 min.   color   1976   SCA
Prod: Laurel Production.   Dist: Counselor
    A sports profile.

BOLEYN, ANNE   See   Anne of a Thousand Days;   Henry VIII and
    his Six Wives;   A Man for all Seasons;   The Private Life of
    Henry VIII (all features); HENRY VIII (The Six Wives of Henry
    VIII)

BOLIVAR, SIMON
    See also   Simon Bolivar (feature)

Bolivar: South American Liberator
11 min.   color   1962   I
Prod. and dist: Coronet.   Rental: Indiana, Syracuse
    Shot in South America, where he liberated five countries
after giving up his fortune, and where he dreamed of uniting the
continent.

BOND, JULIAN

The Angry Negro
30 min.   b&w   1966   SCA
Prod: NET.   Dist: Indiana
        Interviews with black leaders about how they should seek
equality.

World of Julian Bond
11 min.   b&w   1968   SCA
Prod: NET.   Dist: Indiana.   Rental: Association, California
        A review of his political career and his role in the Georgia
State Legislature.

BONHOEFFER, DIETRICH

Dietrich Bonhoeffer (A Third Testament Series)
55 min.   color   1976   SCA
Prod: BBC-TV.   Dist: Time-Life (available on video)
        A teacher, a preacher, and a scholar imprisoned by the
Nazis, he wrote the classic Letters and Papers From Prison during that time.   Malcolm Muggeridge is commentator.

BONNARD, PIERRE

Bonnard
20 min.   color   CA
Dir: Lauro Venturi.   Prod: Flag Films.   Rental: FACSEA
        French dialogue only.   The life and works of this artist.

Bonnard
17 min.   color   1967   JS
Dist: Universal Education and Visual Arts.   Rental: Southern
    California, Syracuse
        A close examination of his development as an artist, the
places he lived and worked.

BOONE, DANIEL
    See also Daniel Boone (feature)

Daniel Boone
18 min.   b&w   1950   IJS
Prod. and dist: Encyclopaedia Britannica (available on video by
    special order).   Rental: Indiana, Michigan, Minnesota, Nebras-
    ka, South Florida, Southern California, Syracuse
        Important episodes as a wilderness scout.

Daniel Boone in America's Story
16 min.   color   1968   IJ
Prod. and dist: Coronet (sale only).   Rental: South Florida

His life is traced from his birth. Emphasis is placed on his roles as an Indian fighter and treaty-maker, explorer, and hunter.

BOOTH, JOHN WILKES

Capture of John Wilkes Booth (You Are There Series)
27 min.   b&w   1956   JS
Prod. and dist: CBS (sale only; no previews or rentals).   Rental: Michigan
A dramatization of his capture.

BORGES, JORGE LUIS

The Inner World of Jorge Luis Borges
28 1/2 min.   color   1969   SC
Prod: Harold Mantell.   Dist: Films for the Humanities (available on 3/4" videocassette)
His inner life as revealed through quotations from his books.

BOSCH, HIERONYMUS
See also VELASQUEZ, DIEGO (Treasures from El Prado)

The Lost Paradise
11 min.   b&w   1952   SCA
Prod. and dist: Pictura
An in-depth examination of his painting "The Garden of Delights." Narrated by Vincent Price, the text is taken from the King James version of the Old Testament.

Three Paintings by Hieronymus Bosch
10 min.   color   1951   SCA
Dir. and prod: J. H. Lenauer. Dist: Macmillan. Rental: South Florida, Southern California
A study of "The Adoration of the Kings," "The Mocking of Christ," and "Ecce Homo."

BOUDIN, EUGENE LOUIS

Boudin
20 min.   color
Dir: Raphael Motte. Prod: Films Démeter. Rental: FACSEA (available in French)
His life and works as well as his research and premonitions.

BOURDELLE, EMILE ANTOINE

Bourdelle

18 min.   1950   SCA
Dir: Rene Lucot.   Prod: Andre Robert.   Rental: FACSEA
    (available in French)
        His youth, his father's furniture creations, his experiences
in art school and in Paris, and the influence of his teacher, Rodin.

BOWEN, CATHERINE DRINKER

Catherine Drinker Bowen: Other People's Lives (Writers on Writ-
    ing Series)
18 min.   color   1972   S
Prod: Davidson Films.   Dist: General Learning Corp.
        A visit to her home, where her daily routine is shown.
She discusses how and why she writes and comments on preparing
and writing biographies, for which she is noted.

BOYD, MALCOLM

Dialogue with Malcolm Boyd
56 min.   b&w   1967   SA
Prod: David Abernathy.   Dist: Sandpiper.   Rental: Mass Media
        A dialogue with young adults.

BRADBURY, RAY DOUGLAS

Ray Bradbury (Sum and Substance Series)
30 min.   b&w   1964   SCA
Prod: Modern Learning Aids.   Dist: Withdrawn.   Rental: Minne-
    sota
        He discusses the creative process of writing.

BRADSHAW, TERRY

Thank God I'm a Country Boy: Terry Bradshaw (The Winners
    Series)
48 min.   color   1976   SCA
Prod: Laurel.   Dist: Counselor
        A sports profile.

BRADY, MATHEW B.

Brady of Broadway (American Civil War Series)
30 min.   b&w   1958   SC
Prod: Westinghouse Broadcasting.   Dist: Association
        His photographs of the Civil War and a portrait.

Mathew Brady
13 min.   b&w

Prod. and dist: Dept. of the Air Force (free loan)
    Documents his work as the first combat photographer.

Mathew Brady: Photographer of an Era
12 min.   b&w   IJSCA
Dir: Lewis Jacobs.   Dist: Texture
    When the Civil War broke out, Brady left his picture studio
and photographed the battlefront, where he trained the world's first
combat camera crew.

BRAHMS, JOHANNES

Brahms and his Music
13 1/2 min.   color   1957   IJSCA
Prod. and dist: Coronet (sale only).   Rental: Indiana, Michigan,
    Minnesota, Nebraska, Syracuse
    The people and places which influenced his music and the
controversies his music aroused.

BRAILLE, LOUIS

The Triumph of Louis Braille (You Are There Series)
26 min.   b&w   1956   JSCA
Prod. and dist: CBS (sale only; no previews).   Rental: Indiana,
    Minnesota
    An "on the scene" dramatization of a news report focusing
on how he developed a method of reading and writing for the blind.

BRANDO, MARLON (MARLON MYERS, JR.)

Meet Marlon Brando
28 min.   b&w   1966   CA
Prod. and dist: Maysles
    A cinéma vérité portrait of a well known actor.

BRAQUE, GEORGES

Hommage à Georges Braque
15 min.   color   SCA
Dir: Jacques Simonnet.   Prod: Sorafilms.   Rental: FACSEA
    (available in French dialogue)
    A commentary on his life and works and the founding of
cubism.

BRAUN, WERNHER VON

Wernher von Braun
25 min.   b&w   1965   IJ

Prod: Metromedia Productions. Dist: Sterling (sale only; available on 8mm). Rental: Syracuse
   The story of a rocket expert, which uses authentic German footage of his research and filmed interviews made when the Allied Armies occupied Germany.

BRESDIN, RODOLPHE

Bresdin
20 min. b&w SCA
Dir: Nelly Kaplan. Rental: FACSEA (available in French dialogue)
   A portrait of the teacher of Odilon Redon and his art work.

BREUGEL see BRUEGEL

BRICO, ANTONIA

Antonia: A Portrait of the Woman
58 min. color 1974 SCA
Prod: Rocky Mountain Productions. Dist: Phoenix. Rental: Michigan, Syracuse
   A warm portrait of her teaching and conducting in Denver, Colorado. She voices her frustration with discrimination against women, which hindered her career.

BROCK, LOU

The Thief--Lou Brock (The Winners Series)
48 min. color 1976 SCA
Prod: Laurel. Dist: Counselor
   A portrait and perspective of the baseball player by journalist Dave Anderson.

BRONOWSKI, JACOB

Jacob Bronowski: 20th Century Man (a series)
30 min. each color 1976 JSCA
Prod. and dist: Great Plains
   Conversations with the late scientist, humanist, playwright, and philosopher.

BRONTÉ, ANNE & CHARLOTTE & EMILY

The Brontë Sisters
19 min. color 1970 SCA
Dir: Terrence Ladlow. Prod: Attico Films in association with

the Brontë Society. Dist: International Film Bureau. Rental: Syracuse

Shot in York, the film presents their lives and personalities set against the background of their times. Excerpts from their novels are included.

BROOKS, GWENDOLYN

Gwendolyn Brooks
30 min. b&w 1966 SCA
Prod: NET. Dist: Indiana. Rental: California
She reads her poetry and talks about her life and work.

BROOKS, VAN WYCK

Van Wyck Brooks (Wisdom Series)
30 min. b&w 1959 SCA
Prod: NBC. Dist: Films Inc. Rental: Minnesota, Southern California
An interview about his life, works, and philosophy.

BROWN, CHRISTY

Triumph of Christy Brown
60 min. b&w 1970 SCA
Prod: NET. Dist: Indiana. Rental: California
Filmed in Dublin, this documentary traces the life of the author of My Left Foot and Down All the Days. Emphasizes how he overcame being afflicted with cerebral palsy.

BROWN, JAMES

James Brown: The Man
15 min. color 1974 IJS
Prod: NBC. Dist: Sterling (sale only; available on 8mm)
Seen at business meetings and at informal talks with students whom he encourages to stay in school.

BROWN, WILLIAM WELLS

Slavery and Slave Resistance
23 1/2 min. color 1973 JSC
Prod: Dynamic Films for Arno Press. Dist: Perspective
Documents the achievements of some famous runaway or former slaves such as Phillis Wheatley, novelist Brown, and Frederick Douglass.

BROWNING, ELIZABETH BARRETT See The Barretts of Wimpole Street (feature); Robert Browning--His Life and
Poetry

BROWNING, ROBERT
See also The Barretts of Wimpole Street

Robert Browning--His Life and Poetry
21 min. color 1972 SCA
Prod: Armada Productions and International Film Bureau. Dist:
International Film Bureau. Rental: California, Syracuse
Photographs and paintings are intercut with scenes of London and Italy to depict important events in his life such as his
courtship of Elizabeth Barrett. Selections from his poetry are
read and his style and use of the first person and dramatic mono-
logues are discussed.

BRUBECK, DAVID WARREN

Brubecks: Dave and Chris
25 min. color SCA
Dist: Modern Talking
A jam session.

The Jazz of Dave Brubeck
26 min. b&w 1961 SCA
Prod: CBS. Dist: Association, Syracuse
His quartet and their unique cooperation.

BRUCE, LENNY

Lenny Bruce on TV
35 min. b&w 1959 SA
Prod: Fred Baker. Dist: New Yorker
Performing several famous routines on two Steve Allen
shows and in an unaired pilot for a show of his own.

BRUEGEL (or BRUEGHEL)

Axe and the Lamp
7 min. color 1971 SCA
Prod: British Film Institute. Dist: Films Inc.
Analysis of his "Nederlandish Proverbs."

BRYAN, WILLIAM JENNINGS
See also Inherit the Wind (feature)

Darrow vs. Bryan (Men in Crisis Series)
25 min.   b&w   1964   SC
Prod: Metromedia Producers.   Dist: Films Inc.   Rental: Michigan, Southern California, Syracuse
    Edmond O'Brien narrates the story of the famous "monkey" trial.

William Jennings Bryan--Fairview (American Life Styles Series)
28 min.   color   1976   IJSCA
Prod: Comco Productions.   Dist: Association
    A tour of his home which gives insight into the man.
Hosted by E. G. Marshall.

BUCK, PEARL

Pearl S. Buck (Wisdom Series)
30 min.   b&w   1959   SCA
Prod: NBC.   Dist: Films Inc.   Rental: Southern California
    In an interview in her home she discusses China, her life there, and its affect on her writing.

BUCKLEY, WILLIAM F.

William F. Buckley (The Dissenters)
30 min.   b&w   1967   SCA
Prod: NET.   Dist: Indiana.   Rental: Minnesota
    He discusses his political and philosophical beliefs with Donald Fouser.

BUDDHA   See   Gautama Buddha

BUFFET, BERNARD

Bernard Buffet
20 min.   color   CA
Dir: Etienne Périer.   Prod: Cinetel.   Rental: FACSEA
    French dialogue only.   All the stages of painting a calf's head.

BULLOCK, WYNN   See   CUNNINGHAM, IMOGEN

BURBANK, LUTHER

Personal History: Great Americans (News Magazine of the Screen Series)
11 min.   JSA
Prod: Warners Pathe News.   Rental: Minnesota

The life story of Luther Burbank and his new species. Also "Portrait of an American Artist," the craft of William Robinson Leigh.

BURCHFIELD, CHARLES

Charles Burchfield
14 min.   color   SCA
Prod: Radio-TV Bureau, University of Arizona. Dist: International Film Bureau. Rental: Southern California
Presents his major paintings of U.S. life and how Beardsley, Oriental art and the novels of Cather and Gorki influenced him.

BURKE, EDMUND

Man and the State: Burke and Paine on Revolution
28 min.   color   1974   JSCA
Prod: Bernard Wilets. Dist: BFA
A dramatization of a debate on political change between Paine, a radical, and Burke, a conservative.

BURKE, ROBERT O'HARA

Burke and Wills (Age of Exploration Series)
52 min. (2 pts)   color   1976   SCA
Prod: BBC-TV and Time-Life. Dist: Time-Life (available on video)
The first overland crossing of Australia, in which 11 men died and one survived.

BURR, AARON

Hamilton-Burr Duel (You Are There Series)
28 min.   b&w   1956   JSA
Prod. and dist: CBS (sale only; no previews). Rental: Michigan, Minnesota, Southern California, Syracuse
A dramatization of the duel in which Hamilton is mortally wounded.

BURTON, SIR RICHARD FRANCIS

The Search for the Nile (a series of 6 films)
52 min. each (2 pts)   color   1976   JSCA
Prod: BBC-TV and Time-Life. Dist: Time-Life (available on video or in Spanish)
The struggle among Burton, Speke, Livingstone and Stanley to discover the Nile and their mutual conflict against Nature is dramatized. "The Dream of the Wanderer" shows the Royal

Geographical Society asking Burton to find the source of the Nile. He asks Speke to go with him. Meanwhile, Dr. Livingstone sets out across the Kalahari. In 'Discovery and Betrayal" Burton and Speke quarrel and Speke returns home and claims he's found the source--Lake Victoria. Then in "The Secret Fountains" Speke returns to confirm his theory and meets the Bakers. "The Great Debate" pits Speke against Burton, who refutes the theory about Lake Victoria. Later Speke is found dead. "Find Livingstone" is the chore set aside for Henry Stanley. "Conquest and Death" traces Stanley's expedition. Burton dies and his wife destroys his manuscripts.

BUTLER, REG See ARMITAGE, KENNETH (Five British Sculptors Work and Talk)

BYRD, RICHARD EVELYN

Admiral Byrd
25 min.   b&w   1965   IJ
Prod: Metromedia Productions. Dist: Sterling (sale only; available on 8mm). Rental: Mass Media
    Recounts his great accomplishments in the Antarctic, beginning with his world trip--at the age of 12.

Byrd vs. Amundsen
25 min.   b&w   1964   SCA
Prod: Metromedia Producers. Dist: Films Inc. Rental: Southern California
    A race between them to be the first to fly over the North Pole.

To the Ends of the Earth
15 min.   b&w   1952-53   JSCA
Prod: Mike Sklar. Dist: Star Film
    Compiled from the Fox Movietone News Library, this shows his exploration of the North Pole.

CABOT, JOHN

Age of Discovery: English, French and Dutch Explorations
11 min.   color or b&w   1956   I
Prod. and dist: Coronet (sale only). Rental: Indiana, Michigan, Nebraska, South Florida, Syracuse
    The routes of early explorers of America.

Age of Discovery: Spanish and Portuguese Explorations
15 min.   b&w   1957   JSC
Prod: Victor J. Jurgens for Young America Films. Dist: McGraw-Hill. Rental: Indiana, Michigan, Syracuse
    Briefly describes conditions in Europe and the voyages of

several explorers including Diaz, Columbus, Vasco Da Gama, Magellan, and Vespucci.

John Cabot: Man of the Renaissance
28 min.   b&w   1966   JS
Prod: National Film Board of Canada.   Dist: Perennial (special order; no previews).   Rental: Michigan
How he sought backing for his explorations in the New World, but was delayed until after Columbus discovered America.

CAESAR, GAIUS JULIUS
See also Caesar and Cleopatra (feature); Julius Caesar (feature; Bradley) Julius Caesar (feature; Burge)

The Assassination of Julius Caesar (You Are There Series)
27 min.   b&w   1955   IJSCA
Prod: CBS.   Dist: Withdrawn by McGraw-Hill.   Rental: Indiana, Michigan
The assassination of March 15, 44 B.C. is dramatized and "reported."

Four Views of Caesar
23 min.   b&w   1964   JSC
Prod: CBS.   Dist: BFA.   Rental: Indiana, Minnesota, Nebraska, Syracuse
Caesar as seen by himself, by Plutarch, by Shakespeare, and by George Bernard Shaw.

Julius Caesar--The Rise of the Roman Empire
22 min.   color or b&w   1964   IJS
Prod. and dist: Encyclopaedia Britannica (available on video by special order or in Spanish).   Rental: California, Indiana, Michigan, Minnesota, South Florida, Southern California
His conquests in Gaul and other significant events of his career are traced and photographed in a full-scale reproduction of the Roman Forum.

CALDER, ALEXANDER

Alexander Calder--From the Circus to the Moon
15 min.   color   1963   SA
Dir: Hans Richter.   Dist: Withdrawn by McGraw-Hill.   Rental: Minnesota
Shown creating mobiles in his studio.

Calder's Circus (Cirque Calder)
19 min.   color   1963   SCA
Prod: Carlos Vilardebo.   Dist: Withdrawn by McGraw-Hill.
Rental: Syracuse
Built in 1929, this toy-art foreshadowed his later mobiles in style and color.

The Great Sail
10 min.   color   1968   JSCA
Prod: Robert Gardner.   Dist: Phoenix
      The erection of his largest sculpture, "La Grande Voile,"
on the MIT campus in 1966.

CALHOUN, JOHN C.

John C. Calhoun
16 min.   b&w   1951   JS
Prod. Encyclopaedia Britannica.   Dist: Withdrawn by EB.
      Rental: Indiana, Michigan, Minnesota, Nebraska, South Florida,
Southern California, Syracuse
      The factors leading to his careers as lawyer and Vice
President of the U. S. and his views on important issues of his
time such as tariff regulations and slavery.

States' Rights: Andrew Jackson vs. John C. Calhoun--1832
      (History Alive! Series)
14 min.   color   1970   JSC
Prod: Turnley Walker.   Dist: Walt Disney (long term license)
      A dramatization of Jackson's and Calhoun's disagreement
over a tariff law.

CALLOT, JACQUES

Jacques Callot, Engraver
11 min.   b&w   1966(?)   SCA
Dist: Films Inc.
      A master French engraver, the film documents his life and
times by animating his work.

CALMETTE, ALBERT

Albert Calmette
27 min.   color   1968   SCA
Dir: Pierre Thévenard.   Prod: Ampho.   Rental: FACSEA
      (available in French)
      The life and works of the discoverer of the tuberculosis
vaccine.

CAMBIER, GUY

Day in Autumn with Guy Cambier
12 min.   color   1974   SCA
Prod. and dist: California
      French painter Cambier works at home on his farm, com-
poses music, and travels through the countryside. He discusses
the influences on his life and modern realism.

CAMPANELLA, ROY

Roy Campanella (Sports Legends Series)
20 min.   color   1975   LJ
Prod. and dist: Sport Legends Inc.   Rental: Southern California
     A review of his career in baseball, an interview, and clips
from some of his games with the Dodgers.

CAMUS, ALBERT

Albert Camus: A Self Portrait
20 min.   color and b&w   1972   JSCA
Dir: Georges Regnier.   Prod: Fred Orjain.   Dist: Learning.
   Rental: Minnesota, Syracuse
     Traces his life with emphasis on his ties with Algeria.   In-
cludes excerpts from his writings and an on-camera appearance in
which he discusses his philosophy.

Le Dernier Matin d'Albert Camus
25 min.   1965   CA
Dir: Harry Fischbach.   Prod: Paris Cité Productions.   Rental:
   FACSEA
     French dialogue only.

Unswerving Arrow--A Tribute to Camus
12 min.   color   1963
Dir. and prod: Babette Newburger.   Dist: Withdrawn by McGraw-
   Hill.   Rental: California
     Michael Redgrave reads excerpts from The Plague, The
Fall, and the essay "The Rebel." Illustrated by paintings done by
Babette Newburger.

CAPONE, AL See Al Capone (feature)

CAPOTE, TRUMAN

A Visit with Truman Capote
29 min.   b&w   1966   SCA
Prod. and dist: Maysles
     A cinéma vérité portrait of a noted author.

CARAVAGGIO, MICHELANGELO (MERISI) DA

Caravaggio and the Baroque
15 min.   color   1962   SA
Prod: unknown.   Dist: Withdrawn by McGraw-Hill.   Rental:
   California, Indiana, Southern California, Syracuse
     A non-conformist artist who rejected the idealism of the
past and added to the Reformation movement.

CARLSEN, KURT

Man Against the Sea
15 min.   b&w   1952-53   JSCA
Prod: Mike Sklar.   Dist: Star Film
  His heroism at sea is recounted through Fox Movietone News Library footage.

CARMICHAEL, STOKELY

Where is Jim Crow? A Conversation with Stokely Carmichael
30 min.   b&w   1967
Prod. and dist: California

CARNEGIE, ANDREW

Andrew Carnegie
19 min.   b&w   1951
Prod. and dist: Encyclopaedia Britannica (available on video by
 special order). Rental: Indiana, Michigan, Minnesota, Nebraska, Southern California, Syracuse
  Covers his poor childhood in Scotland and later outlines his philanthropic activities.

Andrew Carnegie: The Gospel of Wealth
26 min.   color   1974   JSCA
Dir: William Francisco.   Prod: Robert Saudek.   Dist: Learning.
 Rental: Michigan, Southern California, Syracuse
  A dramatization of Carnegie's sale of his steel company to
J. P. Morgan.

CARNEGIE, DALE

Dale Carnegie--A World of Confidence
13 1/2 min.   color   A
Dist: Association-Sterling (free loan)
  A portrait which stresses the methods and techniques he created to help people cope with themselves.

CARROLL, LEWIS (pseudonym for Charles Dodgson)

Lewis Carroll and The Rev. Charles Dodgson--In Defense of Nonsense (Touch of Fame Series)
29 min.   b&w   1962   SCA
Prod: KNXT.   Dist: Southern California
  Emphasizes the philosophy and scientific achievements of Lewis Carroll, author of Alice's Adventures in Wonderland.   A kinescope.

CARTIER, JACQUES
     See also CABOT, JOHN (Age of Discovery: English, French
     and Dutch Explorations)

French Explorations in the New World
10 1/2 min.   color   1956   IJ
Prod. and dist: Coronet (sale only). Rental: Indiana, Syracuse
     Traces the patterns of exploration of Verrazano, Cartier,
Champlain, Marquette, Joliet, and La Salle.

CARUSO, ENRICO See The Great Caruso (feature)

CARVER, GEORGE WASHINGTON

Boyhood of George Washington Carver
12 1/2 min.   color   1973   PIJ
Prod. and dist: Coronet (sale only). Rental: Syracuse
     His early years in Missouri, where he developed his love
of nature and science.

George Washington Carver
12 min.   color   1976   IJSCA
Dir: Carlton Moss. Dist: Pyramid
     An animated biography of the black scientist who discovered
many uses for peanuts and who is now considered a great chemist
and educator.

George Washington Carver
11 min.   b&w   1967   IJS
Prod: Vignette Films. Dist: BFA. Rental: Syracuse
     Historic footage shows him at work in his laboratory,
where he developed hundreds of products.

George Washington Carver
12 min.   color   1959   JSC
Prod: Artisan. Dist: Withdrawn. Rental: Michigan
     His struggle to obtain an education and his experiments at
Tuskegee Institute.

The Story of Dr. Carver
10 min.   b&w   1938   SCA
Prod: MGM. Dist: Films Inc. Rental: Indiana
     His scientific accomplishments.

CASALS, PABLO

Pablo Casals (Wisdom Series)
30 min.   b&w   1965   SCA
Prod: NBC. Dist: Films Inc.   Rental: California, Michigan,
     Minnesota, Nebraska

In an interview he discusses his music and his decision to leave Spain.

Pablo Casals Breaks His Journey
10 min.   b&w   1959
Prod. and dist: United Nations (also available in French and Spanish)
An interview in which he talks about the universality of music.

CASEY, BERNIE

Bernie Casey: Black Artist
21 min.   color   1971   JSCA
Prod: Multi-Cul. Dist: ACI. Rental: California, Minnesota, Nebraska, Syracuse
A painter in touch with nature, he's seen in the woods and fields and later in his studio, where he talks about his art.

CASH, JOHNNY

Johnny Cash
94 min.   color   1969   SCA
Dir: Robert Elfstrom. Prod: Arthur and Evelyn Barron. Dist: Sterling. Rental: California
A cinéma vérité portrait capturing him on the road, performing at a state fair, a prison, and a reservation, and at a recording session. He sings 24 songs.

CASTELLI, LEO See DE KOONING, WILLEM (Painters Painting)

CASTRO, FIDEL
See also BATISTA Y ZALDIVAR, FULGENCIO (Castro vs. Batista)

Castro (Biography Series)
26 min.   b&w   1964   SCA
Prod: David Wolper. Dist: Withdrawn by McGraw-Hill. Rental: Indiana, Michigan, Minnesota, South Florida, Southern California, Syracuse
His life and rise to power after Batista is overthrown.

Cuba and Fidel
25 min.   color   1976
Prod: Focal Point Films. Dist: Churchill
In an interview he talks about Cuba's revolution, social systems, the United States, and changes that occurred after his takeover.

CATHERINE II (THE GREAT)
See also Catherine of Russia (feature); Catherine the Great (feature); Catherine the Great (feature; Korda)

Catherine the Great (Profiles in Power)
30 min.   color   1976   SCA
Prod: McConnell Advertising Co. and Ontario Communications Authority. Dist: Learning
    Played by Zoe Caldwell, Catherine is 'interviewed' by Patrick Watson, who acts as a gadfly.

CATHERINE DE MEDICIS

Pierres pour un duel
22 min.   b&w and color   1973   SCA
Dir: Jean-Marie Isnard.   Prod: Guifrance Film.   Rental: FACSEA
    The argument between Catherine de Médicis and Diane de Poitiers over the ownership of Château de Chenonceau, part of Henry II's estate.

CATHERINE OF ARAGON   See   HENRY VIII (The Six Wives of Henry VIII); Henry VIII and His Six Wives (feature)

CATLIN, GEORGE

Catlin and the Indians (Smithsonian Series)
24 min.   color   1967   SCA
Prod: NBC. Dist: McGraw-Hill.   Rental: Southern California, Syracuse
    Examines his paintings and contributions as a historian interested in Indian culture.

George Catlin and Alfred Jacob Miller
7 min.   color   n.d.   SCA
Prod: Westinghouse Broadcasting.   Dist: Films Inc.   Rental: South Florida
    Paintings of the West done before the Civil War.

CEZANNE, PAUL

Cézanne
17 min.   color   1967   JSC
Dist: Universal Education and Visual Arts (available on super 8).
    Rental: Southern California
    An exploration of his impressionist technique and the places, things, and people he painted as revealed through his home and studio.

Les Chemins de Cézanne
18 min.   color   SCA
Dir: Robert Mazoyer. Prod: Flag Films. Rental: FACSEA
   (available in French)
        Where he lived and painted and his subjects.

Paul Cezanne (Pioneers of Modern Paintings Series)
40 min.   color   1971   SCA
Prod. and dist: Independent Television Corp. Rental: California
        Life and work of the "father of cubism," with a critical
analysis by Sir Kenneth Clark, who also narrates.

CHADWICK, FLORENCE

The Challenge
15 min.   b&w   1952-53   JSCA
Prod: Mike Sklar. Dist: Star Film
        Swimming the English Channel.   Compiled from the Fox
Movietone News Library.

CHADWICK, LYNN See ARMITAGE, KENNETH (Five British
   Sculptors Work and Talk)

CHAGALL, MARC

Marc Chagall
25 min.   color   1965   SA
Prod: Flagg Films. Dist: Withdrawn by McGraw-Hill. Rental:
   Indiana, California, Michigan, Minnesota, Southern California,
   Syracuse
        Traces his life and gives a glimpse of him as he works.
Views his paintings, sculpture, and stained glass windows. Nar-
rated by Vincent Price.

Visite à Marc Chagall
20 min.   color   SCA
Dir: Roland Darbois. Prod: Agence Française d'Images.
   Rental: FACSEA
        While painting, he reminisces about his life.

CHAMPLAIN, SAMUEL DE See CARTIER, JACQUES (French
   Explorations in the New World)

CHAMPOLLION, JEAN FRANÇOIS

Champollion ou l'Egypte dévoilée
26 min.   color   1973   SCA
Dir: Jean Vidal, Julien Pappe. Prod: Magic Films Productions.

Rental: FACSEA (available in French)
The discovery of the key to the hieroglyphics.

CHAPLIN, CHARLES SPENCER

Eternal Tramp
54 min.   b&w   1967   SCA
Dir. and prod: Harry Hurwitz.   Dist: Macmillan.   Rental: Cali-
   fornia, Syracuse
   A biographical study based on early films.   Scenes from
"Rink," "Easy Street," "The Fireman" and other shorts are used
to study the development of the "tramp."   Narrated by Gloria
Swanson.

The Funniest Man in the World
102 min.   b&w   1968(?)   SCA
Dir: Vernon P. Becker.   Dist: Films Inc.
   Narrated by Douglas Fairbanks, Jr., this is an anthology
of his best loved films from 1913, when Sennett brought Chaplin to
Hollywood, until the creation of the Tramp.

The Gentleman Tramp
78 min.   color and b&w   1974   JSCA
Prod: Bert Schneider.   Dist: rbc films
   A tribute as well as his life story told through clips from
his best films, newsreel footage, still photos, and Oona Chaplin's
home movies.

CHARLEMAGNE (or CHARLES THE GREAT or CHARLES I)

Charlemagne and his Empire
13 1/2 min.   color   1961   SC
Prod. and dist: Coronet (sale only).   Rental: Indiana, Michigan,
   Minnesota, Syracuse
   Emphasizes his accomplishments and conquests as well as
his system of government.

Charlemagne: Holy Barbarian (Western Civilization Series)
26 min.   color   1970   JSCA
Prod. and dist: Learning (available in Spanish and French).
   Rental: Indiana, Michigan, Minnesota, Nebraska, South Florida,
   Southern California, Syracuse
   Recreates a crucial moment--Charlemagne must decide how
he will conquer the Saxons.

Charlemagne--Unifier of Europe
13 min.   color or b&w   1964   JS
Prod. and dist: Encyclopaedia Britannica (available on video by
   special order).   Rental: Indiana, Michigan, Minnesota, South
   Florida, Southern California, Syracuse
   Dramatizes his contributions to the development of Europe

and reveals his personal characteristics.   Filmed in France; uses artifacts and settings of the period.

CHARLES II (of England)
See also   CROMWELL, OLIVER (The Puritan Revolution: Cromwell and the Rise of Parliamentary Democracy)

Absolutism and Civil War (English History Series)
12 min.   color   1958   SC
Prod. and dist: Coronet (sale only).   Rental: Indiana
Focuses on the theory of divine right to rule and English history.   Shows Cromwell's rise to power and the subsequent restoration of Charles II.

CHASE, DORIS TOTTEN

Full Circle: The Work of Doris Chase
10 min.   color   1974   SCA
Prod: Doris Chase.   Dist: Perspective.   Rental: Michigan, Syracuse
The artist traces her own development as a painter, sculptor, and filmmaker.

CHATEAUBRIAND, FRANÇOIS RENE DE

Chateaubriand, Combourg visage de pierre
14 min.   1948   SCA
Dir: Jacques de Casembroot.   Prod: Jean Mugeu.   Rental: FACSEA (available in French)
His home during his youth.   Passages from Mémoires d'Outre-tombe are read by Pierre Fresnay.

Souvenance
26 min.   1966   CA
Dir: Jacques de Casembroot.   Prod: Films J. K. Raymond-Millet.   Rental: FACSEA
French dialogue only.   His life as revealed through his well known novel, Mémoires d'Outre-tombe.

CHAUCER, GEOFFREY

Chaucer's England
30 min.   b&w or color   1958   SC
Prod. and dist: Encyclopaedia Britannica.   Rental: Indiana, Michigan, Minnesota, Nebraska, South Florida, Southern California, Syracuse
Dramatizes "The Pardoner's Tale" and gives a brief biographical sketch of Chaucer and an outline of the period.

Chaucer's Tale
30 min.   color   1971   JSC
Prod: Not known.   Dist: BFA.   Rental: Syracuse
    Recreates his life and the traditions and spirit of his times
through music, paintings, and tapestries.   Filmed in England.

CHEEVERS, GERRY

Gerry Cheevers
22 min.   color   1973   SCA
Prod: Tele-Sports.   Dist: Paramount Oxford
    A sports profile.

CHEKHOV (or CHEKOV or TCHEKHOV), ANTON

Anton Chekhov: A Writer's Life
37 min.   b&w   1972   SC
Prod: Mosfilm.   English version adapted by Harold Mantell.
    Dist: Films for the Humanities (available on 3/4" videocas-
    sette)
    A portrait of his energetic life as a writer, physician, es-
tate manager, and traveler.   Excerpts from his plays and stories.
Narrated by Eli Wallach.

CHIANG KAI-SHEK See MAO TSE-TUNG (Mao vs. Chiang)

CHIANG KAI-SHEK, MADAME

Madame Chiang Kai-Shek
27 min.   b&w   1965   IJ
Prod: Metromedia Producers.   Dist: Sterling (sale only; avail-
    able on 8mm).   Rental: Syracuse
    The background of the woman who helped change the history
of China.

CHISHOLM, SHIRLEY ANITA
    See also GIOVANNI, NIKKI (Accomplished Women)

Chisholm: Pursuing the Dream
42 min.   color   1973   SCA
Dir: Tom Werner.   Prod: Bob Denby.   Dist: New Line Cinema.
    Rental: Michigan
    A documentary of her race in the Democratic Florida Presi-
dential primary and at the convention in Chicago in 1972.

CHOPIN, FREDERIC FRANÇOIS
    See also Song to Remember (feature)

Chopin (Great Composers Series)
28 1/2 min.   color   1975   JSA
Prod: Seabourne Enterprises. Dist: International Film Bureau.
   Rental: Syracuse
        An introduction to his life and music. Tamas Vasary plays
"Waltz in A minor, opus 69-2," "Prelude 15" and other selections.

CHURCHILL, WINSTON LEONARD SPENCER
   See also Young Winston (feature)

Churchill the Man
53 min.   color   1973   IJSCA
Dir: Peter Lambert. Dist: Pyramid. Rental: Southern California
        A portrait to commemorate the 100th anniversary of his
birth. His daughter Sarah describes his personal qualities. Narrated by Douglas Fairbanks, Jr.

The Impact of Winston Churchill
26 min.   color   1973   SCA
Prod: Koplin and Grinker. Dist: Pictura
        A visit to his underground headquarters during the War re-
veals much about his leadership. His friend J. Colville relates
many anecdotes about him.

Man of the Century: Churchill
54 min.   b&w   1959   SA
Prod: CBS. Dist: McGraw-Hill, Association. Rental: California,
   Indiana, Michigan, Minnesota, Southern California, Syracuse
        A close-up study of his role in the Boer War, World War I
and the '20s and '30s.

The Other World of Winston Churchill
50 min.   color   1964   SCA
Dir. and Prod: Louis Stoumen. Dist: Macmillan
        A documentary about his paintings, which includes remi-
niscences by Eisenhower. Narrated by Paul Scofield and Patrick
Wymark.

Winston Churchill
50 min.   b&w   1965   IJ
Prod: Metromedia Productions. Dist: Sterling (sale only; available on 8mm). Rental: Mass Media, Syracuse
        Emphasizes the years of World War II and utilizes stills
and newsreel footage.

CLARK, ROBERT

Robert Clark: An American Realist
19 min.   color   1974   SCA
Prod. and dist: California

Rural scenes of America are intercut with his paintings and his own voice-overs are used for the commentary about his art.

CLARK, WILLIAM

The Journal of Lewis and Clark (edited version)
27 min.   color or b&w   1966   IJS
Prod: NBC.   Dist: Encyclopaedia Britannica (available on video by special order; 50-minute version also available).   Rental: California, Indiana, Michigan, Minnesota, Southern California, Syracuse
        A faithful re-enactment of their expedition based on the journals they kept.

Lewis and Clark
17 min.   b&w   1950   IJS
Prod. and dist: Encyclopaedia Britannica (available on video by special order).   Rental: Indiana, Michigan, Minnesota, Nebraska, Southern California, Syracuse
        Their expedition of the land between the Mississippi River and the Pacific Ocean.

Lewis and Clark at the Great Divide (You Are There Series)
22 min.   color   1971   IJ
Prod: CBS.   Dist: BFA.   Rental: Syracuse
        A dramatization of an "on the scene" report.

Lewis and Clark Journey
16 min.   color   1969   IJ
Prod. and dist: Coronet (sale only)
        Using the words from the explorers' "Journals," their voyage is retraced.

CLAY, CASSIUS   See   MUHAMMAD ALI

CLEMENCEAU, GEORGES

Georges Clemenceau
55 min   SCA
Dir: Roland Bernard.   Prod: ORTF.   Rental: FACSEA
        Politician, statesman, Parliamentarian, he negotiated the Treaty of Versailles; here his accomplishments are traced.

CLEMENS, SAMUEL LANGHORNE   See   TWAIN, MARK

CLEOPATRA   See   Anthony and Cleopatra (feature); Caesar and Cleopatra (feature); Cleopatra (feature by De Mille); Cleopatra (feature by Mankiewicz); Cleopatra (silent feature)

CLEVELAND, (STEPHEN) GROVER

President Grover Cleveland (Profiles in Courage Series)
50 min.   b&w   1965   SA
Prod: Robert Saudek Associates.   Dist: IQ Films.   Rental:
   Michigan, Syracuse
      Upholds his belief in sound Federal financing, even though
it jeopardizes his chance for re-election.

COHEN, LEONARD

Ladies and Gentlemen, Mr. Leonard Cohen
44 min.   color   1965
Prod: National Film Board of Canada.   Dist: Center for Mass
   Communication (sale only).   Rental: McGraw-Hill, Minnesota
      Uses a cinéma vérité technique to reveal his life; he re-
cites some of his poetry.

COLERIDGE, SAMUEL TAYLOR

Coleridge: The Fountain and the Cave
50 min. or 32 min.   color   1974   JSCA
Dir: Bayley Silleck.   Dist: Pyramid.   Rental: Southern California
      Filmed on location in England; his life and poetry are visu-
alized.

COLETTE (SIDONIE GABRIELLE CLAUDINE)

Colette
35 min.   b&w   1951   SCA
Dir: Yannick Bellon.   Prod: Jacoupy Films.   Rental: FACSEA
   (available in French), Syracuse
      A day in her life.

Colette, Gabrielle, Sidonie
13 min.   color   1972   CA
Dir: Edouard Berne.   Prod: C.I.T.   Rental: FACSEA
      French dialogue only.   Insights into her writing are re-
vealed by a close look at her surroundings.

COLUMBUS, CHRISTOPHER
   See also CABOT, JOHN (Age of Discovery: Spanish and Portuguese Explorations); Christopher Columbus (feature)

Christopher Columbus
16 min.   b&w   1963   IJ
Prod. and dist: Churchill.   Rental: Indiana, Michigan, Minnesota, South Florida, Syracuse

Dramatizes his voyage and subsequent discovery of America through animation.

Christopher Columbus (Age of Exploration Series)
52 min. (two 26-minute segments)   color   1976   SCA
Prod: BBC-TV and Time-Life.   Dist: Time-Life (available on video)
        Beginning with the discovery of the New World, his explorations of the Caribbean and his return to Spain are retold in this docu-drama.

Columbus and Isabella (You Are There Series)
22 min.   color   1972   IJ
Prod: CBS. Dist: BFA. Rental: Syracuse
        A dramatization of their famous meeting.

The Early Discoverers (Americana Series #16)
15 min.   color   1975   IJSCA
Prod: Norman Foster. Dist: Handel
        A large segment deals with the voyages of Columbus.

Path of Columbus
13 min.   color   1954   JSCA
Prod: Meservey. Rental: Michigan
        The significant places and scenes from his life in Spain.

Story of Christopher Columbus
17 min.   color or b&w   1948   IJ
Prod. and dist: Encyclopaedia Britannica (available on video by special order). Rental: Indiana, Michigan, Nebraska, Southern California, Syracuse
        Dramatizes his boyhood dreams of adventure and his later discovery of America.

CONANT, JAMES B.

James B. Conant (Wisdom Series)
30 min.   b&w   1960   SCA
Prod: NBC. Dist: Withdrawn. Rental: Minnesota
        Together with Nathaniel Ober, principal of a high school, he discusses American education.

CONFUCIUS

Confucianism (Religions of Man Series)
30 min.   b&w   1955   SCA
Prod: NET. Rental: Indiana, Syracuse
        His life as a teacher, statesman, and religious leader.

CONSTABLE, JOHN

John Constable (Romantic Versus Classic Art Series)
26 min.   color   1974   JSCA
Prod: Reader's Digest.   Dist: Pyramid.   Rental: Southern California (listed under the series title)
    A lover of nature, his life is told through his works.   Nar-
rated by Kenneth Clark.

COOK, CAPT. JAMES

James Cook (Age of Exploration Series)
52 min. (two 26-minute segments)   color   1976   SCA
Prod: BBC-TV and Time-Life.   Dist: Time-Life (available on
video)
    A voyage to the Pacific to observe Venus, with a stop at
Tahiti; this docu-drama is based on his journals.

COOLIDGE, (JOHN) CALVIN

United States in the Twentieth Century: 1920-1932
18 min.   b&w   1971   JSC
Prod. and dist: Coronet (sale only)
    Newsreel footage highlights the administrations of Wilson,
Harding, Coolidge and Hoover.

COOPER, JAMES FENIMORE

James Fenimore Cooper
18 min.   b&w   1949   JS
Prod. and dist: Encyclopaedia Britannica (available on video by
special order).   Rental: Indiana, Minnesota, Nebraska, South
Florida, Southern California, Syracuse
    A dramatization of his life at sea and on his farm.

COPLAND, AARON

The Copland Portrait
29 min.   color   1976   SCA
Prod: U.S. Information Agency.   Dist: National Audiovisual
Center
    A sensitive portrait of his life, work and music, he's
shown with his friends discussing his career and significant moments in his life.

CORONADO, FRANCISCO VASQUEZ   See   CABOT, JOHN (Age of
Discovery: Spanish and Portuguese Explorations)

COROT, JEAN BAPTISTE CAMILLE

Corot
18 min.   color   1972   JSCA
Dir. and prod: Roger Leenhardt.   Dist: Roland
    A brief sketch of his life is given.   Describes his experi-
mentation with light and shadow and juxtaposes his works with
those of his contemporaries, Millet and Monet.

CORTES or CORTEZ, HERNANDO
    See also CABOT, JOHN (Age of Discovery: Spanish and Portu-
    guese Explorations)

Cortez and Montezuma: Conquest of an Empire
52 min.   color   1973   JS
Prod: Wolper Organization.   Dist: Films Inc.   Rental: Michigan
    The confrontation between these two men and the shattering
effect it had on the Aztec empire.

Cortez and the Legend (Saga of Western Man Series)
52 min.   color   1968   SCA
Prod: ABC.   Dist: McGraw-Hill (available in Spanish).   Rental:
    California, Indiana, Southern California, Syracuse
    Re-creates the Spanish conquest of the Aztec empire and
the struggle between Montezuma and Cortez as well as showing
how Spain built her empire.

COUNSILMAN, JAMES "DOC"

James "Doc" Counsilman
22 min.   color   1973   SCA
Prod: Tele-Sports.   Dist: Paramount Oxford
    A sports profile.

COURBET, GUSTAVE

Gustave Courbet, The First Realist
16 min.   color   1964   SCA
Dir: Roger Leenhardt.   Dist: Film Images
    Traces his turbulent but successful career and his years in
Ornans and Paris.   Over 40 paintings are shown and analyzed.

L'Homme à la pipe: Gustave Courbet
16 min.   color
Dir: Roger Leenhardt.   Rental: FACSEA (available in French
    dialogue)
    His life as revealed through his paintings.

COUSTEAU, JACQUES

World of Jacques Cousteau
49 min. (2 pts)   color   1966   JSCA
Prod: National Geographic Society. Dist: Films Inc. Rental:
   Minnesota, Southern California
        The story of how and why he and his men spent 27 days
328 feet below the ocean's surface.

COWARD, NOEL PIERCE

This Is Noel Coward
60 min.   color
Dist: Arthur Cantor
        An interview filmed shortly before his death is intercut with
biographical photos, scenes from his plays, reminiscences by
friends and rare footage shot by Coward himself. Narrated by Sir
John Gielgud.

CRANDALL, PRUDENCE

Prudence Crandall (Profiles in Courage Series)
50 min.   b&w   1966   IJSA
Prod: Robert Saudek Associates. Dist: IQ Films. Rental:
   Syracuse
        She insisted on an education for everyone regardless of race.

CRANE, HART

Poetry: In Search of Hart Crane
90 min.   b&w   1966   JSCA
Prod: NET. Dist: Indiana. Rental: California
        His biographer searches Crane's papers, books, and memo-
rabilia for clues to his personality. Crane's friends are interviewed and Gary Merrill narrates and reads several of Crane's
poems.

CREELEY, ROBERT

Poetry: Robert Creeley
30 min.   b&w   1966   JSCA
Prod: NET. Dist: Indiana. Rental: California
        A candid interview on how and why he writes poetry; he
reads several of his own poems.

CROCKETT, DAVID See Davy Crockett, King of the Wild
   Frontier (feature); Davy Crockett and the River Pirates
   (feature); Davy Crockett, Indian Scout (feature)

CROMWELL, OLIVER
See also CHARLES II (Absolutism and Civil War); Cromwell
(feature)

The Puritan Revolution: Cromwell and the Rise of Parliamentary
Democracy (Western Civilization Series)
33 min.   color   1972   JSCA
Prod: Columbia Pictures. Dist: Learning. Rental: Indiana,
Nebraska, Syracuse
    The conflict between Cromwell, who believed in the rights
of the common man, and King Charles II, who believed in "divine
right. " Specially edited from the feature, "Cromwell. "

CUMMINGS, E. E.

e. e. cummings: The Making of a Poet
24 min.   color   1973   SC
Prod: Harold Mantell. Dist: Films for the Humanities (available
on 3/4" videocassette). Rental: California, Indiana, Michigan
    Tells his own story of his childhood, his years at Harvard,
the struggle for self-expression in New York and Paris and the
years spent in Greenwich Village and New Hampshire. He reads
excerpts from his poems. Illustrated by his photos and drawings.

CUNNINGHAM, IMOGEN

Imogen Cunningham, Photographer
20 min.   color   1973   SCA
Dir: John Korty. Prod: American Film Institute. Dist: Time-
Life. Rental: California
    A portrait of this pioneer photographer, who was in her
80's when filmed. Includes interviews with candid footage of her
and examples of her photos.

Never Give Up--Imogen Cunningham
28 min.   color   1975   SCA
Dir: Ann Hershey. Dist: Phoenix. Rental: Viewfinders
    A warm visit with the late photographer, whose wit and
energy are readily apparent.

Two Photographers: Wynn Bullock, Imogen Cunningham
29 min.   b&w   1968
Dir. and prod: Fred Padulla. Dist: Western World Productions
    A candid dialogue between these two photographers. Much
of their work is included.

CUNNINGHAM, MERCE

Merce Cunningham
13 min.   b&w   1964   JSCA

Dir: Patrice Wyerse and Merce Cunningham. Dist: Macmillan
During his six-month tour in 1964 he and his company were filmed backstage and on stage in "Antic" and "Story."

CURIE, MARIE and PIERRE

The Discovery of Radium (You Are There Series)
25 min. b&w 1956 JS
Prod. and dist: CBS (special order sale; no rentals or previews).
Rental: Indiana
An "on the scene" news dramatization of the Curie's discovery of radium.

Madame Curie
23 min. b&w 1950 SA
Prod: MGM, edited by Teaching Film Custodians. Rental: Indiana, Michigan, Minnesota, Syracuse
Excerpts from the feature film of the same title. Shows the discovery of radium despite the many obstacles she and her husband faced.

Monsieur et Madame Curie
13 min. 1953 CA
Dir: Georges Franju. Rental: FACSEA
French dialogue only. The commentary is taken from Pierre's biography of Madame Curie and retraces their lives and their discovery of radium.

CURTIS, EDWARD S.

The Shadow Catcher: Edward S. Curtis and the North American Indian
88 min. color 1975 CA
Dir. and prod: T. C. McLuhan. Dist: Phoenix. Rental: Michigan
His 32 years as a photographer, anthropologist, and filmmaker, who worked among and with the Indians of North America. All the recoverable film footage he shot is included, such as excerpts from film of the Kwakiutl. Set against a background of American history.

CUSTER, GEORGE ARMSTRONG

Custer: The American Surge Westward (Saga of Western Man Series)
33 min. color 1966 JSC
Prod: ABC. Dist: McGraw-Hill. Rental: Indiana, Michigan, Nebraska, Southern California, Syracuse
A dramatization of the westward movement, which recaptures the famous battle between Custer and the Indians.

DAGUERRE, LOUIS JACQUES

Daguerre; The Birth of Photography (or FACSEA Title: Daguerre
  ou la Naissance de la Photographie)
29 min.   b&w   1964   CA
Dir: Roger Leenhardt. Dist: Film Images. Rental: FACSEA
      Centers on Daguerre and his contributions to photography,
but also acknowledges the work of Niepce and Talbot. Lithographs,
drawings, rare photos and examples of their work are used.

DALEY, RICHARD

Mayor Daley: A Study in Power (CBS Reports Series)
49 min.   b&w   1972   JSC
Prod: CBS. Rental: Indiana
      His political machine in Chicago and how he controls it.

DANIEL See JOB (Prophetic Voices of the Bible)

DARRAGH, LYDIA

All's Well with Lydia: Lydia Darragh, Revolutionary War Heroine
15 min.   b&w   1952
Prod: Teaching Film Custodians. Dist: Indiana
      Relates how a Quaker widow outwitted British soldiers and
passed vital information to Washington.

DARROW, CLARENCE SEWARD
  See also BRYAN, WILLIAM JENNINGS (Darrow vs. Bryan);
  Inherit the Wind (feature)

Clarence Darrow
25 min.   b&w   1965   IJS
Prod: Metromedia Productions. Dist: Sterling (sale only; available on 8mm). Rental: South Florida, Syracuse
      His famous cases, especially the Scopes "monkey" trial.

DARWIN, CHARLES ROBERT
  See also The Darwin Adventure (feature)

Charles Darwin (Great Scientists Speak Again Series)
24 min.   color   1974   SCA
Prod. and dist: California
      Through impersonation, the life studies and writings of Dar-
win are revealed. "He" discusses the writing of The Origin of
Species, reads from his autobiography and recounts the trip to the
Galapagos Islands.

Charles Darwin--A Mind, a Concept and a Gift (Touch of Fame
  Series)
29 min.   b&w   1962   SCA
Prod: KNXT-TV.   Dist: Southern California
     A biographical sketch drawing on his diary and presented by
Dr. Herman Harvey, a psychology professor.

Darwin
26 min.   color   1970   JSC
Prod: Canadian Broadcasting Corp.   Dist: Films Inc.   Rental:
  Syracuse
     A brief sketch that re-creates the voyage of the HMS
Beagle.

Darwin and Evolution (AIBS, Life, Time and Change Series)
28 min.   color   1961   SCA
Prod: American Institute of Biological Sciences.   Rental: Minnesota, South Florida
     Summarizes his life and achievements from his days as a
student until the latter part of his life when he evolved his theories.

Darwin and the Theory of Natural Selection
12 1/2 min.   color   1967   JSC
Prod. and Dist: Coronet (sale only).   Rental: Michigan, Minnesota, Syracuse
     His voyage on the H. M. S. Beagle resulted in his discoveries
about evolution and natural selection; this film traces his steps.

Darwin's Bulldog
50 min.   color   1971   SCA
Prod: BBC-TV.   Dist: Time-Life (available on video)
     A dramatization based on eye-witness accounts taken from
the letters of well known Victorians; Huxley spoke in favor of
Darwin's The Origin of Species and Samuel Wilberforce, Bishop of
Oxford and Sir Richard Owen opposed him at the meeting of the
British Association for the Advancement of Science.

DAUGHERTY, JAMES

James Daugherty
19 min.   color   1972   CA
Prod. and dist: Weston Woods
     His home and studio, where he talks about his portraits of
well known Americans.

DAUMIER, HONORE

Daumier
14 min.   b&w   1972   JSCA
Dir: Roger Leenhardt and Henry Sarrade.   Prod: Les Films
  Roger Leenhardt.   Dist: Roland Collection

An account of his life and his prolific output of satirical lithographs; he spent six months in jail after caricaturing the king.

DAVENPORT, THOMAS

The Indomitable Blacksmith: Thomas Davenport
20 min.   b&w   1953   PIJ
Prod: Teaching Film Custodians.   Dist: Indiana (lease)
   In the 1830's he discovered how to run an electric motor, but business leaders did not heed him.

DAVID   See   MOSES (Living Personalities of the Old Testament)

DAVID, JACQUES LOUIS

Jacques Louis David (Romantic Versus Classic Art Series)
26 min.   color   1974   JSCA
Prod: Reader's Digest.   Dist: Pyramid.   Rental: Southern
   California (listed under series title)
   He brought Classicism back to life.   Illustrations of his finest works together with a discussion of the major influences of his life.   Narrated by Kenneth Clark.

DAVIS, ANGELA

Angela: Portrait of a Revolutionary
60 min. (or 35 min. version)   b&w   1971   SA
Dir: Yolande du Luart.   Dist: New Yorker
   Filmed before her arrest; she's shown teaching, relaxing at home, and at demonstrations for the Soledad Brothers.   She talks at length about her political beliefs.

DAVIS, JEFFERSON

What Might Have Been: Jefferson Davis
20 min.   b&w   1954   PIJ
Prod: Teaching Film Custodians.   Dist: Indiana
   His marriage to Knox Taylor's daughter, his life as a planter, and his brother's influence, which directed him toward a political career.   An excerpt from a Cavalcade of America television movie.

DEBUSSY, CLAUDE ACHILLE

Claude Debussy (Great Composers Series)
28 min.   color   1975   JSA
Prod: Seabourne Enterprises.   Dist: International Film Bureau.

Rental: Syracuse
An introduction to his life and music, with excerpts from "Clair de Lune" and other selections.

DEGAS, EDGAR

Ballet by Degas
10 min.   color   1952   JSCA
Dir. and Prod: J. H. Lenauer.   Dist: Macmillan
The camera studies his ballet paintings: "The Ballet Class," "On Stage," "Dancers Practicing at the Bar," and others. A music background without commentary.

Degas
7 min.   color   1973   SCA
Prod. and dist: National Gallery of Art (free loan)
Painting and graphics.

Degas
17 min.   color   1967   JSC
Prod: Not known.   Dist: Universal Education and Visual Arts.
Rental: Southern California, Syracuse
An examination of his works and techniques as an impressionist.

Degas, Master of Motion
17 min.   color   1957   SCA
Prod. and dist: Southern California.   Rental: Indiana, Michigan
His life and experimental art techniques.   Includes his later impressionist works.

Edgar Degas (Romantic Versus Classic Art Series)
26 min.   color   1974   JSCA
Prod. Reader's Digest.   Dist: Pyramid.   Rental: Southern California (listed under series title)
A study of the artist and his works, narrated by Kenneth Clark.

Monsieur Degas
20 min.   color   SCA
Dir: Robert Mazoyer.   Prod: Skira Flag Films.   Rental: FACSEA (available in French dialogue)
The relationship between dancing and his works.

DE GAULLE, CHARLES ANDRE

Charles De Gaulle
15 min.   b&w   1974
Prod: Hearst Corp.   Dist: Withdrawn by E. M. Hale.   Rental: Syracuse
Follows De Gaulle from the '30s through World War II to

his ruling years in France and his downfall and death.

Charles DeGaulle (Biography Series)
26 min.   b&w   1964   JSCA
Prod: David Wolper. Dist: Withdrawn. Rental: Michigan,
   Minnesota, Southern California, Syracuse
      Highlights his military and political careers, especially the
French refusal to adopt his military strategies.

De Gaulle vs. Petain: Struggle for France (Men in Crisis Series)
30 min.   b&w   1964   JSCA
Prod: United Artists. Dist: Films Inc. Rental: Michigan
      Petain's surrender to the Nazis, De Gaulle's victory and
Petain's trial for treason.

DE KOONING, WILLEM

Painters Painting
116 min.   b&w and color   1972   SCA
Dir. and prod: Emile DeAntonio. Dist: New Yorker
      Interviews with the artists, who discuss their art in rela-
tionship to the modern art movement, and the process of creativity;
the critics and dealers discuss their roles in the art world. In-
cludes the following: Willem de Kooning, Helen Frankenthaler,
Hans Hoffman, Jasper Johns, Robert Motherwell, Barnett Newman,
Kenneth Noland, Jules Olitski, Philip Pavia, Jackson Pollock,
Larry Poons, Robert Rauschenberg, Frank Stella, Andy Warhol,
Leo Castelli, Henry Geldzahler, Clement Greenberg, Tom Hess,
Philip Johnson, Hilton Kramer, William Rubin, and Robert Scull.
Their works were filmed at the Metropolitan Centennial Show of
American Painting, 1940-1970.

Willem De Kooning
13 min.   color   SCA
Prod: Hans Namuth and Paul Falkenberg. Dist: Film Images.
   Rental: Minnesota (title: The Painter, Willem De Kooning)
      As he works, this modern American artist comments on
his projects.

DELACROIX, EUGENE

Delacroix
12 min.   b&w   1962   C
Prod: Anthony M. Roland. Rental: Indiana
      Drawings from the Louvre, without commentary.

Delacroix: Peintre de l'Islam
15 min.   color   CA
Dir: C. Malville. Prod: Jean Cotte. Rental: FACSEA
      Excerpts from his diaries and letters during his Algerian
visit. Not to be shown in high schools!

Eugene Delacroix (Romantic Versus Classic Art Series)
26 min.   color   1974   JSCA
Prod: Reader's Digest.   Dist: Pyramid.   Rental: Southern Cali-
    fornia (listed under series title)
    A stimulating discussion of his life and work as a Romantic
artist.   Narrated by Kenneth Clark.

Le Peintre et le Poète
22 min.   color   SCA
Dir: Georges Regnier.   Prod: Fred Orain for Armor Films.
    Rental: FACSEA (available in French dialogue)
    The relationship between him and the poet Baudelaire, based
on excerpts from "Curiosités Esthétiques."

DESCARTES, RENE

René Descartes, une autobiographie
20 min.   1966   CA
Dir: Georges Rebillard.   Prod: Productions de Touraine.
    Rental: FACSEA
    French dialogue only.   Based on his autobiography, Discours
de la Méthode, the film is shot on location where he lived.

de SOTO, HERNANDO   See   CABOT, JOHN (Age of Discovery:
    Spanish and Portuguese Explorations)

DE VALERA, EAMON

Eamon De Valera (Wisdom Series)
29 min.   b&w   1965   SCA
Prod: NBC.   Dist: Films Inc.   Rental: Minnesota
    Recalls the fight for Irish independence and his role in it.

DEWEY, ADMIRAL GEORGE

Admiral Dewey's Victory at Manila (You Are There Series)
27 min.   b&w   1955   JSC
Prod: CBS.   Dist: McGraw-Hill.   Rental: Indiana, Michigan,
    Minnesota, Syracuse
    The background of the Spanish-American War is summarized
and a dramatized "on the scene" report of the victory at Manila
Bay is given by Walter Cronkite.

DEWEY, THOMAS EDMUND

Thomas E. Dewey
27 min.   b&w   1965   IJ
Prod: Metromedia Productions.   Dist: Sterling (sale only; avail-

able on 8mm). Rental: Syracuse
    Covers his political career as a prosecutor, governor, and presidential candidate through newsreel footage.

DIAZ, BARTHOLOMEU See CABOT, JOHN (Age of Discovery: Spanish and Portuguese Explorations)

DICKENS, CHARLES

The Changing World of Charles Dickens (Western Civilization Series)
26 min.   color   1970   JSCA
Prod: Allan King Associates. Dist: Learning. Rental: Indiana, Minnesota, South Florida, Syracuse
    Set against a background of 19th century England, excerpts from David Copperfield, Oliver Twist, Great Expectations and other well-known novels are dramatized.

Charles Dickens: Background for His Work
11 min.   color or b&w   1949   JSC
Prod. and dist: Coronet (special order; no previews). Rental: Indiana, Michigan, Minnesota, South Florida
    His home and haunts in London and their relationship to his works; re-enacts passages from his stories and novels.

The Charles Dickens Show
52 min.   color   1973   JSCA
Dir. and prod: Piers Jessop. Dist: International Film Bureau. Rental: Michigan, Syracuse
    A traveling magic lantern show, intercut with dramatized scenes from events in his life and scenes from Oliver Twist, David Copperfield, The Old Curiosity Shop, presents his life and works.

Dickens Chronicle
54 min.   b&w   1963   JS
Rental: Nebraska, Southern California, Syracuse
    Key events of his life are interwoven with scenes based on his writings. Sam Weller, a character from the Pickwick Papers, acts as "commentator" and discusses Victorian society and its affect on Dickens' novels.

Early Victorian England and Charles Dickens (Humanities Series)
30 min.   color   1962   SC
Prod. and dist: Encyclopaedia Britannica (available on video by special order). Rental: Indiana, Michigan, Minnesota, South Florida, Southern California
    Clifton Fadiman narrates this history of Victorian England and Dickens' place in it. Excerpts from Great Expectations, Little Dorrit, and A Christmas Carol are dramatized.

Mr. Dickens of London
52 min.   color   1968   SA
Prod: ABC.   Dist: Withdrawn by McGraw-Hill
    Sir Michael Redgrave impersonates Dickens on a tour
through London as it was in the 19th century.

DICKEY, JAMES

James Dickey: Poet--Lord, Let Me Die But Not Die Out (Humanities Series)
37 min.   color   1970   SC
Prod. and dist: Encyclopaedia Britannica (available on video by
    special order). Rental: California, Indiana, Michigan, Minnesota, South Florida, Southern California, Syracuse
    The camera follows him on a three-week poetry tour.

From the Encyclopaedia Britannica film, James Dickey: Poet.

DICKINSON, EMILY

Magic Prison: A Dialogue Set to Music (Humanities Series)
35 min.   color   1969   SC
Prod. and dist: Encyclopaedia Britannica (available on video by
    special order). Rental: California, Minnesota, Nebraska,

Southern California, Syracuse
    The letters between her and a stranger, Col. T. W. Higginson, are the basis of this drama.

DIDEROT, DENIS

Diderot
25 min.   CA
Dir: Jean Vidaz.   Prod: Ste Eurodis.   Rental: FACSEA
    French dialogue only.   Pictures representing his time reveal the story of his life and works.

DILLINGER, JOHN

Dillinger
10 min.   b&w   1974   SCA
Prod: Harry Mantel Productions.   Dist: Mar/Chuck Film
    His life, crimes, and death told through news stills.

The Last Days of John Dillinger
52 min.   color   1973   JSCA
Prod: Wolper Organization.   Dist: Films Inc.   Rental: Michigan
    Begins with his first bank robbery in Ohio and chronicles his criminal career and ultimate death at the hands of the FBI. Narrated by the late Rod Serling.

DINE, JIM

Artists: Jim Dine
30 min.   b&w   1966   SCA
Prod: NET.   Dist: Indiana
    The periods of his paintings: "tie," "tool," "bathroom," "child's room," and "palette."   He also tells why he gave up paintings for sculpture.

DISRAELI, BENJAMIN See Disraeli (feature)

DODGSON, CHARLES See CARROLL, LEWIS

DONIPHAN, ALEXANDER WILLIAM, GENERAL

General Alexander William Doniphan (Profiles in Courage Series)
50 min.   color   1965   SA
Prod: Robert Saudek Associates.   Dist: IQ Films.   Rental: Syracuse
    He refuses to obey an order to execute the Mormon prophet, Joseph Smith.

DOSTOEVSKY, FYODOR

Dostoevsky 1821-1881
54 min.　color　1976　SCA
Prod: Nielsen-Ferns.　Dist: Learning
　　　A comprehensive chronological survey of his career and the
emotional and psychological upheavals which influenced novels such
as The Idiot and Crime and Punishment.　Written and narrated by
Malcolm Muggeridge.

DOUGHTY, CHARLES MONTAGU

Charles Doughty (Age of Exploration Series)
52 min.　color　1976　SCA
Prod: BBC-TV and Time-Life.　Dist: Time-Life (available on
　video)
　　　Exploration of Arabia despite Moslem and Bedouin hostility.

From Mr. Justice Douglas (Carousel Films, Inc.)

DOUGLAS, STEPHEN ARNOLD

The Great Debate: Lincoln vs. Douglas
30 min.   color or b&w   1965   JS
Prod. and dist: Encyclopaedia Britannica (available on video by
    special order).   Rental: Indiana, Michigan, Nebraska, South
    Florida, Syracuse
        Hal Holbrook as Lincoln and Jack Bittner as Douglas re-
enact the meat of the debate.

A House Divided: The Lincoln-Douglas Debates
52 min.   color   1971   SCA
Prod: A House Divided Co.   Dist: Time-Life
        A re-enactment based on newspaper accounts of the debate.

DOUGLAS, WILLIAM O.

Mr. Justice Douglas
52 min.   b&w   1972   SCA
Prod: CBS.   Dist: Carousel (sale only).   Rental: California,
    Impact, Michigan, South Florida, Syracuse
        Talks about some of the important issues which came be-
fore the Supreme Court, such as busing, pornography, and The
Bill of Rights.

DOUGLASS, FREDERICK
    See also BROWN, WILLIAM WELLS (Slavery and Slave Re-
    sistance)

The Angry Prophet: Frederick Douglass
24 min.   color   1970   SCA
Prod: WRC-TV.   Dist: Films Inc.
        The story of how and why he became a black spokesman of
his time.

Frederick Douglass
9 min.   color   1971   IJS
Prod. and dist: Encyclopaedia Britannica (available on video by
    special order).   Rental: Syracuse
        His contributions as a champion of freedom for blacks.

Frederick Douglass (Profiles in Courage Series)
50 min.   b&w   1966   JSCA
Prod: Robert Saudek Associates.   Dist: IQ Films.   Rental:
    California, Michigan, Syracuse
        Fights for the freedom of other blacks at great risk to him-
self.

Frederick Douglass: The House on Cedar Hill
17 min.   b&w   1953   SCA
Prod: Carlton Moss. Dist: Withdrawn by McGraw-Hill. Rental:
California (listed by sub-title), Michigan, Southern California
A biography based on Douglass' writings; the musical score
is based on black folk songs.

DOYLE, SIR ARTHUR CONAN

Sir Arthur Conan Doyle Speaks for Movietone News
12 min.   b&w   1927
Prod: Fox Movietone News. Rental: Images
Reconstructed from the only sound film made of him and
from new footage.

DRAKE, SIR FRANCIS
See also CABOT, JOHN (Age of Discovery: English, French,
and Dutch Explorations)

Sir Francis Drake: The Rise of English Sea Power
30 min.   b&w   1957   IJS
Prod. and dist: Encyclopaedia Britannica (available on video by
special order). Rental: Indiana, Michigan, Minnesota, Nebraska, Southern California
Authentic settings are used to recreate events of his life
which helped England rule the sea.

Sir Francis Drake's Life and Voyages
14 min.   b&w   1956   JSC
Prod. and dist: Coronet (officially withdrawn; sale only; no previews). Rental: Indiana, Michigan, Minnesota, Nebraska
His life and exploration of the New World and the obstacles
and difficulties, such as the crude equipment.

DREW, DR. CHARLES

The Hurdler
16 min.   color   1970   JSCA
Prod. and dist: Rediscovery Productions
How the creator of the Blood Bank fought racism.

DREXLER, ROSALYN

Who Does She Think She Is?
60 min.   color   1974   CA
Dir: Patricia Lewis Jaffee and Gaby Rodgers. Dist: New Yorker
A candid documentary about her life as a novelist, playwright, painter, singer, wife and mother, in which she also acts
out her fantasies.

DREYFUS, ALFRED

The Dreyfus Affair
15 min.   b&w   1972   JSCA
Prod. and dist: Texture Films.   Rental: Minnesota, Viewfinders
        Contemporaneous graphics are used to tell the story of this
French army officer accused of treason.

DU BARRY, MARIE JEANNE See   Madame Du Barry (feature)

DUCHAMP, MARCEL

Marcel Duchamp (Wisdom Series)
30 min.   b&w   1958   SCA
Prod: NBC. Dist: Films Inc.   Rental: Minnesota, Nebraska,
    South Florida, Southern California
        Discusses his work, especially "Nude Descending the Stair-
case. "

DUCHIN, EDDY See   The Eddy Duchin Story (feature)

DUFY, RAOUL

The Invisible Moustache of Raoul Dufy
9 min.   color   1955   I
Prod: UPA. Dist: Macmillan
        An amusing, animated biography of painter Dufy.

DUMAS, ALEXANDRE

Alexandre Dumas
53 min.   SCA
Dir: Roland Darbois. Prod: ORTF. Rental: FACSEA
        His life and works, with numerous excerpts from film
adaptations of his novels.

DUNBAR, PAUL LAURENCE

Paul Laurence Dunbar
23 min.   color   1972   JSCA
Dir: Carlton Moss. Dist: Pyramid. Rental: Southern California
        Pictures, paintings, African art, and dramatization are all
utilized to reveal the poet and his poetry.

Paul Laurence Dunbar: American Poet
14 min.   color   1966   IJSA
Prod: Vignette Films. Dist: BFA. Rental: Minnesota, Syracuse

The forces which shaped his life and writings, with excerpts from his poems and plays.

DUNOYER, ANDRE

Dunoyer de Segonzac
18 min.   color   CA
Dir: Francois Reichenback.   Prod: Pierre Braunberger.   Rental: FACSEA
French dialogue only.   An interview with this landscape artist.

DÜRER, ALBRECHT

Albrecht Dürer
10 min.   b&w   1970   SCA
Prod: BBC-TV.   Dist: Time-Life (special sale orders only; no previews or rentals)
Combines a narrative taken directly from his book with an examination of his masterpieces.

Dürer and the Renaissance
15 min.   color   1962   SCA
Prod: Information not available.   Dist: Withdrawn by McGraw-Hill.   Rental: Minnesota, Southern California, Syracuse
How this German painter was greatly influential in the Northern Renaissance movement.

DYER, MARY

In a Violent Time
20 min.   color   1974   JSA
Prod. and dist: Agency for Instructional Television (available on 3/4" videocassette)
A dramatic presentation of Anne Hutchinson and Mary Dyer, both of whom spoke out for religious freedom.

EARHART, AMELIA

Amelia Earhart
25 min.   b&w   1965   PIJS
Prod: CBS.   Dist: Sterling (sale only; available on 8mm).
Rental: Insight Exchange, Syracuse
Begins with her childhood, stresses her accomplishments and feminism and ends with her disappearance on a lone flight. Utilizes some newsreel footage.

The Mystery of Amelia Earhart (You Are There Series)
22 min.   color   1972   IJS

Prod: CBS. Dist: BFA. Rental: Syracuse
      A dramatization of her disappearance over the Pacific Ocean
in 1937 while making an attempt to be the first woman to fly
around the world.

EARL OF ESSEX   See   ELIZABETH I (Elizabeth R.)

EARL OF LEICESTER   See   ELIZABETH I (Elizabeth R.)

EARP, WYATT

Heroes and Villains
30 min.   b&w   1964   IJSCA
Prod: NET. Dist: Indiana. Rental: Minnesota
      The stories of the heroes and villains of the Old West--
Wyatt Earp, Ben Thompson, Bat Masterston, Wild Bill Hickok--
and the realities.

EBAN, ABBA

A Conversation with Abba Eban
27 min.   color   1973   SA
Prod. and dist: Anti-Defamation League
      Israel's foreign minister discusses his country's role in the
world.

EDEN, ANTHONY

Anthony Eden
26 min.   b&w   1964
Prod: CBS. Dist: Association

EDISON, THOMAS ALVA
   See also Edison the Man (feature); Young Tom Edison (feature)

Boyhood of Thomas Edison
14 min.   b&w or color   1964   PI
Prod. and dist: Coronet (sale only). Rental: Indiana, Michigan,
   Minnesota, Syracuse
      Photographed in Greenfield Village and his home in Milan,
Ohio. Incidents from his childhood, which led to his career as an
inventor, are dramatized.

Edison, Persistent Genius
16 min.   color   1965   IJ
Prod: Dave Estes. Dist: Aims. Rental: South Florida, Southern
   California

Stresses his tenacity in developing electric lighting.

The Impact of Thomas Edison
26 min.   color   1973   SCA
Prod: Koplin and Grinker.   Dist: Pictura
A visit to his former home in Glenmont, N.J., where his co-workers talk about him and his inventions such as the light bulb and the phonograph.

Let There Be Light
15 min.   b&w   1952-53   JSCA
Prod: Mike Sklar.   Dist: Star Film
A pictorial account of his many inventions such as the phonograph and moving pictures.   Compiled from the Fox Movietone News Library.

A Man Called Edison
30 min.   b&w   1971
Dir: Dennis Atkinson.   Rental: Kit Parker Films
His early years in cinema with emphasis on the 1890's; film clips of the period are included.

The Man Called Edison
28 min.   b&w   1972   SCA
Prod: Spectra Films.   Dist: Sterling (sale only; available on 8mm)
His contributions to the motion picture industry are shown through early Kinetoscope films.

Thomas Alva Edison (Biography Series)
26 min.   b&w   1963   JS
Prod: David Wolper.   Dist: McGraw-Hill.   Rental: Indiana, Michigan, Minnesota, Southern California
Updated in 1968, the title was changed to Thomas Edison. Both films show his boyhood through his death with emphasis on his inventions.

Thomas Edison
21 min.   b&w   1975   JSCA
Prod: Hearst.   Dist: Counselor
His biography shown through newsreels, feature films and home movies.

The Wizard Who Spat on the Floor: Thomas Alva Edison
60 min.   color   1974   SCA
Prod: BBC-TV.   Dist: Time-Life (available on video or in a 41-minute version)
An interview with his only living daughter and actual footage of famous moments in his life are included in this study.   The drama and philosophy of his inventions such as the stock-ticker and the light bulb come to life.

EDMONDS, WALTER D.

Walter D. Edmonds: The Presence of the Past (Writers on Writing Series)
18 min.   color   1972   S
Prod: Davidson Films. Dist: General Learning
     He talks about how he used the history of New York to
write such books as Drums Along the Mohawk and how he overcame a series of problems suffered in mid-career, including writer's block.

EDWARD III See EDWARD II (feature)

EDWARD VIII (DUKE OF WINDSOR)

For Love of a Woman
15 min.   b&w   1952-53   JSCA
Prod: Mike Sklar. Dist: Star Film
     The story of how and why he gave up his throne; compiled
from the Fox Movietone News Library.

The Windsors
26 min.   b&w   1965   SA
Prod: CBS. Dist: Association. Rental: Syracuse
     His childhood, his romance with Wallis Warfield Simpson,
whom he married, and his abdication of the throne.

EDWARDS, JONATHAN

A Gathering of One
60 min.   color
Prod: NBC. Dist: National Council of Churches
     A dramatization about Jonathan Edwards, who is considered
to be America's first theologian. He fought against religious dog-
ma.

EIFFEL, ALEXANDRE GUSTAVE

The Unknown Eiffel
28 min.   color   1975   JSC
Dir: Joan Laskoff. Prod: Lenox Art Corp. Dist: Films Inc.
  (available in French)
     The life of Gustave Eiffel, the man who created the world-
famous Tower in Paris. Also shows the viaducts, bridges, cathedrals and buildings he designed.

EINSTEIN, ALBERT

Albert Einstein (Biography Series)
16 min.   color   1970   IJSCA
Prod: McGraw-Hill in collaboration with Project 7 Films.   Dist:
   McGraw-Hill.   Rental: Indiana, Minnesota
      His life including his childhood in Germany, where his
teachers thought him "slow." Discusses his famous theories and
their implications.

From Albert Einstein in the Biography Series (McGraw-Hill Films)

Albert Einstein--People, Humanity and Science (Touch of Fame
   Series)
29 min.   b&w   1962   SCA
Prod: KNXT-TV. Dist: Southern California
      An analysis of Einstein and his theories and accomplish-
ments, by Dr. Herman Harvey of USC. A kinescope.

Albert Einstein: The Education of a Genius
44 min.   color   1975   SC
Prod: Harold Mantell. Dist: Films for the Humanities (available on 3/4" videocassette)
      Emphasizes his childhood, when he established a reputation
as a non-conformist, who later dropped out of high school. Uses
his own recollections to describe his scientific accomplishments.
Narrated by Peter Ustinov.

Dr. Einstein Before Lunch (Human Dimension Series)
50 min.   color   1974   JSCA
Prod: NBC. Dist: Graphic Curriculum (may be shown on closed
    circut television)
        The young Einstein; his theory of relativity and a defense
of his role in the development of the atomic bomb.

Einstein: The Story of the Man Told by Friends
42 min.   b&w   1969   CA
Prod: BBC-TV. Dist: Time-Life (available on video)
        The first full-length biographical film on him, it features
interviews with his friends and colleagues. Banesh Hoffman, an
aide, clearly explains the theory of relativity.

EISENHOWER, DWIGHT DAVID

America Elects a New President--Dwight D. Eisenhower
12 min.   b&w   1952   JSCA
Prod: Hearst. Dist: Counselor
        Newsreel footage of the elections, his meeting with Truman,
and his visit to Korea.

Dwight David Eisenhower
14 min.   b&w   1975   JSCA
Prod: Hearst. Dist: Counselor
        A portrait, as military leader and as President.

Dwight David Eisenhower (Biography Series)
26 min.   b&w   1963   JSC
Prod: David Wolper. Dist: McGraw-Hill. Rental: Indiana,
    Michigan, Minnesota, Southern California, Syracuse
        His career, beginning with his student days at West Point
and following him through two terms as President.

Dwight D. Eisenhower: From Soldier to President (The History
    Makers Series)
19 min.   b&w   1974   JSCA
Prod: American School and Library Films. Dist: ACI
        A brief sketch of his early life, his career as a soldier
and his election to the Presidency.

Dwight D. Eisenhower: The Presidential Years (The History
    Makers Series)
19 min.   b&w   1974   JSCA
Prod: American School and Library Films. Dist: ACI
        Ike's handling of important events, such as the integration
of Little Rock's schools, and his re-election.

The Eisenhower Years
22 min.   b&w   1963   SCA
Prod: Teaching Film Custodians. Dist: Indiana. Rental: Cali-
    fornia, Michigan, Minnesota

From Dwight D. Eisenhower: From Soldier to President (ACI Media, Inc.)

Newsreel footage of the important events and accomplishments of his administration.

Famous Generals (a series)
28 min. each   1963
Prod. and dist: Dept. of the Army (cleared for television; free loan)
Eisenhower traces his military career but not the Presidency. MacArthur emphasizes World War II. Marshall traces his career including his assignment as Secretary of State. Patton emphasizes his military career during World War II. Pershing traces his career from 1900 to retirement. Stilwell shows his military leadership in the Far East during World War II.

Five Presidents on the Presidency
24 min.   color   1974   JSCA
Prod: CBS. Dist: BFA. Rental: Michigan, Southern California
Eisenhower, Kennedy, Wilson and Truman and Nixon talk

about the duties, limitations and problems of the Presidency, with varying degrees of candor.

The Impact of Eisenhower (2 parts)
26 min. each   color   1973   SCA
Prod: Koplin and Grinker.   Dist: Pictura
        The Military Man (part I) reviews his military career; his wife Mamie recalls his early years and Charles Blair also talks with his colleagues.   In The Statesman (part II) Mamie talks about his days as a college president and his decision to run for President.

EISENSTEIN, SERGEI

Eisenstein: His Life and Times
50 min.   b&w   1958   SCA
Prod: BF. Dist: Cinema Eight
        An in-depth portrait is combined with scenes from several of his classic films including "Alexander Nevksy" and "Ivan the Terrible."

Sergei Eisenstein
50 min.   b&w   1958   JSCA
Prod: V. Katanyan at the Central Documentary Film Studios,
    Moscow. Dist: Macmillan (life of print lease). Rental: California, Kit Parker, Syracuse
        A biography dealing with his life, his theatrical productions such as "Bezhin Meadow," and his major films, which are excerpted.

EL GRECO See GRECO

ELEANOR OF AQUITAINE See The Lion in Winter (feature)

ELIJAH See JOB (Prophetic Voices of the Bible)

ELIOT, THOMAS STEARNS

The Mysterious Mr. Eliot
62 min. (2 pts)   color   1973   SCA
Prod: BBC and WNET. Dist: McGraw-Hill. Rental: Michigan,
    Southern California
        A blend of documentary footage, interviews, and dramatic episodes reveals the connection between his life and poetry.
Scenes from Murder in the Cathedral and highlights from the plays Sweeney Agonistes and The Family Reunion. Robert Lowell and Stephen Spender reminisce about him.

From The Mysterious Mr. Eliot (McGraw-Hill Films)

ELIZABETH I
See also Mary of Scotland; Mary, Queen of Scots; The Virgin Queen; Young Bess (all features)

Elizabeth R (6 pts)
90 min. each color 1976 SCA
Prod: BBC-TV. Dist: Time-Life (available on video)
    Stars Glenda Jackson and follows Elizabeth's transition from a young, pretty princess to an old unattractive woman. The Lion's Club (pt. 1) portrays her during the brief reigns of her brother and sister and her imprisonment in the Tower. The Marriage Game (pt. 2) is her romance with the Earl of Leicester. Shadow in the Sun (pt. 3) dramatizes her flirtation with the Duke of Alençon, heir to the throne of France. Horrible Conspiracies (pt. 4) covers the plot against her and Mary's execution. The Enterprise of England (pt. 5) is the defeat of the Armada, and Sweet England's Pride (pt. 6) depicts her romance with the Earl

of Essex and her death.

Elizabeth: The Queen Who Shaped an Age (Western Civilization Series)
27 min.   color   1971   JSCA
Prod: John Secondari and Helen Jean Rogers. Dist: Learning.
  Rental: Indiana, Michigan, Minnesota, Nebraska, South Florida, Syracuse
      The incredible half-century reign of a woman who trans-
formed England into a power nation, and who uncovered many plots
against her.   Played by Frances Cuka, the film was shot at Hever
Castle, home of her mother, and the dialogue is based on actual
documents.

Hamlet: The Age of Elizabeth (Humanities Series)
31 min.   color   1959   SC
Prod: and dist: Encyclopaedia Britannica (special order only; no
  previews). Rental: Indiana, Michigan, Nebraska
      A history of the period combined with a study of her per-
sonality, the life of Shakespeare, and the history of the Elizabethan
theater.

Tudor Period (English History Series)
10 min.   color or b&w   1954   JS
Prod. and dist: Coronet. Rental: Indiana, Michigan, Minnesota,
  Nebraska
      The highlights of the reigns of Henry VII, Henry VIII, and
Elizabeth I.

ELLINGTON, EDWARD KENNEDY (DUKE)

Duke Ellington Swings Through Japan
26 min.   b&w
Prod: CBS. Dist: Association
      A musical portrait of the well-known musician on tour.

ELLIS, ALBERT

Three Approaches to Psychotherapy (3 parts)
32-50 min.   b&w
Prod. and dist: Psychological Films. Rental: Minnesota
      Carl Rogers, Founder of Client-Centered Therapy (pt. 1,
48 min.), Frederick Perls, Founder of Gestalt Therapy (pt. 2,
32 min.) and Albert Ellis, Founder of Rational-Emotive Therapy
(pt. 3, 50 min.) are the three parts; in each the therapist treats
a 30-year old divorced woman according to his method.

ELLISON, RALPH

Novel: Ralph Ellison on Work in Progress

30 min.   b&w   1966   JSCA
Prod: NET. Dist: Indiana. Rental: California
    An interview in which he discusses his philosophy of writing, the black church and American literature in general.

ELLSBERG, DANIEL

The Pentagon Papers: Conversations with Daniel Ellsberg
30 min.   b&w   n. d.
Dir. and prod: Jerry Stoll. Dist: Impact
    Ellsberg's change from a dedicated government worker to a concerned public citizen.

The Pentagon Papers and American Democracy: Conversations
   with Daniel Ellsberg
40 min.   b&w   1972   CA
Prod: Tony Grutman. Dist: Macmillan
    Reveals his involvement with the growing military-industrial complex and the reasons he disclosed the secret Pentagon Papers.

ELY, RICHARD T.

Richard T. Ely (Profiles in Courage Series)
50 min.   b&w   1964   IJSA
Prod: Robert Saudek Associates. Dist: IQ Films. Rental:
   Michigan, Syracuse
    Challenges his students to think for themselves.

EMERSON, RALPH WALDO

Books Alive: Ralph Waldo Emerson
6 min.   color   1969   SCA
Prod: Turnley Walker. Dist: BFA. Rental: Syracuse
    Actor Eduard Franz portrays Emerson in a lecture hall, where he answers questions posed by an offscreen actor.

ERIC THE RED

Vanished Vikings: Eric the Red
15 min.   color   1973   JSCA
Prod. and dist: Journal Films. Rental: Minnesota
    Traces his voyages. Toynbee and other historians comment on the Viking explorations. Emphasizes the Viking way of life.

ERIKSON, ERIK

Interview with Professor Erik Erikson (2 parts)

50 min. each   b&w   1971   C
Prod: Dr. Richard Evans. Dist: Macmillan (sale only). Rental:
  Association, South Florida, California (title is Professor Erik
  Erikson)
          In part 1 he talks about his eight stages of psychosocial de-
velopment; in part 2, the libido theory, ego, leadership qualities,
man's survival.

ERNST, MAX

Max Ernst--Journey into the Subconscious
11 1/2 min.   color   1972   JSCA
Dir: Peter Schamoni and Dr. Carl Lamb.   Prod: Peter Schamoni.
  Dist: Roland Collection
          Commentary by Ernst himself; the film focuses on his in-
ner world and surreal paintings.

ESCHER, MAURITS C.

Adventures in Perception
21 min.   color   1973   JSCA
Prod: Hans Van Gelder Film Production.   Dist: BFA.   Rental:
  Syracuse
          An introduction to some of his most important paintings.

Maurits Escher: Painter of Fantasies
26 1/2 min.   color   1970   SCA
Prod: Document Associates.   Dist: Perspective (sale only).
  Rental: California, Indiana, Michigan, Syracuse
          His art and his philosophy.

ESTHER

Queen Esther
50 min.   b&w   1947   JSCA
Prod: Cathedral.   Rental: Catholic Film Center
          Based on the Biblical Book of Esther, it shows how Esther
asks for and receives mercy for the Jews.

EVANS, WALKER

Walker Evans--His Time, His Presence, His Silence
22 min.   b&w   1970   SCA
Dir: Sedat Pakay.   Dist: Film Images
          Filmed at his home in Old Lyme, Connecticut, this out-
standing American photographer talks about America, past and
present, about his earlier years, and about photography.

EVERGOOD, PHILIP

Philip Evergood
19 min.   color   1952   CA
Dir: Howard Bird. Dist: Macmillan.   Rental: Indiana, Syracuse
        The scope of his art work.

EYCK, HUBERT VAN

Van Eyck: Father of Flemish Painting
26 1/2 min.   color   1974   SCA
Dir: Jean Cleinge. Prod: Rosobel and the International Film
    Bureau. Dist: International Film Bureau
        "The Arnolfini Wedding" and "The Adoration of the Lamb"
and the personal style of his paintings.

EZEKIEL See JOB (Prophetic Voices of the Bible)

EZRA See MOSES (Living Personalities of the Old Testament)

FAULKNER, WILLIAM

Faulkner's Mississippi--Land Into Legend
32 min.   color   1965   JSC
Prod. and dist: University of Mississippi.   Rental: South Florida
        Scenes of Mississippi, pictures of Faulkner and his home
are shown as Joseph Cotten reads quotations from Faulkner's works.

William Faulkner
17 min.   b&w   n.d.   IJSCA
Prod: Robert Saudek. Dist: IQ Films
        At home in Oxford, Mississippi he speaks to high school
students.   This is the only film record of him.

William Faulkner's Mississippi
49 min.   b&w   1967   JSCA
Prod: Metro Media TV. Dist: Benchmark. Rental: California,
    Michigan, Minnesota, Syracuse, Viewfinders
        Recreates his background and his mixed feelings towards
the South.   Includes readings from several of his books: Intruder
in the Dust, Requiem for a Nun, The Hamlet, The Sound and the
Fury, and The Town. Narrated by Montgomery Clift.

FELLINI, FEDERICO

Ciao Federico!
60 min.   color   1970   SCA
Dir: Gideon Bachmann. Prod: Victor Herbert. Dist: Macmillan.

Rental: California, Syracuse
Filmed during the shooting of "Satyricon." Includes interviews with him and the cast and footage of the film. Italian and English dialogue.

Federico Fellini: The Director as Creator
29 min.   b&w   1969   SC
Prod: Harold Mantel and RAI.   Dist: Films for the Humanities
    (available on 3/4" videocassette)
    At work on "Juliet of the Spirits."

Fellini: A Director's Notebook
52 min.   color   1969   SCA
Prod: NBC.   Dist: Films Inc.   Rental: California, Indiana,
    Pyramid, Twyman

FENELON, FRANÇOIS DE SALIGNAC DE LA MOTHE-

Fénelon
48 min.   SCA
Dir: Roland Bernard.   Prod: ORTF.   Rental: FACSEA
    Traces his life and emphasizes his free spirit.

FERLINGHETTI, LAWRENCE

Allen Ginsberg and Lawrence Ferlinghetti (Poetry Series)
30 min.   b&w   1966   SCA
Prod: NET.   Dist: Indiana.   Rental: California
    Two poets depicted in their San Francisco environment.
Readings from their poetry are included.

FERMI, ENRICO

Enrico Fermi (Biography Series)
15 min.   color   1970   IJSCA
Prod: McGraw-Hill in collaboration with Project 7 Films.   Dist:
    McGraw-Hill
    Traces his life from childhood in Italy to his achievements
in nuclear energy, which won him a Nobel Prize.

FIELD, CYRUS W.

Great Gamble: Cyrus W. Field
20 min.   b&w   1954
Prod: Teaching Film Custodians.   Dist: Indiana (lease)
    How he tried to organize the Transatlantic cable.

FISH, HAMILTON

Secretary of State Hamilton Fish (Profiles in Courage Series)
50 min.   b&w   1965   SA
Prod: Robert Saudek Associates.   Dist: IQ Films.   Rental:
    Syracuse
        Defends his no-war policy over Cuba, which jeopardized his
political career.

FITZGERALD, FRANCIS SCOTT   See   Beloved Infidel (feature)

FLACK, ROBERTA

Roberta Flack (Artists in America Series)
30 min.   color   1971   SCA
Prod: Public Television Library.   Dist: Indiana.   Rental: Cali-
    fornia, Impact
        A portrait which includes several of her songs such as
"Ain't No Mountain High." She also reveals the problems of a
mixed marriage and dual careers.

Roberta Flack (Artists in America Series)
11 min.   color   1971   SCA
Prod: FilmFair Communications.   Rental: Indiana
        She and her husband discuss the problems of a mixed mar-
riage.   She sings at the Newport Jazz Festival and at a nightspot
in Washington, D.C.

FLAHERTY, FRANCES

Frances Flaherty: Hidden and Seeking
56 min.   b&w   1972   SCA
Dir: Peter Werner.   Dist: Withdrawn.   Rental: Michigan
        The wife of filmmaker Robert Flaherty at home on her
farm.

FLAHERTY, ROBERT   See   FLAHERTY, FRANCES (Frances Fla-
    herty: Hidden and Seeking)

FONG, HIRAM

Hiram Fong (Biography Series)
15 min.   color   1970   IJSCA
Prod: McGraw-Hill in collaboration with Project 7 Films.   Dist:
    McGraw-Hill
        The story of how he overcame his poverty to become the
first Oriental Senator.

From <u>Hiram Fong</u> in the Biography Series (McGraw-Hill Films).

FONTEYN, MARGOT

<u>Margot Fonteyn</u>
53 min.   color   1976   JSCA
Dir: Keith Money.   Prod: Degamo Productions.   Dist: Audley
   Square
        The only film of her, it combines specially filmed dance
sequences with a portrait of her.   She and Rudolf Nureyev perform
a pas de deux, she dances the "Birthday Offering" with Viktor Rona
and she also performs a sequence from "Sleeping Beauty."

FORD, HENRY

<u>Henry Ford</u> (Biography Series)
26 min.   b&w   1963   IJSCA
Prod: David Wolper.   Dist: Withdrawn by McGraw-Hill.   Rental:

Michigan, Minnesota, Southern California, Syracuse
Emphasizes his contributions to mass production via the assembly line.

Henry Ford
24 min.   b&w   1975   JSCA
Prod: Hearst. Dist: Counselor
His story and the impact he had on our society.

The Mark of a Man
15 min.   b&w   1952-53   JSCA
Prod: Mike Sklar. Dist: Star Film
His life as told through Fox Movietone News Library footage.

FORD, JOHN

Directed by John Ford
102 min.   color   1973   SCA
Prod: American Film Institute. Dist: Films Inc. (lease or
    rental)
A study of Ford and his films. Interviews with Ford,
Henry Fonda, James Stewart and John Wayne are combined with
segments from his films beginning with "Straight Shooting."

FORMAN, MILOS

Meeting Milos Forman
30 min.   color   1972   SCA
Prod: Miriam Hetlar Weingarten. Dist: Macmillan. Rental:
    Syracuse
An interview in which he tells several anecdotes. Filmed
shortly after he completed "Taking Off," his first American film;
clips from it and "Loves of a Blonde" and "The Fireman's Ball"
are included.

FOSTER, STEPHEN COLLINS

Stephen Foster and His Songs
16 1/2 min.   color   1960   JSCA
Prod. and dist: Coronet (sale only). Rental: Indiana, Michigan,
    Nebraska, Syracuse
A portrait of his life which highlights his disappointments
and the backgrounds of his best known songs.

Stephen Foster's Footprints in Dream and Song
14 1/2 min.
Dist: Florida Dept. of Commerce (free loan)
His story filmed at Stephen Foster Memorial at White
Springs, Florida. Includes his songs.

FRANCIS OF ASSISI See Brother Sun, Sister Moon (feature);
 Francis of Assisi (feature); St. Francis of Assisi (feature)

FRANCIS I (OF FRANCE)

François 1er
31 min.   SCA
Dir: Michel Ayats.   Prod: ORTF.   Rental: FACSEA
 His reign, the Renaissance and the famous Chateauxes.

FRANCO, FRANCISCO

Francisco Franco
13 1/2 min.   b&w   1974
Prod: Hearst. Dist: Withdrawn by E. M. Hale.   Rental: Syracuse
 Begins in 1936 with his rebellion and ultimate rise to power.

Franco (Biography Series)
26 min.   b&w   1963   SCA
Prod: David Wolper. Dist: Withdrawn by McGraw-Hill.   Rental:
 Minnesota, Southern California, Syracuse
 His rise to power, and the conditions in Spain during the
early '60s.

FRANK, ANNE
 See also Diary of Anne Frank (feature)

Legacy of Anne Frank
29 min.   color   1968   JSCA
Prod: NBC. Dist: McGraw-Hill.   Rental: Michigan
 Combines on-location shots with documentary footage to tell
her story as a young girl.

FRANKENTHALER, HELEN See DE KOONING, WILLEM (Painters
 Painting)

FRANKLIN, ARETHA

Aretha Franklin, Soul Singer
25 min.   color   1969   JSCA
Prod: ABC. Dist: McGraw-Hill.   Rental: Michigan
 A behind-the-scenes profile of her at rehearsals, rap ses-
sions with friends, on stage and at home.   Based on the ABC News
Special "The Singers: Two Profiles."

Aretha Franklin, Soul Singer (McGraw-Hill Films)

FRANKLIN, BENJAMIN

Benjamin Franklin
17 min.   b&w   1962   IJS
Prod. and dist: Encyclopaedia Britannica (available on video by
    special request). Rental: Indiana, Michigan (1949 version),
    Minnesota, Nebraska, South Florida, Southern California, Syra-
    cuse
        Highlights his roles as statesman, scientist, inventor and
writer.

Benjamin Franklin: Scientist, Statesman, Scholar and Sage (Ameri-
    cana Series #5)
30 min.   color   1969   IJSCA
Prod: Leo A. Handel. Dist: Handel. Rental: Syracuse
        Emphasizes his versatility by explaining his role in the de-
velopment of the postal system, his many inventions, and his roles
as an ambassador and a revolutionary.

Crisis in Paris: Franklin's Diplomatic Mission
20 min.   b&w   1955   JS
Prod: Teaching Film Custodians. Dist: Indiana (lease)
        A dramatization of how and why Franklin maintained cordial
relationships with the French, though at first they refused him aid.
Excerpt from the Cavalcade of America television movie.

In All Cases Whatsoever (Decades of Decision: The American
    Revolution Series)
35 min.   color   1975   IJS
Prod: WQED, Pittsburgh. Dist: National Geographic Society
    (available on videocassette)
        He argues for repeal of the Stamp Act before the British
Parliament.

Poor Richard: Benjamin Franklin
10 min.   b&w   1952   PIJS
Prod: Teaching Film Custodians. Dist: Indiana (lease)
        Franklin stalls the British long enough for Washington to
withdraw from a possible British encirclement. An excerpt from
a Cavalcade of America television movie.

FREMONT, JOHN CHARLES

John Charles Frémont
18 min.   b&w   1950   JS
Prod. Encyclopaedia Britannica. Dist: Withdrawn by EB.
    Rental: Indiana, Michigan, Minnesota, Nebraska, Southern
    California, Syracuse
        A dramatization of the key events of his life: his work as
an explorer and map-maker, his association with Kit Carson, his
role in the Mexican and Civil Wars, his run for the Presidency,
and his appointment as governor of the territory of Arizona.

FREUD, SIGMUND
See also JUNG, CARL GUSTAV (Discussion with Dr. Carl G.
Jung; and Jung Speaks of Freud); Freud (feature)

Freud: The Hidden Nature of Man (Western Civilization Series)
29 min.   color   1970   SCA
Dir: George Kaczender. Dist: Learning (available in Spanish).
    Rental: Indiana, Minnesota, South Florida, Southern California,
    Syracuse
        His theories are explored as the film cuts back and forth
between live action and photographs. He talks about his own
dreams.

Sigmund Freud: His Offices and Home, Vienna 1938
17 min.   color   1974   SCA
Prod: Gene Friedman. Dist: Filmmakers Library
        Photographs and stock footage are used to explore the
premises where he lived and worked for over 45 years.

Sigmund Freud--The View from Within (Touch of Fame Series)
29 min.   b&w   1962   SCA
Prod: KNXT-TV. Dist: Southern California
        Dr. Herman Harvey, a psychology professor, traces
Freud's life and the inner thoughts which prompted his theories.
A kinescope.

FRIEDAN, BETTY

Women Talking
80 min.   b&w   1971   CA
Dir: Midge MacKenzie. Dist: Impact
        Several women talk about their experiences and analyze the
sexual bias existing in society.

FROBISHER, SIR MARTIN See CABOT, JOHN (Age of Discovery:
    English, French, and Dutch Explorations)

FROMM, ERICH

Interview With Dr. Erich Fromm.   2 pts.   (Notable Contributors
    Series)
50 min. each   b&w   1971   C
Prod: Dr. Richard Evans. Dist: Macmillan (sale only). Rental:
    Association, California, South Florida, Syracuse
        In part 1 he discusses what makes individuals productive
and escape devices; the second part presents his approach to psychotherapy.

FROST, ROBERT

Autumn: Frost Country
9 min.   color   1969   JSCA
Prod: Pyramid Films. Dist: BFA.   Rental: Nebraska
    A film essay of "The Road Not Taken" and "Reluctance,"
read by Frost.

A Lover's Quarrel with the World
40 min.   b&w   1967   SCA
Prod: WGBH-TV and Holt, Rinehart and Winston.   Dist: BFA.
  Rental: California, Indiana, Michigan, Minnesota, Nebraska,
  Southern California, Syracuse, Twyman

Robert Frost
28 min.
Prod: U.S. Information Agency.   Rental: Pyramid

Robert Frost (Wisdom Series)
30 min.   b&w   1958   SCA
Prod: NBC. Dist: Films Inc.   Rental: Michigan (Title: Conversation with Robert Frost), Minnesota, Nebraska, Syracuse
    He discusses his personal experiences as a mill worker,
as a teacher, cobbler, small-town editor, and farmer and how they
affected his poetry.   He reads "Stopping by the Woods on a Snowy
Evening" and "The Drumlin Woodchuck. "

Robert Frost (Poetry by Americans Series)
10 min.   color   1972   JSC
Prod: Art Evans. Dist: Paramount Oxford.   Rental: Nebraska,
  Syracuse
    Actor Leonard Nimoy reads the poem "Mending Wall" fol-
lowing a short biographical sketch.

Robert Frost: A First Acquaintance
16 min.   color   1975   IJSA
Prod: Harold Mantell. Dist: Films for the Humanities (available
  on 3/4" videocassette)
    Scenes of Frost reading his poems are intercut with scenes
of his daughter Lesley in a classroom, where she talks about her
father and the origins and locales of his poems.

FRY, HAYDEN

Hayden Fry
22 min.   color   1973   SCA
Prod: Tele-Sports. Dist: Paramount Oxford
    A sports profile.

FULLER, R. BUCKMINSTER

Buckminster Fuller
90 min.   color   1971   CA
Dir. and prod: Robert Synder.   Dist: Center for Learning Re-
    sources
    A record and lecture of his philosophy.

I Seem to Be a Verb
23 min.   color   1975   SCA
Prod: Lester Berman and Arden Rynew.   Dist: Texture
    A film interpretation of the book of the same title, which
features Fuller and presents his basic ideas.

R. Buckminster Fuller: Prospects for Humanity
30 min.   b&w   1967   CA
Prod: NET.   Dist: Indiana.   Rental: California, Nebraska
    His predictions as expressed in three college speeches.

FULTON, ROBERT

Persistent Mr. Fulton (Meet the Inventors)
7 min.   color   1968   PI
Prod: UPA.   Dist: Macmillan.   Rental: Syracuse
    An old river boat captain tells a small girl how Fulton
persisted in his efforts to build a steamboat despite initial failure.
Animated.

GAINES, ERNEST J.

Ernest J. Gaines: Bloodlines in Ink (Writers on Writing Series)
18 min.   color   1972   S
Prod: Davidson Films.   Dist: General Learning Corp.
    The black author of The Autobiography of Miss Jane Pitt-
man tells how his early background influenced his work and how
Hemingway, Faulkner, Flaubert and others helped him learn about
the craft of writing.   Concretely explains his steps in writing.

GAINSBOROUGH, THOMAS

Gainsborough
37 min.   color   1971   SCA
Prod: BBC-TV.   Dist: Time-Life (special purchase only; no
    rentals or previews)
    The famous painting "Lady Howe" is the focal point of
William Thompson's (Canadian artist) critique of his work.

GALE, ZONA

Some Will Be Apples
15 min.   color   1974   SCA
Dir: Phyllis Poullette Macdougal and Kathleen Laughlin.   Dist:
    Odeon, Serious Business
        A film essay on the life and writing of Pulitzer Prize-
winning playwright.   She observed and recorded the life of women
at the turn of the century.

GALILEO

Galileo (Men of Science Series)
14 min.   color   1959   JS
Prod. and dist: Coronet (sale only).   Rental: Indiana, Michigan,
    Nebraska, Syracuse
        Stresses how he fought traditional theories of his time.

Galileo and His Universe (You Are There Series)
22 min.   color   1972   IJ
Prod: CBS.   Dist: BFA
        An "on the scene" news report of his experiments.

Galileo: The Challenge of Reason (Western Civilization Series)
26 min.   color   1970   JSCA
Prod. and dist: Learning (available in Spanish).   Rental: Indiana,
    Michigan, Nebraska, South Florida, Syracuse
        His story and his trial before the Inquisition are dramatized.
Shows the conflict between him and the established authority of the
time--the Church.

GAMA, VASCO DA See CABOT, JOHN (Age of Discovery:
    Spanish and Portuguese Explorations)

GANCE, ABEL

Abel Gance: The Charm of Dynamite
52 min.   b&w   1968   SCA
Dir: Kevin Brownlow.   Dist: Images
        Utilizes footage shot during the making of "Napoleon" to
show his extraordinary early work.   Also clips from "J'Accuse"
and "La Roue."

Abel Gance: Yesterday and Tomorrow
28 min.   color   1962   SCA
Prod: J. Ruault and The Office de Documentation par le Film.
    Dist: Withdrawn by McGraw-Hill.   Rental: Indiana, South
    Florida
        Focuses on his life and contributions to motion picture
technology.

GANDHI, INDIRA

Indira Gandhi: A Heritage of Power
21 min.   color   1976   IJSA
Dir: Paul Saltzman.   Dist: Eccentric Circle
    An interview which took place in 1975 in her office in New
Delhi and at home with her family; her countrymen comment about
her and recent political events in India.

Indira Gandhi of India
52 min.   color   1967   SCA
Prod: BBC-TV.   Dist: Time-Life (available in Spanish).   Rental:
  Minnesota
    An autobiographical conversation in which she talks about
Mahatma Gandhi, her father Nehru, her imprisonment by the
British, and the problems of India.   Historic film clips are inter-
woven.

Mrs. Indira Gandhi
26 min.   b&w   1966   JSA
Prod: CBS.   Dist: Association.   Rental: Syracuse
    A portrait of her personality and office.

Our Indira
16 min.   b&w
Dist: Information Service of India (free loan)
    Her personality and leadership of India.

GANDHI, MAHATMA
  See also GANDHI, INDIRA (Indira Gandhi of India)

Gandhi (Twentieth Century Series)
27 min.   b&w   1959   JSCA
Prod: CBS.   Dist: Withdrawn by McGraw-Hill.   Rental: California, Indiana, Michigan, Minnesota, Southern California, Syracuse
    His rise to importance in India, his struggle for inde-
pendence for his country, and his assassination in 1948.

Gandhi (Biography Series)
26 min.   b&w   1964   SCA
Prod: David Wolper.   Dist: Withdrawn by McGraw-Hill.   Rental:
  Syracuse
    How he used non-violence to lead India to independence.

Gandhi's India
58 min.   b&w   1969   SCA
Prod: BBC-TV.   Dist: Indiana.   Rental: California, Minnesota
    His life and influence on India; footage of Gandhi and inter-
views with his associates and followers.

Gandhi's India (New Nations Series)
20 min.   b&w   1970   JSCA
Prod: BBC-TV.   Dist: Time-Life (available in Spanish)
     His emergence as a leader.

Mahatma Gandhi
82 min.   b&w
Dist: Macmillan
     Emphasizes his philosophy of love and truth.   Narrated by
Quentin Reynolds.

Mahatma Gandhi
19 min.   b&w   1955   JSA
Prod: Encyclopaedia Britannica.   Dist: Withdrawn by EB.
     Rental: California, Indiana, Minnesota, Nebraska, South Florida
     Utilizes film clips to highlight his life and efforts to gain
equality and freedom for his people through non-violence.

Mahatma Gandhi (Profiles in Power)
30 min.   color   1976   JSCA
Prod: McConnell Advertising Co. and Ontario Communications
     Authority.   Dist: Learning
     As played by Louis Negin, Gandhi is 'interviewed' by
Patrick Watson, who challenges his accomplishments from a
modern-day perspective.

A Night at Maritzburg
30 min.   b&w   1970
Prod: ABC.   Rental: National Council of Churches
     On a trip to South Africa he was forced from his first-class
apartment and then protested by spending the night sitting in a cold
train station.   Combines newsreel footage with live action.

Non-Violence--Mahatma Gandhi and Martin Luther King; the Teach-
     er and the Pupil (Turning Points: America in the 20th Century
     Series)
15 min.   color and b&w   1971   JSCA
Prod: Koplin and Grinker.   Dist: Pictura
     The parallels between the philosophies of the two men.

GARLAND, HAMLIN

Hamlin Garland: Historian of the Midwest
10 min.   b&w   1965   SCA
Dist: Withdrawn.   Rental: Minnesota
     How his early life influenced his writings; also describes
his literary contributions and achievements, including the Pulitzer
Prize.

GAUDI, ANTONIO

Antonio Gaudí

21 1/2 min.　color　1973　SCA
Prod: William Thomson.　Dist: International Film Bureau.
　　Rental: Syracuse
　　　His major architectural events, such as "Casa Vicens,"
"Palacio Guell," and "Casa Battlo," and what influenced their de-
sign.

Antonio Gaudí
27 min.　color　1964　JSC
Prod: Ira Latour.　Dist: Center for Mass Communication (sale
　　only).　Rental: California, Michigan
　　　Traces the major developments in his career, beginning
with "Casa Vicens." Explores much of his architecture.

GAUGUIN, EUGENE HENRI PAUL

Gauguin in Tahiti: Search for Paradise
54 min.　color　1968　SA
Prod: CBS.　Dist: Withdrawn by McGraw-Hill.　Rental: Southern
　　California
　　　Why he went to Tahiti, the effect on his painting, and his
life in France.

Paul Gauguin
13 min.　b&w　1952　SCA
Dir: Alain Resnais.　Dist: Pictura.　Rental: Michigan
　　　His escape to the islands of the South Sea, together with
autobiographical paintings and a commentary drawn from his own
writings.

GAUTAMA BUDDHA
　　See also　Buddha (feature)

Buddhism (Great Religions Series)
16 min.　b&w　1962　JSCA
Prod: National Film Board of Canada.　Dist: McGraw-Hill.
　　Rental: Minnesota
　　　The film is divided into three parts; one deals with the life
of Buddha and the other two with the religion and its spread.

Buddhist World
10 1/2 min.　color　SC
Prod. and dist: Coronet (sale only).　Rental: Minnesota
　　　Shows how the life, work, and philosophy of Buddha led to
the growth of the Buddhist religion.　Gives a history of Buddism
and how it grew.

GEHRIG, HENRY LOUIS (LOU)
　　See also　Pride of the Yankees (feature)

King of Diamonds
15 min.   b&w   1952-53   JSCA
Prod: Mike Sklar.   Dist: Star Film
     His touching farewell at Yankee Stadium on July 4, 1939.
Compiled from the Fox Movietone News Library footage.

Lou Gehrig's Greatest Day (You Are There Series)
30 min.   IJSCA
Prod. and dist: CBS (special sale; no rentals or previews).
     Rental: Minnesota
     A dramatized "on the scene" newscast of his fans' tribute
to him in Yankee Stadium.

GELDZAHLER, HENRY See DE KOONING, WILLEM (Painters
     Painting)

GEORGE III (OF ENGLAND)

The Last King of America
60 min.   color   1974
Dist: Travelers Film Library, West Glen Films (free loan)
     An "interview" of King George III, played by Peter Ustinov;
the reporter is Eric Sevareid.

GERICAULT, THEODORE

Géricault--The Raft of the Medusa
20 min.   color   1973   JSCA
Prod: Institute Pédagogique National.   Dist: Roland Collections
     A brief biographical sketch is presented with a detailed
analysis of his celebrated work, "The Raft of the Medusa," which
introduced the Romantic movement to the public.

Théodore Géricault (Romantic Versus Classic Art Series)
26 min.   color   1974   JSCA
Prod: Reader's Digest.   Dist: Pyramid.   Rental: Southern Cali-
     fornia (listed under series title)
     A study of the artist and the works he produced.   Narrated
by Kenneth Clark.

GESINUS-VISSER, BOB

Gésinus in California
8 min.   color   1974   SCA
Prod: Black Lion Productions.   Dist: California
     Holland's leading expressionist painter was filmed when he
visited California for the first time at the age of 74.   He talks
about his early days in Paris, his friend Picasso, and other impressionist painters.

GIACOMETTI, ALBERTO

Alberto Giacometti
29 min.   color   C
Dist: Embassy of Switzerland (distribution restricted to colleges)
        At work in his Paris and Stampa studios.

Alberto Giacometti
29 min.   color   1966   SCA
Prod: Ernst Scheidegger. Dist: Film Images. Rental: Michigan
        As he sculpts a head, he talks to a friend about his art
works.

Alberto Giacometti
12 min.   color   1967
Dir: Stuart Chasmar. Prod: Sumner Glimcher. Dist: Center
    for Mass Communication (sale only)
        A presentation of the works exhibited just before his death
in a major retrospective.

Giacometti
14 min.   b&w   1972   SCA
Prod: Arts Council of Great Britain. Dist: Films Inc.
        He comments on his life and sculptures.

Giacometti
20 min.   color   1970   SCA
Prod: BBC-TV. Dist: Time-Life (special order purchase; no
    previews or rentals)
        Centers on one of his portraits of Caroline, the model
whom he painted over and over again. Paintings, drawings, and
sculpture are represented and the influence of ancient Egyptian art
is highlighted.

GIDE, ANDRE

Avec André Gide
40 min.   CA
Rental: FACSEA
        French dialogue only. Gide himself narrates the story of
his life. Shown with Mallarmé, Valéry and other friends, and at
home with his grandchildren.

GIFFORD, FRANK

Frank Gifford (Sports Legends Series)
20 min.   color   1975   IJ
Prod. and dist: Sports Legends, Inc. Rental: Southern California
        His years as a football player at USC and with the New
York Giants as well as his experiences as a sportscaster.

GINSBERG, ALLEN See FERLINGHETTI, LAWRENCE (Allen Ginsberg and Lawrence Ferlinghetti)

GIOVANNI, NIKKI

Accomplished Women
26 min.   color   1974   JSC
Prod: Charles Braverman. Dist: Films Inc.
        Katharine Graham, Dr. Virginia Apgar, LaDonna Harris, founder of Americans for Indian Opportunity, Shirley Chisholm and Giovanni talk about sexual discrimination and how they overcame it.

Black Woman
52 min.   b&w   CA
Prod: NET. Dist: Indiana. Rental: Impact, Michigan
        Poet Giovanni, singer Lena Horne and others talk about the role of black women in our society.

GLEIZES, ALBERT

Albert Gleizes
16 min.   color
Prod: Les Films du Cypres. Dist: International Film Bureau
        Traces the development of his cubist art.

GLENN, JOHN

John Glenn
25 min.   b&w   1965   IJ
Prod: Metromedia Productions. Dist: Sterling (sale only; available on 8mm). Rental: Mass Media, Syracuse
        From his interest in aviation as a child through his flight on Friendship Seven in 1962.

John Glenn Story
30 min.   color   1963   JSA
Prod: Warner Bros. for NASA. Rental: Nebraska, Syracuse
        A biography in which his hometown friends and family talk about his childhood. Traces his education and service career. Footage of pre-flight training and the Mercury capsule in orbit are included. Narrated by Jack Webb.

GODDARD, MARY KATHERINE

Mary Kate's War (Decades of Decision: The American Revolution Series)
25 min.   color   1975   JSCA
Prod: WQED, Pittsburgh. Dist: National Geographic Society (available on videocassette)

As the publisher of the Maryland Journal, she published a satirical letter urging the colonies to accept England's peace offer. The Whigs took it seriously and demanded to know the author. Dramatized.

GODDARD, ROBERT

The Impact of Robert Goddard
26 min.   color   1973   SCA
Prod: Koplin and Grinker.   Dist: Pictura
A conversation between Charles Blair and Goddard's widow. Includes her unique films of his rocketry during the '20s; his patents were the basis of all space flight.

The Dream That Wouldn't Down (Space--Man's Greatest Adventure
Series)
27 min.   b&w   1965   JSC
Prod. and dist: NASA (free loan)
Mrs. Goddard's reminiscences about his dreams of flight; includes historic footage of some of his experiments.

GOEBBELS, JOSEF PAUL

Josef Goebbels
27 min.   b&w   1965   IJ
Prod: Metromedia Productions.   Dist: Sterling (sale only; available on 8mm).   Rental: Mass Media, Syracuse
Master of propaganda for Hitler; his life, personality and career are set against the background of Germany.

Minister of Hate
26 min.   b&w   1959   SCA
Prod: CBS.   Dist: McGraw-Hill.   Rental: Association, Indiana, Michigan, Southern California
His work as Germany's Minister of Propaganda and how he controlled the media.   Fritz Lang and H. R. Trevor Roper describe him.

GOERING, HERMANN WILHELM

Goering (Twentieth Century Series)
26 min.   b&w   1960   SCA
Prod: CBS.   Rental: Association, Minnesota
The career of Hitler's number two man.

GOGH, VINCENT VAN

Van Gogh
6 min.   color   1969   PI

Prod: Corsair. Dist: BFA. Rental: Syracuse
A narrative song provides the story of his life. His major
works are also presented.

Van Gogh
14 min.   b&w   1970
Dist: Time-Life (special purchase only; no previews or rentals)
The backbone of the narrative is based on letters to his
brother; he wrote about his days as a theology student, his years
at Hague, the impressionists and Gauguin.

Van Gogh
17 min.   b&w   1952   JSCA
Dir: Alain Resnais. Dist: Pictura. Rental: California, Michigan
His own paintings are utilized to tell the story of his life,
his years among the miners, his years in Paris and Province,
and his eventual madness and death.

Van Gogh: A Self Portrait
54 min.   color   1968   SA
Prod: NBC. Dist: McGraw-Hill
The work, the life, and the influences which drove him to
artistic greatness and also to self-destruction.

Vincent Van Gogh
25 min.   color   1959   JSC
Prod: Jan Hulsker. Dist: Coronet (sale only). Rental: Michigan, Minnesota, Nebraska, Syracuse
As the camera scans his paintings, excerpts from his
letters to his brother Theo provide a narrative thread.

Vincent Van Gogh--To Theo, With Love (Touch of Fame Series)
29 min.   b&w   1962   SCA
Prod: KNXT-TV. Dist: Southern California
What prompted him to kill himself is explored by psychology
professor Dr. Herman Harvey.

GOLDWATER, BARRY

The Making of the President, 1964
80 min.   b&w   1966   SC
Prod: Metromedia Producers. Dist: Films Inc. Rental: Indi-
ana, Michigan, South Florida, Southern California, Syracuse
A behind-the-scenes look at the race between Johnson and
Goldwater.

GOODALL, JANE

Miss Goodall and the Wild Chimpanzees
28 min.   color   1966   JSCA

Prod: National Geographic Society. Dist: Films Inc. Rental: Minnesota, South Florida, Southern California (also 52-min. version)
 Her life among the chimpanzees of East Africa.

GOODMAN, BENNY See The Benny Goodman Story (feature)

GOODYEAR, CHARLES

The Story of Charles Goodyear
11 min. b&w 1941 JSCA
Prod: Teaching film Custodians. Rental: Minnesota
 A dramatization of his efforts to make India rubber commercially acceptable.

GORES, JOE

Joe Gores: A Penny a Word (Writers on Writing Series)
21 min. color 1973 S
Prod: Davidson Films. Dist: General Learning
 How this freelance writer gets his ideas.

GORKI, MAXIM See Gorky Trilogy (feature)

GOULD, GLENN

Glenn Gould--Off the Record
30 min. b&w 1960 SA
Prod: National Film Board of Canada. Dist: Withdrawn by McGraw-Hill. Rental: Syracuse
 Concert pianist Gould at his lakeside cottage. A cinéma vérité portrait.

Glenn Gould--On the Record
30 min. b&w 1960 SA
Prod: National Film Board of Canada. Dist: Withdrawn by McGraw-Hill. Rental: Syracuse
 A companion piece to "Glenn Gould--Off the Record," this film focuses on a recording session.

GOYA Y LUCIENTES, FRANCISCO JOSE DE
 See also VELASQUEZ, DIEGO (Treasures from El Prado)

Francisco Goya (Romantic Versus Classic Art Series)
26 min. color 1974 JSCA
Prod: Reader's Digest. Dist: Pyramid. Rental: Southern California (listed under series title)

The clash between the two artistic movements is evident in Goya's work and by his life. Narrated by Kenneth Clark.

The Glory of Goya
17 min.　b&w　1952　SCA
Prod. and dist: Pictura
　　　A record of his work and era. Rapid editing recreates a bull fight from his art work.

Goya
11 min.　color　1952　SCA
Prod: No-Do Productions. Dist: Pictura
　　　A look at the world in which he lived as shown through his paintings, including "A Self-Portrait," "Family of King Charles IV," and "Disasters of War."

Goya
7 min.　color　1973　JSCA
Prod. and dist: National Gallery of Art (free loan)
　　　His satiric portraits and his war and bullfight paintings are shown.

Goya
20 min.　b&w　1957　SCA
Prod: McGraw-Hill. Rental: Nebraska, Southern California
　　　Traces his life within the framework of his times. Shows selections of his work.

Goya
30 min.
Dist: Southern Baptist Radio-TV Commission
　　　A look at his drawings, etchings, and oils.

Goya
29 min.　color　1975　SCA
Prod: Scala Art Films. Dist: Macmillan
　　　A look at the paintings from his early, middle, and late periods.

GRAHAM, KATHARINE　See　GIOVANNI, NIKKI (Accomplished
　　Women)

GRAHAM, MARTHA

A Dancer's World
30 min.　b&w　1957　JSCA
Dir: Peter Glushanok.　Prod: Nathan Kroll.　Dist: Macmillan,
　　Phoenix.　Rental: California, Michigan, Minnesota, South
　　Florida, Syracuse, Viewfinders
　　　As members of her company perform, she talks about her world, her experiences, and her years of training. A classic.

GRANT, ULYSSES S.

Grant and Lee at Appomattox (You Are There Series)
26 min.   b&w   1956   JSCA
Prod. and dist: CBS (sale only; no previews).   Rental: Indiana,
   Minnesota, South Florida, Southern California
      A dramatized "on-the-scene" news story of Lee's surrender.

Grant and Lee 1864-1865
27 min.   b&w   1958   JSCA
Prod: Westinghouse Broadcasting.   Rental: Indiana
      Grant's appointment as head of the Union army and his sub-
sequent clashes with Lee.

Surrender at Appomattox
52 min.   color   1974   SC
Prod: Wolper Organization.   Dist: Films Inc.
      Part 1, The Union Triumphant, deals with Lee's defeat and
withdrawal at Gettysburg, and part 2, Appomattox Court House,
with the meeting when they agree to the terms to end the Civil
War.

U. S. Grant--An Improbable Hero
27 min.   b&w   1962   JS
Prod: NBC.   Dist: McGraw-Hill.   Rental: Minnesota, Nebraska,
   Southern California, Syracuse
      Photos and dramatic incidents portray Grant as a man who
disliked the career which made him famous.

GRASS, GÜNTER

Günter Grass
30 min.   b&w   1967   SCA
Prod: NET.   Dist: Indiana.   Rental: California
      He reads a portion of his novel The Tin Drum, gives a po-
litical speech, and an interview in his studio.

GRECO, EL (Domenikos Theotocopoulos)
   See also El Greco (feature); VELASQUEZ, DIEGO (Treasures
from El Prado)

El Greco
5 min.   color   1975   SCA
Prod. and dist: National Gallery of Art (free loan)
      His life and art, with emphasis on his search for the "light
within."

El Greco (Human Dimension Series)
30 min.   color   1971   SCA
Prod: Wiley Hance.   Dist: Graphic Curriculum (may be shown on
   closed circuit television)

His life is interwoven with a detailed exploration of his masterpieces.

El Greco
11 min.   color   1952   SCA
Prod: No-Do Productions. Dist: Pictura
A study of the personality who painted "The Cardinal," "Burial of the Count of Orgaz," and "The Martyrdom of St. Maurice."

GREELEY, HORACE

One Nation Indivisible: Horace Greeley--Editor
20 min.   b&w   1953   S
Prod: Teaching Film Custodians. Dist: Indiana (lease)
Lincoln's appeal to him to support restoration of the South in his editorials for the New York Tribune. An excerpt from the Cavalcade of America television movie.

GREENBERG, CLEMENT See DE KOONING, WILLEM (Painters Painting)

GREY, LADY JANE

The Last Day of an English Queen (You Are There Series)
30 min.   1956   JSCA
Prod. and dist: CBS (special sale only; no previews or rentals).
Rental: Minnesota
Her ten-day reign is dramatized as an "on the scene" report.

GRIEG, EDVARD
See also Song of Norway (feature)

Music Experiences--Edvard Grieg--The Man and His Music
17 min.   color   1972   IJSC
Prod: J. P. Stevens Co. Dist: Aims
Shows his love of nature, his life and his music.

GRIERSON, JOHN

Grierson
58 min.   color   1973   SCA
Prod. and dist: National Film Board of Canada. Rental: California, Indiana, McGraw-Hill
Personal interviews with the "father of documentary film" and his friends. Focuses on his years in Canada, especially his work with the National Film Board. Includes excerpts from his films.

I Remember, I Remember
56 min.　color　1972　SCA
Prod: Films of Scotland.　Dist: Films Inc.　Rental: Viewfinders
　　　Film clips of his documentaries and an on-camera commentary by him tell the story of his craft in this tribute.

GRIFFITH, DAVID WARK

D. W. Griffith--An American Genius
55 min.　color　1970　CA
Prod: WAVE-TV.　Dist: Killiam Shows
　　　His life from birth through his years as an actor and then
as a director.

D. W. Griffith Interview
10 min.　b&w　1930
Rental: Images (title: D. W. Griffith Prologue, 6 min.), Kit
　Parker
　　　Apparently the only surviving sound interview, it was shot
while he was producing "Abraham Lincoln" and was conducted by
Walter Huston.

The Great Director
50 min.　color　1967　SCA
Prod: BBC-TV.　Dist: Withdrawn.　Rental: Minnesota
　　　The life and work of Griffith, with comments by Lillian
Gish.　Excerpts from "Birth of a Nation," "Intolerance," and "Way
Down East."

GROPIUS, WALTER

Walter Gropius (Wisdom Series)
30 min.　b&w　1962　SCA
Prod: NBC.　Dist: Films Inc.　Rental: Michigan (title: Conver-
　sation with Walter Gropius), Minnesota, South Florida
　　　An interview with the founder of the Bauhaus School of
architecture.

GUEVARA, CHE
　See also Che! (feature)

Che
10 min.　b&w　1972　SCA
Dir: Miguel Torres.　Dist: Tricontinental
　　　In Spanish with English sub-titles.　A Cuban Film Institute
Newsreel utilizing archival footage and photos.　Includes speeches
about him by Castro.

GUIMARD, HECTOR

Hectorologie--Hector Guimard
13 min.   color   1973   SCA
Dir: Yves Plantin and Alain Blondel.   Prod: Films ABC.   Dist:
    Roland Collection
        A survey of his life and works; he was a highly controversi-
al architect-designer while alive.

GUGGENHEIM, PEGGY

Peggy Guggenheim: Art in Venice
44 min.   color   1975   SC
Prod: Raffaele Andreassi.   Dist: Films for the Humanities
        Filmed in Venice at Palazzo Venier dei Leoni, which houses
one of the greatest art collections in the world.   Focuses on her
relationship with Jackson Pollock, whom she allegedly discovered.

GUTHRIE, TYRONE

Tyrone Guthrie
30 min.   b&w   1967   SCA
Prod: NET.   Dist: Indiana
        At home in Ireland, rehearsing in New York, talking to
American students, Guthrie presents his ideas and methods of
working in the theater.

HALSEY, WILLIAM FREDERICK

Admiral William Halsey
25 min.   b&w   1965   IJ
Prod: Metromedia Producers.   Dist: Sterling (sale only; avail-
    able on 8mm).   Rental: Mass Media
        His heroic role during World War II as a military leader
and as captain of the aircraft carrier Enterprise.

HAMER, FANNIE LOU

Fannie Lou Hamer
10 min.   color   1972   IJ
Prod. and dist: Rediscovery Productions; Sterling (sale only;
    available on 8mm).   Rental: Indiana
        Her struggle for non-violence and black rights in Missis-
sippi.

HAMILTON, ALEXANDER
    See also BURR, AARON (Hamilton-Burr Duel); Alexander
    Hamilton (feature)

Alexander Hamilton
18 min.   b&w   1951   JSC
Prod: Emerson Film Corp.   Dist: Encyclopaedia Britannica
   (available on video by special order).   Rental: Indiana, Michigan, Minnesota, Nebraska, South Florida
      Begins with his childhood in the West Indies, highlights his
achievements, and ends with his duel with Aaron Burr.

From the Encyclopaedia Britannica film, Alexander Hamilton.

Democracy--Equality or Privilege?   Thomas Jefferson vs. Alexander Hamilton--1790's (History Alive! Series)
13 min.   color   1970   JSC
Prod: Turnley Walker.   Dist: Walt Disney (long term license)
      A dramatization of these two leaders disagreeing on how
the people should be governed.

Man and the State: Hamilton and Jefferson on Democracy
26 min.   color   1974   JSCA
Prod: Bernard Wilets.   Dist: BFA.   Rental: Syracuse
      A dramatization in which Hamilton and Jefferson are brought
to life in order to react to crises in American history.

HAMMARSKJÖLD, DAG HJALMAR AGNE CARL

Dag Hammarskjöld
27 min.   b&w   1965   IJ
Prod: David L. Wolper.   Dist: Sterling (sale only; available on
    8mm).   Rental: Mass Media, Michigan, Syracuse
        His career as Secretary General of the U.N. until his death
in the Congo in 1961.

Portrait of Dag Hammarskjöld
28 min.   b&w   1961
Prod: Alistair Cooke.   Dist: United Nations
    A conversation with Alistair Cooke.

HANDEL, GEORGE FREDERICK

Handel and His Music
14 min.   color   1957   IJSCA
Prod. and dist: Coronet (sale only).   Rental: Indiana, Michigan,
    Minnesota, Nebraska, Syracuse
        Filmed in Germany, Italy, and London, which were the
places he became well-known.   Includes musical selections from
"Messiah. "

HANDY, WILLIAM CHRISTOPHER
    See also   St. Louis Blues (feature)

W. C. Handy
14 min.   color   1967   JSA
Prod: Vignette Films.   Dist: BFA.   Rental: Southern California,
    Syracuse
        The contributions made by him to the world of music.   This
black composer is known as the "Father of the Blues. "   The film
also reflects the economic, social and political conditions from
1890 to 1950.

HANSBERRY, LORRAINE

Lorraine Hansberry: The Black Experience in the Creation of
    Drama
35 min.   color   1975   JSCA
Prod: Ralph J. Tangney and Harold Mantell.   Dist: Films for the
    Humanities (available on 3/4" videocassette)
        From her childhood through her death at the age of 34; her
growth as an artist and excerpts from "A Raisin in the Sun," "The
Sign in Sidney Brustein's Window" and "Les Blancs. "   Narrated by
Lorraine Hansberry and Claudia McNeil.

To Be Young, Gifted and Black
90 min.   color   1972   SCA

Lorraine Hansberry (Films for the Humanities, Inc.)

Prod: NET.   Dist: Indiana
    Her struggles, her first visit to the South, and her experi-
ences in Harlem are dramatized by a cast comprised of Ruby Dee,
Al Freemen, Jr. and Claudia McNeil.   Much of the script is
based on her own letters, plays, and diaries.

HANSEN, ARMAUER

Armauer Hansen: Discoverer of the Leprosy Bacillus
10 min.   color   1975   IJS
Prod: Svekon Films. Dist: BFA
    How he worked to discover the leprosy bacillus.

HARDING, WARREN See COOLIDGE, (JOHN) CALVIN (United
    States in the Twentieth Century: 1920-1932)

HARDY, OLIVER

Hardy-Lugosi Interview
8 min.   1953   JSCA
Rental: Kit Parker
    Separate interviews in which they discuss their careers.

HARRIS, FRANCO

Good Luck on Sunday Franco Harris (The Winners Series)
48 min.   color   1976   JSCA
Prod: Laurel. Dist: Counselor
    An in-depth profile of the football player with comments by
Steeler coach Chuck Noll and others.

HARRIS, LA DONNA See GIOVANNI, NIKKI (Accomplished Wo-
    men)

HARRISON, WILLIAM HENRY

Tippecanoe and Tyler, Too
12 min.   b&w   1960   JSC
Prod: Virginia State Board of Education.   Rental: Indiana
    Profiles of the education, childhoods, and political achieve-
ments of Harrison and John Tyler, with emphasis on the 1840
campaign.

HART, NANCY MORGAN

Breakfast at Nancy's: Nancy Morgan Hart

20 min. b&w 1953
Prod: Teaching Film Custodians. Dist: Indiana
A dramatization of how she outwitted the Tories to protect a militia dispatch rider. An excerpt from the motion picture series, Cavalcade of America.

HARTUNG, HANS

Hartung
15 min. b&w or color 1964
Dir: Camille Bourniquel, Guy Suzuki. Prod: Sorafilms. Rental: FACSEA (available in French)
His life and expressionist art work.

HARVEY, WILLIAM

William Harvey (Great Scientists Speak Again Series)
19 min. color 1974 SCA
Prod. and dist: California
An impersonation in which Harvey returns to life to discuss his discoveries and theories.

HAYES, HELEN

Helen Hayes: Portrait of an American Actress
90 min. color 1974 SCA
Dir. and prod: Nathan Kroll. Dist: Phoenix. Rental: Syracuse, Viewfinders
Her personal recollections and re-enactments recall the history of the theater and her triumphs on the stage. Clips from her greatest roles: Queen Victoria in Housman's "Victoria Regina," Mary Stuart in Anderson's "Mary of Scotland," and Catherine in Hemingway's "A Farewell to Arms."

HEANEY, SEAMUS

Seamus Heaney: Poet in Limboland
28 1/2 min. color 1974 SCA
Prod: Humphrey Burton. Dist: Films for the Humanities (available on 3/4" videocassette)
He recites his poetry against the background of battle-torn Ireland. Narrated by Heaney and Denys Hawthorne.

HEARST, WILLIAM RANDOLPH

William Randolph Hearst--San Simeon (American Life Styles Series)
28 min. color 1976 IJSCA
Prod: Comco Productions. Dist: Association

E. G. Marshall hosts a tour of his home, which reveals much about the personality of Hearst.

HEMINGWAY, ERNEST

Hemingway
54 min.   b&w   1962   SA
Prod: NBC. Dist: McGraw-Hill. Rental: California, Indiana, Minnesota, Nebraska, South Florida, Southern California, Syracuse
      A large collection of photographs and rare motion picture footage tell the story of his life from boyhood to his death. Other famous people are also included, such as Picasso, Fitzgerald, and Gertrude Stein. Emphasizes how the events of his life influenced his novels.

HENRY II See BECKET, THOMAS A (Becket); Becket (feature); The Lion in Winter (feature); Murder in the Cathedral (feature)

HENRY V See Henry V (feature)

HENRY VII See ELIZABETH I (Tudor Period)

HENRY VIII
      See also ELIZABETH I (Tudor Period); Henry VIII and His Six Wives (feature); A Man for All Seasons (feature); The Private Life of Henry VIII (feature)

Matter of Conscience: Henry VIII and Thomas More (Western Civilization Series)
28 min.   color   1972   SA
Prod: Columbia. Dist: Learning. Rental: Michigan, South Florida, Syracuse
      Extracted from "A Man for All Seasons," it shows the conflict between him and More over the divorce he wanted from Anne Boleyn.

The Six Wives of Henry VIII (six parts)
90 min. each   color   1976   SCA
Prod: BBC-TV. Dist: Time-Life (available on video)
      A dramatization of the courtly and private lives of Henry and his wives, beginning with Catherine of Aragon, with whom he lived for 18 years and with whom he had a daughter, Mary. Hoping to have a boy, he marries Anne Boleyn, mother of Elizabeth (pt. 2); she's later beheaded and he marries Jane Seymour (pt. 3), who dies giving birth. His fourth marriage is to Anne of Cleaves, a German princess (pt. 4). Catherine Howard, his next wife is

also executed (pt. 5) and he marries Catherine Parr, who outlives
him (pt. 6).

HENRY, PATRICK

Patrick Henry's Liberty or Death
15 min.   color   1973   JSC
Prod: Art Evans.   Dist: Paramount Oxford
        Graphics tell the story of the times.   Barry Sullivan de-
livers this famous speech.

Resolve of Patrick Henry (You Are There Series)
27 min.   b&w   1956   JSC
Prod. and dist: CBS (sale only; no previews or rentals)
        A dramatization of his famous speech.

HENRY THE NAVIGATOR, PRINCE
        See also CABOT, JOHN (Age of Discovery: Spanish and Portu-
        guese Explorations)

The Exploration of Prince Henry
13 min.   color   1959   IJS
Prod: Jan Juta.   Rental: Indiana, Nebraska
        Summarizes his contributions to navigation.

Henry, the Navigator
33 min.   color
Dist: Portuguese National Tourist Office (free loan)
        Show the development of nautical equipment and the advances
he made.

HENSON, MATTHEW

Peary and Henson: North to the Pole (Biography Series)
15 min.   color   1969   IJSCA
Prod: McGraw-Hill in collaboration with Project 7 Films.   Dist:
        McGraw-Hill
        Traces the historic events within perspective and ack-
knowledges the role of Henson, a black.

HENZE, HANS WERNER

Hans Werner Henze
30 min.   b&w   1967   SCA
Prod: NET.   Dist: Indiana
        German composer Henze discusses the social meanings of
his compositions, and excerpts from his opera "The Bassarides"
and his concerts "The Muses of Sicily" are played.   W. H. Auden
and others comment on his background and music.

HEPWORTH, BARBARA
See also ARMITAGE, KENNETH (Five British Sculptors Work and Talk)

Barbara Hepworth
30 min.   b&w   1969   SCA
Prod: BBC-TV.   Dist: Time-Life (special order purchase; no previews or rentals)
An in-depth study narrated largely by herself in which she explains her artistic perceptions as revealed through her sculpture.

Barbara Hepworth at the Tate
13 min.   color   1971   SCA
Prod: Arts Council of Great Britain.   Dist: Films Inc.
A retrospective exhibition.

Figures in a Landscape
16 min.   color   1972   SCA
Prod: Arts Council of Great Britain.   Dist: Films Inc.
Outdoor display of her sculpture.

HESS, RUDOLF

The Strange Case of Rudolph Hess (20th Century Series)
26 min.   SCA
Prod: CBS.   Dist: Association

HESS, THOMAS   See   DE KOONING, WILLEM (Painters Painting)

HEYWOOD, BILLIE

I'm the Prettiest Piece in Greece
30 min.   b&w   1974   SCA
Prod: Richard Wedler.   Dist: Wombat.   Rental: Syracuse, Viewfinders
Reminisces about her career as a black jazz singer in the '30s and '40s. She also worked as wardrobe mistress for Mae West.

HICKOK, JAMES BUTLER (WILD BILL)   See   EARP, WYATT (Heroes and Villains)

HILGARD, ERNEST R.

Interview with Dr. Ernest R. Hilgard (2 pts)
27-30 min.   b&w   1968   C
Prod: Dr. Richard Evans.   Dist: Macmillan (sale only).   Rental: Association, South Florida

In the first part he discusses his learning theory; in the second, hypnosis.

HIROHITO, EMPEROR OF JAPAN

Emperor Hirohito
26 min.   b&w   1964   SCA
Prod: David L. Wolper.   Rental: Michigan, Minnesota
His life, his objections to military growth, his leadership of Japan before and after the War.

The Immaculate Emperor: Hirohito of Japan
60 min.   color   1972   SCA
Prod: BBC-TV and Time-Life.   Dist: Time-Life (available in
    Spanish and on video)
Newsreel footage shows him as a young boy, as a university student, as a conqueror, and as a defeated leader.

HITLER, ADOLF
See also Hitler: The Last Ten Days (feature)

Adolf Hitler (Profiles in Power)
30 min.   color   1976   JSCA
Prod: McConnell Advertising Co. and Ontario Communications
    Authority.   Dist: Learning
Hitler, played by Robin Gammell, is 'interviewed' by Patrick Watson.

From Kaiser to Fuehrer (Twentieth Century Series)
26 min.   b&w   1960   JSC
Prod: CBS.   Rental: Indiana, Minnesota, Southern California
The conditions in Europe, the ups and downs of his career are depicted in newsreel footage.

Hitler 2 pts. (Biography Series)
26 min. each   b&w   1963   SCA
Prod: David Wolper.   Dist: McGraw-Hill.   Rental: California,
    Indiana, Minnesota, Southern California, Syracuse
The Rise to Power (pt. 1) deals with his boyhood and early life, including his role in leading the National Socialist Party.
The Fall of the Third Reich (pt. 2) shows the early German victories and then the eventual defeat.   Each part is available separately.

Hitler: Anatomy of a Dictatorship
22 min.   b&w   1970   JSCA
Prod. and dist: Learning (available in Spanish).   Rental: Nebraska, Southern California, Syracuse
Documentary footage plus a narrative cover his career from 1923 to the end of World War I.

Hitler vs. Hindenburg
25 min.   b&w   1964   SCA
Prod: Metromedia Producers.   Dist: Films Inc.
    Hitler becomes Chancellor.

Mein Kampf
119 min.   b&w
Dir: Edward Leiser.   Prod: Columbia.   Rental: McGraw-Hill,
    Macmillan, Twyman
    Hitler's rise to power and the story of the Third Reich are
told through the words and photographs of the Germans themselves.
Some gory scenes.

Parallels: The President and the Dictator
47 min.   b&w   1969   JSCA
Prod: Reaction Films.   Rental: Indiana
    The backgrounds of Hitler and Roosevelt are set within the
historical developments.   Contrasts the leadership roles of the
two men.   Utilizes newsreel footage.   Available in two parts.

The Rise and Fall of the Third Reich (a series)
28-31 min.   b&w   1972   SC
Prod: MGM.   Dist: Films Inc.   Rental: Syracuse (The Rise of
    Hitler, Götterdämmerung: Fall of the Third Reich)
    The four films trace his rise, the triumphant years, the
fall, and the Nuremberg Trial.   The titles are Rise of Hitler,
Nazi Germany: Years of Triumph, Götterdämmerung: Fall of the
Third Reich, Nuremberg Trial.

From The Rise of Adolph Hitler (McGraw-Hill Films)

The Rise of Adolph Hitler (You Are There Series)
27 min.   b&w   1955   SCA
Prod: CBS. Dist: McGraw-Hill.   Rental: Indiana, Michigan,
    Minnesota, Nebraska, Syracuse
        The climax of his rise to power--September 9, 1938, in a
dramatized "on the scene" news report.

The Rise of Hitler (War and Peace in Europe Series)
20 min.   b&w   1970   JSCA
Prod: BBC-TV. Dist: Time-Life (available in Spanish)
        Europe from the early '30s to the attack on Poland in 1939.

The Twisted Cross
55 min.   b&w   1958   SC
Prod: NBC. Dist: McGraw-Hill.   Rental: Indiana, Michigan,
    Minnesota, Nebraska, South Florida, Southern California
        Previously impounded German footage is used to tell the
story of Hitler's rise to power, his defeat, and his suicide.

HO CHI MINH

Ho Chi Minh (Twentieth Century Series)
26 min.   b&w   1966   SCA
Prod: CBS. Dist: Association. Rental: Minnesota
        His career and personality are analyzed.   Stills and footage
dating from 1916 and interviews with noted scholars and journalists
reveal his political power.

Interview with Ho Chi Minh
8 1/2 min.   color   1970
Rental: Impact
        Made several months before his death during a conversation
he had with soldiers and Pham Van Dong, Prime Minister.

HODLER, FERDINAND

Ferdinand Hodler--Vision of the Land
11 min.   color   CA
Dist: Embassy of Switzerland (free loan; restricted to colleges
    and adult groups)
        His landscape drawings, 1871-1918; the commentary is based
on his own words.

HOFFER, ERIC

Eric Hoffer: The Passionate State of Mind
52 min.   b&w   1967   JSCA
Prod: CBS. Dist: Carousel (sale only).   Rental: California,
    Indiana, Mass Media, Michigan, South Florida, Syracuse
        Eric Sevareid conducts this interview in which Hoffer states

his views on hippies, hawks, drugs, automation, politics, and race.

HOFFMAN, HANS See DE KOONING, WILLEM (Painters Painting)

HOGARTH, WILLIAM

The London of William Hogarth
27 min.   b&w   1956   JS
Dir: Phil Barnard. Dist: Withdrawn by McGraw-Hill. Rental: Southern California
How he captured London through his engravings.

William Hogarth
30 min.   b&w   1969   SCA
Prod: BBC-TV. Dist: Time-Life (special purchase only; no previews or rentals)
His passionate commitment to realism is evident in his engravings and paintings, which were not valued highly while he lived. Tells the story of his life and why he chose to be a painter.

HOKUSAI

Hokusai: Thirty-Six Views of Mt. Fuji
30 min.   color   1973   SC
Prod: NHK International. Dist: Films Inc.
The foremost "ukiyoe" artist, his views of Mt. Fuji, his cartoons, and his life as revealed through his art.

HOLBEIN, HANS, THE YOUNGER

At the Turn of the Age--Hans Holbein
14 min.   color   1972   JSCA
Dir: Herbert E. Meyer. Prod: Film-Studio Walter Leckebusch. Dist: Roland Collection. Free loan: Embassy of Switzerland (title reversed; college and adult groups only)
Begins with a description of the Renaissance and the development of his painting, etching, and drawing. Describes his life as a court painter for Henry VIII.

HOLIDAY, BILLIE See The Lady Sings the Blues (feature)

HOLMES, OLIVER WENDELL
See also The Magnificent Yankee (feature)

Oliver Wendell Holmes
18 min.   b&w   1950   JS

Prod. and dist: Withdrawn by Encyclopaedia Britannica.   Rental:
   Indiana, Michigan, Minnesota, Nebraska
      Through dramatization his importance as an American writ-
er and lecturer is shown.   Highlights how and why he came to
write Old Ironsides, Autocrat of the Breakfast Table and other
works.

HOMER, WINSLOW

Yankee Painter--The Work of Winslow Homer
26 min.   color   1964   CA
Prod: Radio-TV Bureau, University of Arizona.   Dist: International Film Bureau.   Rental: Southern California
      A commentary on his life is enhanced by his drawings, oils,
and watercolors, which are shown in detail.

HONEYMAN, JOHN

In This Crisis: Trenton, 1776
21 min.   b&w   1952   IJS
Prod: Teaching Film Custodians.   Dist: Indiana (lease)
      A Revolutionary War spy, he gathered the information
Washington needed to cross the Delaware and surprise the British.

HONNECOURT, VILLARD DE

Villard de Honnecourt, Builder of Cathedrals
15 min.   b&w   1973   SCA
Dir: Georges Rebillard and Yves Thaleer.   Prod: Les Films du
   Touraine.   Dist: Roland Collection
      A brief biographical sketch and a tour of the cathedrals he
designed, intercut with his drawings of them.

HOOVER, HERBERT
   See also The Election of 1932; COOLIDGE, CALVIN (U. S. in
   the Twentieth Century: 1920-1932)

Herbert Hoover
55 min.   b&w   1958   SCA
Prod: NBC.   Dist: Films Inc.   Rental: Michigan, Minnesota,
   Nebraska
      An interview in which he discusses his career, his child-
hood and education, and his other activities in and out of politics.

Herbert Hoover (Biography Series)
26 min.   b&w   1964   SCA
Prod: David Wolper.   Dist: Withdrawn by McGraw-Hill.   Rental:
   Michigan, Minnesota, Southern California, Syracuse

His political career, beginning with his job as an international miner.

Man and the State: Roosevelt and Hoover on the Economy
25 min.   color   1975   JSC
Prod: Bernard Wilets.   Dist: BFA
A dramatization of FDR and Hoover debating their economic policies during the Depression.

A Tribute to President Herbert Clark Hoover, 1874-1964
11 min.   b&w   1964
Prod: U.S. Dept. of Defense.   Dist: National Audiovisual Center
Highlights his work as a food administrator during World Wars I and II, as Secretary of Commerce, and as elder statesman.

HOPKINS, GERARD MANLEY

Gerard Manley Hopkins
30 min.   color   1974   SCA
Prod: BBC-TV.   Dist: Time-Life (available on video)
An intense study of his religious conflicts and his poetry.

HOPKINS, SAM

Sam "Lightnin" Hopkins (Artist in America Series)
30 min.   color   1971   SCA
Prod: Public Television Library.   Dist: Indiana
His folk songs reflect the lives of many blacks.

HORNE, LENA   See   GIOVANNI, NIKKI (Black Woman)

HORNER, MATINA

Matina Horner: Portrait of a Person
16 min.   color   1975   SCA
Dir. and prod: Joyce Chopra.   Dist: Phoenix.   Rental: California
Flashback shots of her earlier years in high school, of her wedding day, her children's Christening, and her inauguration as Radcliffe's President.   Her famous research about why women fail is presented in an animated sequence.   She's also shown on campus and at home.

HOSEA   See   JOB (Prophetic Voices of the Bible)

HOUSTON, JAMES

James Houston: The Vision Beyond the Mask (Writers on Writing

Series)
18 min.   color   1972   S
Prod: Davidson Films.   Dist: General Learning
    This writer-artist talks about his 12 years in the Canadian Arctic, where he lived with the Eskimos; he's the author of The White Dawn.

HOUSTON, SAMUEL

Governor Sam Houston (Profiles in Courage Series)
50 min.   b&w   1960   IJSCA
Prod: Robert Saudek Associates.   Dist: IQ Films.   Rental:
    Syracuse
    He was embroiled in the conflict over whether or not slavery should be allowed in the territories.

A Matter of Honor: Sam Houston
27 min.   b&w   1953   S
Prod: Teaching Film Custodians.   Dist: Indiana (lease)
    A re-enactment of Houston's disagreement with his wife and subsequent departure for Texas.   An excerpt from a Cavalcade of America television picture.

HOWARD, CATHERINE   See   HENRY VIII (The Six Wifes of Henry VIII); Henry VIII and His Six Wives (feature)

HOWE, ELIAS

Story of Elias Howe
11 min.   b&w   1939   PIJ
Prod: Columbia, edited by Teaching Film Custodians.   Dist:
    Indiana
    How he invented and marketed the sewing machine.   Dramatization.

HOWE, OSCAR

Oscar Howe: The Sioux Painter
27 min.   color   1974   SCA
Prod: Telecommunications Center, University of South Dakota.
    Dist: Centron (prefers sales only).   Rental: Syracuse
    He recalls how his cultural heritage dominated his paintings, for which he won over 15 grand or first awards in national contests.   Vincent Price narrates.

HUBBARD, BERNARD

The Glacier Priest

15 min.   b&w   1952-53   JSCA
Prod: Mike Sklar.   Dist: Star Film
His exploration of Alaska; compiled from the Fox Movietone News Library footage.

HUDSON, HENRY
See also CABOT, JOHN (Age of Discovery: English, French, and Dutch Explorations)

The Last Voyage of Henry Hudson
28 min.   b&w   1965   IJSC
Prod: National Film Board of Canada.   Dist: Perennial (special order; no previews).   Rental: Michigan
A dramatization of the voyage.   Also includes a history of exploration and equipment.

HUGHES, CHARLES EVANS

Chief Justice Charles Evans Hughes (Profiles in Courage Series)
50 min.   b&w   1965   IJSCA
Prod: Robert Saudek Associates.   Dist: IQ Films.   Rental: Syracuse
Risks his career to uphold the principle of representative government.

HUGHES, LANGSTON

Harlem Renaissance: The Black Poets
20 min.   color   1971   SCA
Prod: CBS.   Dist: Carousel (sale only).   Rental: Impact
Captures black experiences during the '20s and '30s and includes excerpts from well-known poems.

Langston Hughes
24 min.   color   1970   JSCA
Prod: CBS.   Dist: Carousel (sale only).   Rental: Association, Impact
A comprehensive biography and introduction to his work. Selections from "The Negro Mother," "The Best of Simple," and "The Big Sea" are read.

HUGO, VICTOR

Victor Hugo
37 min.
Dir: Roger Leenhardt.   Dist: Film Images

HULL, CORDELL

The Good Neighbor
15 min.   b&w   1952-53   JSCA
Prod: Mike Sklar.   Dist: Star Film.
His appointment as Secretary of State by Franklin Roosevelt; compiled from the Fox Movietone News Library footage.

HUMBOLDT, ALEXANDER VON

Alexander von Humboldt (Age of Exploration Series)
52 min.   color   1976   SCA
Prod: BBC-TV and Time-Life.   Dist: Time-Life (available on video)
The hazards of exploring the interior of Venezuela are dramatized.   Based on his 30-volume report.

HUMPHREY, HUBERT

Hubert Humphrey: New Man on Campus
59 min.   b&w   1969   SCA
Prod: NET.   Dist: Indiana
The former Vice President meets with his class of college students.

The Making of the President, 1968
82 min.   color or b&w   1969   SC
Prod: Metromedia Producers.   Dist: Films Inc.   Rental: Southern California, Syracuse
How the events of the '60s--the Vietnam War, student demonstrations, riots, King's and Kennedy's assassinations--affected the race between him and Nixon.

My Childhood: Hubert Humphrey's South Dakota (pt. 1)
51 min. (both parts)   b&w   1968   JSCA
Prod: Metromedia TV.   Dist: Benchmark.   Rental: Indiana, Michigan, Southern California, Syracuse, Viewfinders
He recalls his childhood as a very happy time and recounts how much his family meant to him.   Part 2 focuses on James Baldwin, a black writer who grew up in Harlem.

Primary: Humphrey vs. Kennedy
54 min.   b&w   1967   SCA
Prod: Drew Associates and Time-Life.   Dist: Time-Life.
Rental: Indiana
A cinéma vérité close-up of the historic Wisconsin primary.

HUNT, RICHARD

Richard Hunt--Sculptor

14 min.   color or b&w   1970   JSC
Prod. and dist: Encyclopaedia Britannica (available on video by
    special order).   Rental: Southern California, Syracuse
        The camera follows this black artist as he collects "junk"
and then welds it into a sculpture.

HURD, PETER

Painters of America: Peter Hurd
16 min.   color   1970   SC
Prod: MFC Film Productions.   Dist: Perspective (sale only)
        He talks about life as an artist at his ranch home in New
Mexico.

HUS (or HUSS), JAN (or JOHN)

Jan Hus
30 min.   b&w   1965
Prod: ABC.   Rental: National Council of the Churches of Christ
        A dramatic re-enactment of his hearing before the Inquisi-
tion Council of Constance in 1414 and of his conflicts with Pope
John.

HUSA, KAREL

Serenade pour Quintette
55 min.   CA
Dir: André Leroux.   Prod: ORTF.   Rental: FACSEA
        French dialogue only.   Bernard Gavoty interviews Czech
composer Husa, and his work "Serenade" is performed by the National Orchestra of the French Broadcasting System.

HUSTON, JOHN

Life and Times of John Huston, Esq.
60 min.   b&w   1966   SCA
Prod: NET.   Dist: Indiana.   Rental: California
        A portrait filmed at his castle in Ireland, where he dis-
cusses his successes and failures in the film world.   He talks
about theater and film personalities.   He's shown at work in Milan
and in London, making "Reflections in a Golden Eye."

HUTCHINSON, ANNE
    See also DYER, MARY (In a Violent Time)

Anne Hutchinson (Profiles in Courage Series)
50 min.   b&w   1965   IJSCA
Prod: Robert Saudek Associates.   Dist: IQ Films.   Rental:

Michigan, Minnesota, Syracuse
Dramatizes her fight for religious freedom and her banishment from Massachusetts.

IKEDA, MASUO

Masuo Ikeda: Printmaker
14 min.   color   1973   JSCA
Prod: KEI.   Dist: ACI.   Rental: Syracuse, Viewfinders
A modern Japanese artist demonstrating his art.

INGRES, JEAN-AUGUSTE DOMINIQUE

Jean-Auguste Dominique Ingres, Parts I and II (Romantic versus Classic Art Series)
26 min. each   color   1974   JSCA
Prod: Reader's Digest.   Dist: Pyramid.   Rental: Southern California (listed by series title)
The forces which shaped his life.   An analysis of some of his major works is given by narrator Kenneth Clark.

Monsieur Ingres
26 min.   color   1971   SCA
Dir. and prod: Roger Leenhardt.   Dist: Film Images
Traces his life in Paris, where he studied with David, and his years in Rome, where he painted many famous nudes.

IRVING, WASHINGTON

Spain: A Journey with Washington Irving
25 min.   color   1973
Prod. and dist: National Geographic Society (available in Spanish or videocassette or in the 50-min. television version)
Based on his diary, written during the 1820's, the camera re-visits the places he traveled to in Spain.

Washington Irving
18 min.   b&w   1949   JS
Prod. and dist: Encyclopaedia Britannica (available on video by special order).   Rental: Indiana, Michigan, Minnesota, Nebraska, South Florida, Syracuse
Both his early life in New York and his life abroad.

Washington Irving's World
12 min.   color   1966   IJSC
Prod: Walter P. Lewisohn.   Dist: Coronet (sale only).   Rental: Indiana, Michigan, Syracuse
Narrated from his literary works and letters.   The visuals are paintings, prints, and scenes from his home, "Sunnyside."

Masuo Ikeda: <u>Printmaker</u> (ACI Media, Inc.)

IRWIN, JAMES B.

Highflight
30 min.
Dist: Southern Baptist Radio-Television Commission
Astronaut Irwin recalls his role on the historic Apollo 15 moon mission and how it changed his life. He resigned his NASA post to head Highflight, a religious organization.

ISABELLA I See COLUMBUS, CHRISTOPHER (Columbus and Isabella)

ISAIAH, FIRST See JOB (Prophetic Voices of the Bible)

ISAIAH, SECOND See JOB (Prophetic Voices of the Bible)

IVAN IV VASILIEVICH (THE TERRIBLE) See Ivan the Terrible (feature)

JABBAR, KAREEM ABDUL- See ABDUL-JABBAR, KAREEM

JACKSON, ANDREW
See also CALHOUN, JOHN C. (States' Rights)

Andrew Jackson
18 min.   b&w   1951   IJS
Prod. and dist: Encyclopaedia Britannica (available on video by special order). Rental: Indiana, Michigan, Minnesota, Nebraska, South Florida, Southern California, Syracuse
Re-enacts boyhood incidents and stresses his military career and presidential years when he was the symbol of the common man.

Andrew Jackson at the Hermitage
16 min.   color   1964   JSC
Prod. and dist: Coronet (sale only). Rental: Indiana, Michigan, Minnesota, Syracuse
Re-creates his visit to his home in Nashville during his re-election campaign in 1832. Told through his own words.

Andrew Jackson's Hermitage (American Life Styles Series)
23 min.   color   1975   JSA
Prod: Comco Productions. Dist: ACI. Rental: Syracuse
He planned his mansion and farm building and had them built in Tennessee. Host E. G. Marshall discusses Jackson's life as reflected by his home.

Andrew Jackson's Hermitage (ACI Media, Inc.)

Era of the Common Man--The Age of Jackson (1828-1848)
30 min.   b&w   1966   JSCA
Prod: NBC. Dist: Graphic Curriculum (available for closed circuit television). Rental: Minnesota

The Jackson Years: The New Americans (American Heritage
  Series)
27 min.   color   1971   JSCA
Dir: Dennis Azzarella. Prod. and dist: Learning. Rental:
  Southern California, Syracuse.
    Dramatizations from real life incidents explore the "com-
mon man" image associated with him.

The Jackson Years: Toward Civil War (American Heritage Series)
27 min.   color   1971   JSCA
Dir: Dennis Azzarella. Prod. and dist: Learning. Rental:
  Syracuse
    The major events of his administration--Turner's slave re-
bellion, the clash between the men who favored states' rights and
those who favored Federal law--are dramatized.

Young Andy Jackson
20 min.   b&w   1954   PIJ
Prod: Teaching Film Custodians. Dist: Indiana (lease)
    He and his brother enlist in the South Carolina militia;
they are captured by the British, but later released. An excerpt
from the Cavalcade of America television movie.

JACKSON, JESSE

Conversation with Jesse Jackson
30 min.   b&w
Prod: ABC.   Rental: National Council of Churches
    An interview with Frank Reynolds about civil rights.

JACKSON, MAHALIA

Got to Tell It: A Tribute to Mahalia Jackson
34 min.   color   1974   SCA
Dir. and prod: Jules Victor Schwerin.   Dist: Phoenix.   Rental:
    Syracuse, Viewfinders
    A portrait of the Queen of the gospels.   Old photos tell the
story of her childhood and footage of her funeral is also included.
She sings 11 songs.

JACKSON, REGGIE

One Man Wild Bunch--Reggie Jackson (The Winners Series)
48 min.   color   1976   SCA
Prod: Laurel.   Dist: Counselor
    A sports portrait with comments by sports journalist Dave
Anderson.

JACKSON, THOMAS JONATHAN (STONEWALL)
    See also LEE, ROBERT EDWARD (Lee, the Virginian)

The Death of Stonewall Jackson (You Are There Series)
26 min.   b&w   1955   IJSCA
Prod. and dist: CBS (sale only; no previews or rentals).   Rental:
    Indiana, Michigan, Minnesota, Southern California
    An "on the scene" news dramatization of the Civil War and
the death of Jackson, whose own men mistakenly shot him.

JEFFERS, ROBINSON

Robinson Jeffers
30 min.   b&w   1967   SCA
Prod: NET.   Dist: Indiana
    The poetry, philosophy, home, and family of Jeffers.   Dame
Judith Anderson presents a passage from "The Power Beyond
Tragedy. "

JEFFERSON, THOMAS
    See also HAMILTON, ALEXANDER (Democracy--Equality or
    Privilege? Thomas Jefferson vs. Alexander Hamilton); (Man
    and the State: Hamilton and Jefferson on Democracy)

The Absent Host: Jefferson, 1781
18 min.   b&w   1954   S
Prod: Teaching Film Custodians.   Dist: Indiana
    Dramatizes Jack Jovett's warning to Jefferson that British
soldiers were planning to capture him.

Administration of Thomas Jefferson
13 1/2 min.   color   1972   JS
Prod. and dist: Coronet (sale only)
    Uses his own words to describe his eight years in office
and the conflicts between his political philosophies and the realities
of the Presidency.

Dilemma of Thomas Jefferson
29 min.   b&w   1956   C
Prod: University of Michigan.   Rental: Michigan
    Based on his ideas, universal education was developed in
America.

Experiment at Monticello: Thomas Jefferson and Smallpox Vacci-
    nation
18 min.   b&w   1953   JS
Prod: Teaching Film Custodians.   Dist: Indiana (lease)
    A dramatization of Jefferson's support of Dr. Benjamin
Waterhouse, who wanted to introduce the vaccination developed by
Dr. William Jenner in England.

Jefferson--The Architect
11 min.   b&w   1949   SC
Dist: Withdrawn by IFB.   Rental: Indiana
    His architectural designs with emphasis on Monticello.

Jefferson's Monticello
25 min.   color   1970   IJSA
Prod: WRC-TV.   Dist: Films Inc.   Rental: Syracuse
    The planning and construction of his home.   Jefferson's own
words are spoken by actor Peter Lombard from the Broadway production, "1776."

Thomas Jefferson (Americana Series #3)
28 min.   color   1966   IJSCA
Prod: Leo A. Handel.   Dist: Handel.   Rental: Indiana, Syracuse
    Traces his career from his student days to his election as
President; includes his role in the purchase of the Louisiana terri-
tory, his creation of Monticello, his development of the Library of
Congress and West Point.

Thomas Jefferson
18 min.   b&w   1949   IJS
Prod. and dist: Encyclopaedia Britannica (available on video by
    special order).   Rental: Indiana, Michigan, Minnesota, Nebras-
    ka, South Florida, Southern California, Syracuse
    His roles as statesman, diplomat, and farmer.

Thomas Jefferson's Monticello (American Life Styles Series)
23 min.   color   1975   IJSA
Prod: Comco Productions.   Dist: ACI
        A tour of Jefferson's home which he designed.   Hosted by
E. G. Marshall.

Thomas Jefferson's Monticello (ACI Media, Inc.)

JEFFRIES, JAMES J.   See   JOHNSON, JACK (Jeffries-Johnson
    1910)

JENNER, WILLIAM

Story of Dr. Jenner
11 min.   b&w   1940   JSCA
Prod: MGM, edited by Teaching Film Custodians.   Rental:
    Michigan, Minnesota, South Florida
        His development of the smallpox vaccine.

JEREMIAH   See   JOB (Prophetic Voices of the Bible)

JESUS
    See also   Day of Triumph (feature)

Christ Is Born
52 min.   color   1969   JSCA
Prod: John Secondari. Dist: Learning. Rental: Nebraska,
Southern California, Syracuse, United Church of Christ
Filmed on location, it traces the events of his birth including the history of the Hebrew people. Excerpts from the Bible
are read by John Huston.

The Coming of Christ
28 min.   color   1963   SCA
Prod: NBC. Dist: Films Inc. Rental: Michigan, Minnesota,
Nebraska, Southern California
His early life as shown through paintings and scenes of the
Apostles. This is a companion film to He Is Risen, which tells
about his early life.

The Crucifixion of Jesus
40 min.   color   1973   PIJSCA
Prod: David Wolper. Dist: American Educational Films
A re-creation of his last six days, narrated by John Huston.

The Face of Jesus
8 min.   color   1969   SCA
Prod: CBS. Rental: United Church of Christ
An excerpt from "60 Minutes" in which Harry Reasoner
narrates a tour of masterpieces by well known artists such as
Gauguin and Rembrandt on their conceptions of Christ. A six-
minute version without narration is also available.

He Is Risen
30 min.   color   1963   JSCA
Prod: NBC. Dist: Films Inc. Rental: Minnesota, Nebraska,
South Florida, Southern California
The Passion of Christ as shown through famous paintings.

Life of Christ
22 min.   color   1954
Prod: United Church of Christ. Rental: United Church of Christ
The Biblical story of his life illustrated by the paintings of
Jacques Barosin.

Living Christ (series)
30 min. each   color or b&w   1951-57   JSCA
Prod: Cathedral Films. Rental: Christian Church, Yale Divinity
School
The 12 films in the series are based on the accounts of his
life as told in the Scriptures. His birth, boyhood, teachings, min-
istry, death and resurrection are dramatized. The individual
titles are the following: Holy Night, Escape to Egypt, Boyhood
and Baptism, Men of the Wilderness, Challenge of Faith, Disciple-
ship, Return to Nazareth, Conflict, Fate of John the Baptist, Retreat and Decision, Triumph and Defeat, Crucifixion and Resurrection. All are also available in Spanish; all except episodes 3, 4,

11, and 12 are available in Portuguese. Episode 5 is available in Japanese, Mandarin, Cantonese; episode 7 in all of the above plus French, Hindi, Korean, and Indonesian.

The New Testament in the Light of Archeology: In the Steps of John and Jesus (a series)
30 min. each   b&w   1964
Prod: NBC. Rental: National Council of the Churches of Christ
      Dr. Jack Finegan conducts a tour of the Holy Land. Two of the four films deal with the life and ministry of Jesus: Bethlehem and Nazareth, and Capernaum and Jericho.

JOAN OF ARC
   See also   Joan of Arc (feature); The Passion of Joan of Arc (feature)

The Final Hours of Joan of Arc (You Are There Series)
26 min.   b&w   1956   SCA
Prod. and dist: CBS (sale only; no previews). Rental: Indiana, Minnesota, Nebraska, Syracuse
      An "on the scene" news dramatization of her trial and execution.

Histoire de Jeanne
13 min.   color   SCA
Prod: Francis Lacassin. Rental: FACSEA
      Manuscript illustrations from such sources as the Bibliothèque Nationale trace her story.

Jeanne de France
33 min.   color   CA
Dir: Jean Lehérissey. Rental: FACSEA
      French dialogue only. Shot on location, peasants, priests, townsmen, princes, etc. at her rehabilitation trial (25 years after her death) say how they saw her.

Joan of Arc
8 min.   color   1970   S
Prod: Concept Films of Australia. Dist: Macmillan (sale only). Rental: Association, South Florida, Syracuse
      Elementary French version. (Also available in an Advanced French version, 10 min.). Her life shown by artwork and maps.

Joan of Arc (Profiles in Power)
30 min.   color   1976   JSCA
Prod: McConnell Advertising Co. and Ontario Communications Authority. Dist: Learning
      Sandy Dennis as Joan of Arc is "interviewed" by Patrick Watson, who challenges her accomplishments.

The Secret Mirror: Joan of Arc's France
53 min.   color   1973

Prod: James Gloege Productions. Dist: Viacom International
(available in French and Spanish)
Traces her journey across France, with commentary taken
from her own words and spoken by Julie Harris.

The Torment of Joan of Arc (You Are There Series)
22 min.   color   1972   IJ
Prod: CBS. Dist: BFA. Rental: Syracuse
The torture and the trial are reported.

JOB

Prophetic Voices of the Bible (a series)
30 min. each   b&w   1965
Prod: NBC. Rental: National Council of the Churches of Christ
Dr. Hagen Staack presents information about the lives and
significance of each prophet in these 12 films: Introduction to the
Prophets, Elijah, Amos, Hosea, First Isaiah, Jeremiah, Ezekiel,
Second Isaiah, Job, Jonah, Daniel, and The Revelation to St. John.

JONAH See JOB (Prophetic Voices of the Bible)

JOHN

"I, John"
30 min.
Prod. and dist: Southern Baptist Radio-Television Commission
Retraces the steps of the exile John, who wrote the last
book of the New Testament.

JOHN XXIII, POPE See Man Named John (feature)

JOHNS, JASPER
See also DE KOONING, WILLEM (Painters Painting)

Artists: Jasper Johns
30 min.   b&w   1966   SCA
Prod: NET. Dist: Indiana
A series of interviews in his South Carolina studio and a
lithographic workshop.

JOHNSON, ANDREW
See also Tennessee Johnson (feature)

Andrew Johnson (Profiles in Courage Series)
50 min.   b&w   1966   JSCA
Prod: Robert Saudek Associates. Dist: IQ Films. Rental:

Michigan, Minnesota
The only Senator to retain his seat when his state (Tennessee) left the Union.

The Arrow and the Bow: Andrew Johnson
20 min.   b&w   1953
Prod: Teaching Film Custodians. Dist: Indiana
A dramatization of his early years, and his marriage to Eliza McCardle. An excerpt from the Cavalcade of America television movie.

Johnson and Reconstruction
33 min.   b&w   1950   SC
Prod: MGM, edited by Teaching Film Custodians. Rental: California, Minnesota, South Florida, Syracuse
Abridged from the feature Tennessee Johnson, this dramatization shows his refusal to join Tennessee when the state left the Union.

Impeachment of a President: Andrew Johnson vs. Thaddeus
Stevens--1868 (History Alive! Series)
14 min.   color   1970   JSC
Prod: Turnley Walker. Dist: Walt Disney (long-term lease)
A dramatization of Stevens' clash with Johnson after Johnson dismissed a Cabinet member over the objections of Congress.

JOHNSON, JACK

Jack Johnson
90 min.   b&w   1970   rated PG
Dir: William Cayton. Rental: Macmillan
The battles he fought in and out of the ring as the first black heavyweight champion of the world. A documentary.

Jeffries-Johnson 1910
21 min.   b&w   1971   SA
Dir: William Kimberlin. Dist: Withdrawn by McGraw-Hill
Before this heavyweight championship fight was fought, a racist campaign was waged against Johnson. This is a re-creation of the match shot from old photos and footage.

JOHNSON, JAMES WELDON

James Weldon Johnson (Poetry by Americans Series)
12 min.   color   1972   JSC
Prod: Art Evans. Dist: Paramount Oxford. Rental: Minnesota, Nebraska (listed by series title), Syracuse
His poem "The Creation" is read following a brief biographical sketch. Captioned for the deaf.

JOHNSON, LYNDON BAINES
See also GOLDWATER, BARRY (The Making of the President, 1964)

The Journey of Lyndon Johnson
51 min.   color   1975   JSC
Prod: Lyndon Baines Johnson Productions. Dist: Films Inc.
    Rental: Syracuse
        Traces his political career, especially the burdens of the
Presidency and his dream for the "Great Society."

LBJ: The Last Interview
43 min.   b&w   1973   SCA
Prod: CBS. Dist: Carousel (sale only)
        An interview in which he talks about the Vietnam War and
the "Great Society."

The President at Work
31 min.   b&w   1966   JSCA
Prod: NBC. Dist: Films Inc. Rental: Minnesota, Southern
    California
        The camera records him at his daily work. Televised as
"Seven Days in the Life of the President."

Seven Days in the Life of a President
50 min.   b&w   1965   SCA
Prod: Metromedia Productions. Dist: Films Inc.
        A behind the scenes look at him during one week. The
President at Work is a shortened version.

JOHNSON, PHILIP See DE KOONING, WILLEM (Painters Paint-
    ing)

JOLLIET (or JOLIET), LOUIS See CARTIER, JACQUES (French
    Explorations in the New World); MARQUETTE, JACQUES (Mar-
    quette and Jolliet: Voyage of Discovery)

JOLSON, AL See The Jolson Story (feature)

JONES, BEN

Monarchs of the Turf
15 min.   b&w   1952-53   JSCA
Prod: Mike Sklar. Dist: Star Film
        A thoroughbred trainer at work. Compiled from the Fox
Movietone News Library footage.

JONES, JAMES

Private World of James Jones
30 min.   b&w   1967   SCA
Prod: NET.   Dist: Indiana
     Shown at his daily activities, he discusses his past, his political ideas, and writing.

JONES, JOHN PAUL
  See also John Paul Jones (feature)

Night Strike: John Paul Jones
20 min.   b&w   1953   PIJ
Prod: Teaching Film Custodians.   Dist: Indiana (lease)
     A raid on the coast of England, which convinces the French to provide him with a warship.   Adapted from the Cavalcade of America television movie.

JONES, ROBERT (BOBBY)

Old Man Par
15 min.   b&w   1952-53   JSCA
Prod: Mike Sklar.   Dist: Star Film
     His rise within the golf world.   Compiled from the Fox Movietone News Library.

JOPLIN, JANIS

Janis: The Way She Was
96 min.   color   1974   SCA
Dir: Howard Alk.   Prod: Universal.   Dist: Swank
     A documentary of her and her music.

JOSHUA   See   MOSES (Living Personalities of the Old Testament)

JOSIAH   See   MOSES (Living Personalities of the Old Testament)

JOYCE, JAMES

James Joyce's Dublin
22 min.   color   1967   SCA
Prod: Michael and Ulick O'Connor.   Dist: Carousel (sale only).
  Rental: Association
     His life as a young man in Edwardian Dublin and on the continent after his self-exile, and in Zurich where he died.

Silence, Exile and Cunning: The World of James Joyce
30 min.   b&w   1969   SCA
Prod: BBC-TV.   Dist: Time-Life (available on video)
        Shot in Dublin; the viewer sees many of the places about
which he wrote.   Anthony Burgess' commentary is about the man
and his works.

JUAREZ, BENITO

Juarez
32 min.   b&w   1930   JSCA
Prod: Warner Bros., edited by Teaching Film Custodians.   Dist:
    Indiana (lease; available on 8mm cartridge)
        He led Mexico against Louis Napoleon III.   An excerpt from
a feature film of the same title.

JUDAH, THEODORE DEHONE

Crazy Judah: The Transcontinental Railroad
20 min.   b&w   1954   JS
Prod: Teaching Film Custodians.   Dist: Indiana
        Dramatized events in his life which show his efforts to uni-
fy the U.S. by a railroad system.   An excerpt from the Cavalcade
of America television movie.

JUNG, CARL GUSTAV

Carl Gustav Jung
38 min.   b&w   1972   CA
Prod: BBC-TV.   Dist: Time-Life (available on video)
        An in-depth interview in his home, where he talks about his
childhood, his work, and his relationship with Freud.

Discussion with Dr. Carl G. Jung (Notable Contributors Series)
32 min.   b&w   1971   C
Prod: Dr. Richard Evans.   Dist: Macmillan (sale only).   Rental:
    Association, Syracuse
        An interview in which he discusses his relationship with
Freud, the unconscious, and introversion-extroversion.

Face to Face
39 min.   b&w   1959   CA
Prod: BBC-TV.   Dist: Withdrawn.   Rental: California, Michigan
        In an interview done when he was 84 he discusses his fam-
ily, his school years, his career, his split with Freud, and his
philosophical ideas.

Jung Speaks of Freud
29 min.   b&w   1957
Dist: Pennsylvania State University

An interview in his home in Zurich; the accent makes listening hard.

The Story of Carl Gustav Jung (a series)
30 min. each   color   1972   SCA
Prod: BBC-TV. Dist: Time-Life (available on video). Rental: California, Michigan
Shot primarily in Switzerland, but also includes unique footage of him on safari in Africa. In Search of the Soul (part 1) traces his childhood, his years at the University and his first years as a psychiatrist. 67,000 Dreams (part 2) focuses on the building of Bollingen, a stone tower that served as his retreat. The Mystery That Heals (part 3) shows him as an old man, who broke with Freud.

KAFKA, FRANZ

The Trials of Franz Kafka
15 min.   b&w   1968   SC
Prod: Kratky Film and Harold Mantell. Dist: Films for the Humanities (available on 3/4" videocassette)
Shot in Prague. His childhood, his young adult years, and the tragedies of his last years are revealed.

KAHLO, FRIDA

The Life and Death of Frida Kahlo
40 min.   color   1975 (release)   CA
Dir: Karen and David Crommie. Dist: Serious Business
Traces the flamboyant life of this painter with comments on her surrealist art. She was married to Diego Rivera.

KANDINSKY, WASSILY

Kandinsky
15 min.   color   1972   JSCA
Dir. and prod: H. G. Zeiss. Dist: Roland Collection
His tortured life as an artist is documented with emphasis on his Russian origins, which made a deep impression upon him. Examples of his pictures are analyzed.

KANE, PAUL

Paul Kane Goes West
16 min.   color   1972   JSCA
Prod: National Film Board of Canada. Dist: Encyclopaedia Britannica (available on video by special order)
Throughout the late 1840's he traveled in Canada, where he painted and sketched the Indians.

KEATON, BUSTER

Buster Keaton Rides Again
55 min.   b&w   1966   SA
Prod: National Film Board of Canada.   Dist: Withdrawn by
   McGraw-Hill.   Rental: California, Michigan, Minnesota, Kit
   Parker
         A film about how he made a Canadian travel film entitled
"The Railroader." He tells several anecdotes about his life in
show business and excerpts from some of his silent movies are
used.

The Great Stone Face
110 min.   color
Prod. and dist: Productions Unlimited
         A biography plus scenes from "The General," "Limelight,"
"Slapstick" and "The Railroader."

KEATS, EZRA JACK

Ezra Jack Keats
17 min.   color   1970   SCA
Prod. and dist: Weston Woods
         How his life and environment affect the children's books he
writes.   Concludes with an iconographic motion picture of A Letter
to Amy.

KEATS, JOHN

John Keats: Poet (Humanities Series)
31 min.   color   1973   SC
Prod. and dist: Encyclopaedia Britannica (available on video by
   special order).   Rental: Michigan (55-minute version), Minnesota, Southern California, Syracuse
         A dramatization of his early life in England until his death
at the age of 26 in Rome.   Excerpts from his letters and poetry
are interspersed.   A longer version, John Keats: His Life and
Death, explores more fully his love affair with Fanny Brawne.
Both were written by Archibald MacLeish.

KELLER, HELEN
   See also Miracle Worker (feature)

Helen Keller
24 min.   b&w   1965   IJ
Prod: Metromedia Producers.   Dist: Sterling (sale only; available on 8mm).   Rental: Mass Media, Syracuse
         Her childhood, her college career and her work with the
blind are told primarily through newsreel footage.

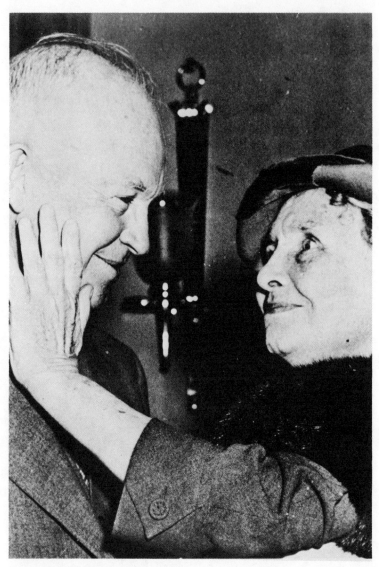

Helen Keller (McGraw-Hill Films)

Helen Keller (Biography Series)
15 min.   color   1969   IJSCA
Prod: McGraw-Hill in collaboration with Project 7 Films. Dist:
    McGraw-Hill. Rental: Indiana
        How she overcame her handicaps with the aid of her teach-
er, Anne Sullivan.

Helen Keller and Her Teacher
27 min.   color   1970   IJSCA
Prod: McGraw-Hill in collaboration with Project 7 Films. Dist:
    McGraw-Hill. Rental: California, Minnesota
        An expanded version of Helen Keller, it more thoroughly
reveals the relationship between her and her teacher, Anne Sullivan.

Helen Keller in Her Story
45 min.   b&w   1956   JSCA
Prod: Louis de Rochemont Associates. Dist: Phoenix (sale only).
    Rental: American Foundation for the Blind, Mass Media, Michi-
    gan, Minnesota, Nebraska
        From her birth until '56 her struggles and victories are
told. Compiled from actual footage, newsreels, and silent films.
Narrated by the late Katharine Cornell.

KELLY, GRACE

Grace Kelly
26 min.   b&w   1965   SC
Prod: Metromedia Producers. Dist: Sterling (sale only; avail-
    able on 8mm). Rental: Syracuse
        How she became a star only to relinquish stardom for
marriage.

KENDRICKS, EDDIE

Eddie Kendricks
7 min.   color   1975   SCA
Dir: Andrew Chiaramonte. Dist: Phoenix Films
        The rock music of a star, his background, and his rela-
tionship to the audience.

KENNEDY, EDWARD See KENNEDY, ROSE (The Impact of the
    Kennedys: The Past; Rose Kennedy Remembers; Rose Kennedy
    Remembers--The Best of Times ... The Worst of Times)

KENNEDY, JOHN FITZGERALD
    See also EISENHOWER, DWIGHT DAVID (Five Presidents on
    the Presidency); HUMPHREY, HUBERT (Primary: Humphrey vs.
    Kennedy); KENNEDY, ROSE (The Impact of the Kennedys: The

Past; Mother of the Kennedys; and Rose Kennedy Remembers)

The Age of Kennedy: The Early Years
46 min.   b&w   1967   JSCA
Prod: NBC. Dist: McGraw-Hill. Rental: Indiana, Michigan,
    Minnesota, Nebraska, Southern California, Syracuse
        Home movies and newsreel footage record his life from his
Harvard days to his years in Congress as a Senator.

Age of Kennedy: The Presidency
52 min.   b&w   1966   JSCA
Prod: NBC. Dist: McGraw-Hill. Rental: Indiana, Michigan,
    Minnesota, Nebraska, Southern California, Syracuse
        His policies and programs, his confrontations and con-
ferences during his 1,000 days as President. Uses newsreels.

America Buries a President
21 min.   b&w   1975   JSCA
Prod: Hearst. Dist: Counselor Films. Rental: Southern Cali-
    fornia
        Begins with a look at his early life, reviews the challenges
of his administration, and ends with his assassination.

The Burden and the Glory of John F. Kennedy
52 min.   b&w   1964   SCA
Prod: CBS. Dist: Carousel (sale only). Rental: Association,
    Michigan, Minnesota, Syracuse
        Kennedy himself comments on some of the significant events
of his administration, and so do Hubert Humphrey, Averill Harri-
man, and the late Adlai Stevenson.

Inauguration of John F. Kennedy--35th President of the United
    States
18 min.   color   1961   JSCA
Prod: U.S. Information Agency. Rental: National Audiovisual
    Center
        His inaugural address, in which he said the famous line,
"Ask not what your country can do for you, but what you can do
for your country."

JFK: Challenges and Tragedy
18 min.   b&w   1975   JSA
Prod: American School and Library Films. Dist: ACI. Rental:
    Syracuse
        The problems he confronted during office, such as the
Russian missile crisis and the civil rights disputes. Taken from
newsreel footage.

JFK: The New Generation
22 min.   b&w   1975   JSA
Prod: American School and Library Films. Dist: ACI. Rental:
    Syracuse
        Newsreel footage shows him being sworn in, and important

events from his first year in office such as U. S. Steel's price reversal.

John F. Kennedy--Man and President
10 min.   b&w   1963
Prod: Castle Films. Dist: Creative Film Society
      His private and political lives.

John F. Kennedy: Years of Lightning, Day of Drums
84 min.   color   JSCA
Prod: George Stevens, Jr. Dist: Avco Embassy
      Opens with his Inauguration and then shows the programs he
initiated. The personal JFK is shown through vignettes of him
with his wife and children. Narrated by Gregory Peck.

John Fitzgerald Kennedy: A History of Our Times
50 min.   b&w   1964
Prod: Official Films. Dist: Macmillan (7-year lease). Rental:
      Syracuse
      The highlights of his life, such as his years at Harvard,
and the key events of his administration, such as the Cuban crisis.
Emphasizes his public life. Narrated by Cliff Robertson.

John Fitzgerald Kennedy, 1917-1963
21 min.   b&w   1964   SCA
Prod: 20th Century-Fox. Dist: Films Inc. Rental: Michigan,
      Minnesota, Nebraska, Southern California, Syracuse
      Highlights of his life. Opens with his funeral and flashes
back to trace his rise within the political world. Uses newsreel
footage.

Kennedy vs. Khrushchev
25 min.   b&w   1965   SC
Prod: Metromedia Producers. Dist: Films Inc.
      The conflict over the missiles in Cuba. Narrated by Edmond O'Brien.

Kennedy: What Is Remembered Is Never Lost
23 min.   b&w   1966   SC
Prod: NBC. Dist: Films Inc. Rental: California, Minnesota
      A memorial tribute in which correspondents who knew him
comment about him. Adapted from "J. F. K. Remembered. "

The Making of the President, 1960
80 min.   b&w   1963   SC
Prod: Metromedia Producers. Dist: Films Inc. Rental: Indi-
      ana (2 pts.), Michigan, Minnesota, South Florida, Southern
      California, Syracuse
      The presidential campaigns of Kennedy and Nixon, which
utilizes newsreel footage and footage of the famous debates.

Parallels in History: Kennedy and Lincoln
10 1/2 min.   color   1974   JSCA

Prod. and dist: Doubleday (available on super 8 sound)
The uncanny similarities between the lives and political careers of these two Presidents.

A Thousand Days
25 min.   b&w   1964   JSCA
Prod: David Wolper.   Rental: Mass Media
The presidential career of JFK interspersed with light personal moments. Narrated by Richard Basehart.

KENNEDY, ROBERT   See   KENNEDY, ROSE (The Impact of the
Kennedys: The Past; Rose Kennedy Remembers; and Rose Kennedy Remembers--The Best of Times ... The Worst of Times)

KENNEDY, ROSE

The Impact of the Kennedys: The Past
26 min.   color   1973   SCA
Prod: Koplin and Grinker.   Dist: Pictura
Rose Kennedy talks about her family--their disappointments and their achievements.

Mother of the Kennedys
57 min.   color   1974   SCA
Prod: Radharc Inc.   Dist: Mass Media
A portrait filmed at her Hyannis home, emphasizing her spiritual beliefs. In interviews her daughter Eunice Shriver and son Ted describe her as a mother.

Rose Kennedy Remembers
24 min.   color   1975   SCA
Prod. and dist: Doubleday (available on super 8 sound)
Based on her manuscript of the same title.

Rose Kennedy Remembers--The Best of Times ... The Worst of
Times
52 min.   color   1975   SCA
Prod: BBC-TV.   Dist: Time-Life
Incorporates photos and film clips as she reveals her emotional feelings about being a Kennedy, the events which shaped her life, and the ups and downs of her family.

KENYATTA, JOMO

Kenyatta
51 min.   color   1973   SCA
Prod: Anthony-Davis Productions.   Dist: Films Inc.
The life of Kenyatta and how he led Kenya to independence.
Also available in a 28-minute version.

KEY, FRANCIS SCOTT

Song of a Nation (Our American Heritage Series)
19 min.   color   n. d.
Dist: Macmillan
    A re-enactment of circumstances which led Key to write the
"Star-Spangled Banner. "

KHRUSHCHEV, NIKITA

Khrushchev and the Thaw (Revolution in Russia Series)
20 min.   b&w   1970   JSCA
Prod: BBC-TV.   Dist: Time-Life (available in Spanish)
    The de-Stalinization period.

The Khrushchev Era (The Red Myth Series)
29 min.   b&w   1960   SCA
Prod: NET.   Rental: Indiana, Minnesota, Syracuse
    His rise to power and the policies of his regime.

Leninism, Stalinism, Khrushchevism (Communism--Myth vs. Reality
   Series)
29 min.   b&w   1962   SCA
Prod. and dist: Southern California
    The life and influences that molded each man and the mark
of each on Russia.

Nikita Khrushchev (Biography Series)
26 min.   b&w   1964   JS
Prod: David Wolper.   Dist: Withdrawn by McGraw-Hill.   Rental:
   Indiana, Michigan, Minnesota, Southern California
    His rise from a minor party worker to the top leader.

The Rise of Khrushchev
52 min.   b&w   1963   JSCA
Prod: McGraw-Hill.   Rental: Indiana, Southern California, Syracuse
    Traces his career from the time of Stalin's death until his
successful climb to the top of the Communist hierarchy.

KIERKEGAARD, SOREN

Kierkegaard--Sounds of Alienation
30 min.   b&w   1966
Prod: CBS.   Rental: National Council of the Churches of Christ
    Emphasizes his struggle with organized religion.   Jerry
Orbach reads excerpts from his writings.

Soren Kierkegaard (A Third Testament Series)
55 min.   color   1976   SCA
Prod: BBC-TV.   Dist: Time-Life (available on video)

His ugliness and gloomy home were largely responsible for the introspective life he led. His existentialist religious thought is explored.

KING, BILLIE JEAN

Billie Jean King
22 min.   color   1972   SCA
Prod: Tele-Sports. Dist: Paramount Oxford
    Her portrait and sports philosophy.

KING, MARTIN LUTHER
    See also GANDHI, MAHATMA (Non-Violence--Mahatma Gandhi
    and Martin Luther King: The Teacher and the Pupil)

The Heritage of Martin Luther King
30 min.   b&w   1972
Prod: ABC. Rental: National Council of the Churches of Christ
    A memorial tribute to King narrated by Frank Reynolds,
with remembrances by his friends and colleagues.

"I Have a Dream...": The Life of Martin Luther King
35 min.   b&w   1968   JSCA
Prod: CBS. Dist: BFA. Rental: Indiana, Michigan, Minnesota,
    Southern California, Syracuse
    The story of his life told through actual news footage.

King: A Filmed Record, Montgomery to Memphis
3 hrs. , 103 min. or 81 min.   SCA
Prod: Ely Landau. Dist: Film Images (available on 35mm)
    A record of the civil rights movement and King's role.
Newsreel and television footage chronicle the historic Montgomery
bus boycott, the sit-ins, the Freedom Rides, and other key events.
Excerpts from his well known speeches. The 103-minute version
is an abridged version of the 3-hour film; the 81-minute version is
the first 81 minutes of the original.

Legacy of a Dream
29 min.   color   1974   SCA
Dir. and prod: Richard Kaplan for the Martin Luther King Founda-
    tion. Dist: Film Images
    The struggles of King during the '50 and '60s and how those
struggles relate to today's society. Historic footage from the civil
rights campaigns is combined with new footage of the '70s.

Martin Luther King
30 min.   b&w   1970   JSCA
Prod: BBC-TV. Dist: Time-Life (available on video)
    An interview in which he talks about segregation, the bus
boycott and his hopes and feelings.

Martin Luther King, Jr.
10 min.   color   1972   IJS
Prod. and dist: Encyclopaedia Britannica (available on video by
  special order).   Rental: Syracuse
     His role as spokesman for blacks, his fight for civil rights
through peaceful sit-ins and marches.

Martin Luther King, Jr.: A Man of Peace
29 min.   b&w   1968   JSCA
Prod: Walter Schwimmer, Inc.   Dist: Journal.   Rental: Michigan, Minnesota, South Florida, Syracuse
     Expresses his philosophy of non-violence and his role in the
civil rights movement.

Martin Luther King, Jr.: Montgomery to Memphis
27 min.   b&w   1969   IJSCA
Prod. and dist: BFA.   Rental: Anti-Defamation League, Indiana,
  Nebraska, South Florida, Syracuse
     The highlights of his career as a civil rights leader from
1954 until 1968 when he was assassinated.   Includes excerpts from
his speeches.

Martin Luther King: The Man and the March
83 min.   b&w   1968   SCA
Prod: NET.   Dist: Indiana.   Rental: California
     A documentary recording King's "Poor People's March. "

KINGSLEY, MARY

Mary Kingsley (Age of Exploration Series)
52 min.   color   1976   SCA
Prod: BBC-TV and Time-Life.   Dist: Time-Life (available on
  video)
     Her journey on the coast of West Africa.   Dramatized.

KISSINGER, HENRY

Kissinger: An Action Biography
52 min.   1974
Prod. and dist: ABC.   Free loan: Aetna
     His early years, his role in foreign policy and an in-depth
interview with Howard K. Smith and Ted Koppel.

KLEE, PAUL

Paul Klee: The Act of Creation
24 min.   color
Dir: Rene Micha.   Dist: Film Images

Paul Klee: Child of Creation
7 1/2 min.   color   1970   PIJSCA
Prod: King Screen.   Dist: BFA.   Rental: California, Syracuse
     In this portrait youngsters comment on his paintings.

KOCH, ROBERT

The Vision of Dr. Koch (You Are There Series)
22 min.   color   1972   IJ
Prod: CBS.   Dist: BFA.   Rental: Syracuse
     A re-enactment of an incident intended to disprove his
theory that a single germ could cause disease.

KOKOSCHKA, OSKAR
  See also ADENAUER, KONRAD (Kokoschka Paints Adenauer)

Kokoschka
11 min.   color   1973   SCA
Prod: Giorgio Patara.   Dist: Roland Collection
     His paintings from 1910 to 1940 reveal his tortured life.

KORBUT, OLGA

Olga: A Film Portrait
47 min.   color   1975   JSCA
Prod: Granada International Productions.   Dist: Carousel (sale
   only).   Rental: Michigan, Syracuse
     A beautifully photographed behind-the-scenes look at one of
the world's greatest gymnasts.   Many of her exercises are seen.

KOSCIUSZKO, THADDEUS

Kosciuszko: An American Portrait
58 min.   color   1976
Prod: Reader's Digest.   Dist: Pyramid
     The young Polish officer who helped defeat the British dur-
ing the Revolutionary War.

KRAMER, HILTON See DE KOONING, WILLEM (Painters Painting)

KRUPA, GENE See The Gene Krupa Story (feature)

KUHN, WALT

The Clowns Never Laugh: The Work of Walt Kuhn

Olga: A Film Portrait (Carousel Films, Inc.)

20 min.   color   1967   SA
Prod: Harry Atwood.   Dist: Withdrawn by McGraw-Hill.   Rental:
   Southern California
      How his work was influenced by European painting and the
American Realist school.

KUPECKY, JAN

Kupecky

12 min.   color   1974   JSA
Prod: Československý Film Bratislava.   Dist: International Film
   Bureau.   Rental: Syracuse
   The major events of the life of this Eastern European por-
trait painter, such as his travels and the death of his son.   Empha-
sis is on his portraits.

LABISSE, FELIX

Les Matins d'Impanéma
15 min.   color   1966   CA
Dir: Robert Hessens.   Prod: Les Films du Méridien.   Rental:
   FACSEA
   French dialogue only.   The life and works of the surrealistic
painter Labisse.

LAFAYETTE, MARQUIS DE
   See also   Lafayette (feature)

Lafayette and Washington
19 min.   color   1963   JSA
Prod: Productions Unlimited.   Dist: Macmillan.   Rental: Syracuse
   An excerpt from the feature Lafayette, which shows the
desperate plight of Washington, Congress' deliberations about Lafayette and the battle won together at Brandywine.

Lafayette--Soldier of Liberty
16 min.   b&w   1955   IJS
Prod: Encyclopaedia Britannica.   Dist: Withdrawn by EB.
   Rental: Indiana, Minnesota, Nebraska, Southern California,
   Syracuse
   Highlights his life and career, with emphasis on his ser-
vice to America.

Victory at Yorktown
21 min.   color   1963   JSA
Prod: Productions Unlimited.   Dist: Macmillan
   An excerpt from the feature Lafayette.   He returns to
France for supplies and comes back in time to help defeat the
British at Yorktown.

The Young Patriot
16 min.   color   1963   JSA
Prod: Productions Unlimited.   Dist: Macmillan.   Rental: Syracuse
   An excerpt from the feature Lafayette, it opens at the beginning of the Revolutionary War and ends with Lafayette sailing
for America.

LA GUARDIA, FIORELLO HENRY

The Crusader
15 min.   b&w   1952-53   JSCA
Prod: Mike Sklar.   Dist: Star Film
Shown as mayor of New York.   Compiled from the Fox Movietone News Library.

La Guardia
26 min.   b&w   1960
Prod: CBS. Dist: Macmillan. Rental: Association
The years as mayor of New York.

The La Guardia Story
26 min.   b&w   1965   IJ
Prod: Metromedia Producers.   Dist: Sterling (available on 8mm)
His three terms as a Republican mayor in New York from 1934 to 1945; uses footage from his speeches and public appearances.

LAING, RONALD DAVID

Interview with Dr. R. D. Laing 2 pts. (Notable Contributors Series)
30 min. each   color   1976   SCA
Prod: Dr. Richard Evans. Dist: Macmillan. Rental: Association
In The Dilemma of Mental Illness (pt. 1) he discusses the problem of classifying mental illnesses.   In Reactions and Reflections (pt. 2) he discusses his treatment methods.

LANGE, DOROTHEA

Photography--Dorothea Lange: The Closer for Me
30 min.   b&w   1965   JSCA
Prod: NET. Dist: Indiana. Rental: California, Michigan, Museum of Modern Art (title: Dorothea Lange)
An interview plus her photographs from the Depression, World War II, and the present.

Photography--Dorothea Lange: Under the Trees
30 min.   b&w   1965   JSCA
Prod: NET. Dist: Indiana. Rental: California, Michigan, Museum of Modern Art (title: Dorothea Lange)
A view of her preparing for a one-woman exhibit of her photographs, on which she comments.   She died shortly after filming.

LARSEN, HENRY

Henry Larsen, Arctic Explorer

16 min.   b&w   1966   IJSCA
Prod: National Film Board of Canada. Dist: Perennial (sale
  only; no previews).   Rental: Michigan
      Biography of this Norwegian explorer who traveled from
Vancouver to Halifax via an Arctic water route.

LA SALLE, RENE ROBERT CAVELIER, SIEUR DE
  See also   CARTIER, JACQUES (French Explorations in the New
  World)

Robert Cavelier, Sieur de La Salle
17 min.   b&w   1950   JS
Prod: Encyclopaedia Britannica.   Dist: Withdrawn by EB.
  Rental: Indiana, Michigan (title: La Salle), Minnesota, Nebraska, Southern California
      His association with Frontenac, the Indians, and his explora-
tion of the Mississippi.

LASORDA, THOMAS (TOM)

Tom Lasorda
22 min.   color   1973   SCA
Prod: Tele-Sports.   Dist: Paramount Oxford
      A sports profile of baseball coach Lasorda, recently ap-
pointed manager of the Dodgers.

LA TOUR, GEORGES DE

Résurrection d'un peintre oublié
22 min.   b&w or color   1956
Dir: J. Faurez.   Prod: Armor Films.   Rental: FACSEA
      French dialogue only. His life set against the historical
background.

LAVAL, PIERRE

Laval: Portrait of a Traitor (20th Century Series)
26 min.   b&w   1962   SCA
Prod: CBS.   Dist: Association
      The premier of the Vichy government who collaborated with
the Germans.

LAWRENCE, DAVID HERBERT

D. H. Lawrence in Taos
41 min.   color   1970   SA
Dir: Peter Davis.   Dist: Withdrawn by McGraw-Hill.   Rental:
  Michigan

Based on recollections by friends and neighbors in Taos, especially his wife Frieda, painter Dorothy Brett, and patroness Mabel Dodge Luhan.

LAWRENCE, THOMAS EDWARD (OF ARABIA) See Lawrence of Arabia (feature)

LEAKEY, LOUIS SEYMOUR

Dr. Leakey and The Dawn of Man
51 min.   color   1967   JSCA
Prod: National Geographical Society.   Dist: Films Inc.   Rental: South Florida
    He discovers evidence of early man in Tanzania.   An edited version (28 min.) is also available (rentals: Southern California, South Florida).

LEAN, DAVID

David Lean: A Self-Portrait
60 min.   color   1971   JSCA
Dir: Thomas Craven.   Dist: Pyramid.   Rental: Indiana, California, Michigan, Minnesota, Southern California, Syracuse
    Personal interviews are intercut with scenes of Lean directing his own films.

LEDBETTER, HUDDIE

Three Songs by Leadbelly
8 min.   color   1945 (released 1973)   SCA
Prod: Folklore Research.   Dist: Film Images
    Singing "Pick a Bale of Cotton," "Grey Goose," and "Take This Hammer."

LEE, ROBERT EDWARD
    See also GRANT, ULYSSES S. (Grant and Lee at Appomattox; Grant and Lee 1864-1865; Surrender at Appomattox)

Lee, the Virginian
27 min.   b&w   1966   JSCA
Prod: NBC.   Dist: Withdrawn by McGraw-Hill.   Rental: Indiana, Michigan, Minnesota, Nebraska, Southern California, Syracuse
    A portrait which includes his most famous battles, and his relationships with his lieutenants, especially Stonewall Jackson.

Robert E. Lee: A Background Study
16 min.   color   1953   JSCA
Prod. and dist: Coronet (sale only).   Rental: Michigan, Minnesota

Nebraska, South Florida, Syracuse
The morals and ethics which shaped his life and led to his decision to lead the Confederacy are stressed.

Robert E. Lee--Stratford Hall (American Life Styles Series)
28 min.   color   1976   IJSCA
Prod: Comco Productions. Dist: Association
A tour of his home, conducted by E. G. Marshall, reveals the life and personality of the man.

Sunset at Appomattox
21 min.   b&w   1953   JS
Prod: Teaching Film Custodians. Dist: Indiana (lease)
The nine days preceding Lee's surrender, based on the eyewitness accounts of 14 people, are dramatized. An excerpt from the Cavalcade of America television movie.

LEGER, FERNAND

Fernand Léger
14 min.   color   1972   JSCA
Dir: Jacques Berthier. Dist: Roland Collection
A brief biographical sketch is included in this analysis of his art.

LE MOAL, JEAN

Le Moal
14 min.   b&w or color   1963   SCA
Dir: Guy Suzuki, Jacques Simmonet. Prod: Sorafilms. Rental: FACSEA (available in French dialogue)
Life and work.

LENIN, NIKOLAI
See also KHRUSHCHEV, NIKITA (Leninism, Stalinism, and Khrushchevism); Nicholas and Alexandra (feature); NICHOLAS II (Nicholas and Alexandra) (series)

Lenin and Trotsky
26 min.   b&w   1964   SCA
Prod: CBS. Dist: McGraw-Hill. Rental: Association, Michigan, Minnesota, Southern California, Syracuse
The development of the Russian revolution and the men behind it.

Lenin Prepares for Revolution
22 min.   b&w   1971   JSCA
Prod: Granada/Novosti. Dist: Films Inc. Rental: Michigan, Minnesota, Syracuse
His early years in exile in Siberia, England, Switzerland, and Poland. Adapted from Ten Days that Shook the World.

Lenin's Revolution (Revolution in Russia Series)
20 min.   b&w   1970   JSCA
Prod: BBC-TV.   Dist: Time-Life (available in Spanish)
      The triumph of the Communist Party.

LEON, PONCE DE See CABOT, JOHN (Age of Discovery:
      Spanish and Portuguese Explorations)

LEONARDO DA VINCI See VINCI, LEONARDO DA

LEVINE, JACK

Jack Levine
23 min.   color   1964   SCA
Dir: Zina Voynow, Peter Robinson, and Herman J. Engel.   Prod:
      Zina Voynow.   Dist: Texture.   Rental: California, Southern
      California
      A profile of him and his work, including "Witches' Sabbath,"
a painting of the McCarthy era.

LEWIS, JOHN LLEWELLYN

John L. Lewis (History Makers of the Twentieth Century Series)
26 min.   b&w   1965   IJ
Prod: David Wolper.   Dist: Sterling (available on 8mm).   Rental:
      Mass Media, Syracuse
      1920-60, when the labor movement was at its peak.

John L. Lewis
26 min.   b&w   1962
Prod: CBS.   Dist: Association.   Rental: Southern California
      A biography of the organizer of the coal industry.

John L. Lewis
24 min.   b&w   1975   JSCA
Prod: Hearst.   Dist: Counselor
      Significant moments as a union leader.

LEWIS, MERIWETHER See CLARK, WILLIAM (The Journal of
      Lewis and Clark; Lewis and Clark; Lewis and Clark at the
      Great Divide; Lewis and Clark Journey)

LILLY, ELI

How Much Is a Miracle
25 min.   color   1966   SCA
Prod: Eli Lilly Co.   Rental: Indiana
      Traces his career as a pharmacist-soldier during the Civil

War and as a drug manufacturer. Also presents a history of medicine.

LINCOLN, ABRAHAM
See also Abe Lincoln in Illinois (feature); Abraham Lincoln (feature); DOUGLAS, STEPHEN ARNOLD (The Great Debate and A House Divided: The Lincoln-Douglas Debates); GREELEY, HORACE (One Nation Indivisible: Horace Greeley--Editor); KENNEDY, JOHN F. (Parallels in History: Kennedy and Lincoln); SANDBURG, CARL (Carl Sandburg Discusses Lincoln); Young Mr. Lincoln (feature)

Abe Lincoln in Illinois: Politician or Hero (American Challenge Program Series)
24 min.   b&w   1975   JSA
Prod: RKO.   Dist: Films Inc.
    A reconciliation between the man and the myth. An excerpt from the Robert Sherwood feature film starring Raymond Massey.

Abraham Lincoln
19 min.   b&w   1951   IJS
Prod. and dist: Encyclopaedia Britannica (available on video by special order). Rental: Michigan, Minnesota, Nebraska, Southern California, Syracuse
    Dramatizes incidents which reveal his principle of human freedom; uses famous quotations.

Abraham Lincoln (a series)
17 min. each   color   1959   IJS
Prod: Francis R. Line.   Rental: Indiana, Michigan, Minnesota
    Lincoln's Youth (pt. 1) is about the important events of his boyhood in Kentucky, Indiana, and finally Illinois; the effect of the death of his mother and the influence of his stepmother are noted. The Illinois Years (pt. 2) dramatizes his life from the time he moved to Illinois until his election as President. The War Years (pt. 3) highlights his inaugural and Gettysburg addresses, the death of his son, the surrender of Lee and his assassination.

Abraham Lincoln (a series)
27-33 min.   b&w   1952-53   IJSCA
Prod: Robert Saudek Associates.   Dist: IQ Films.   Rental: Michigan (pts. I, II, and IV), Minnesota
    The End and the Beginning (pt. I, 27 min.) begins with his last days and goes backwards to his birth. Frontier Family (pt. II, 28 min.) dramatizes the loss of his mother and the role of his step-mother. Lincoln as a Pioneer Youth (pt. III, 27 min.) shows his young adult years. The Young Lawyer in New Salem (pt. IV, 30 min.) dramatizes his first election; reveals the Ann Rutledge legend. A Future President (pt. V, 33 min.) is when he loses the election but retains his faith in himself.

Abraham Lincoln: A Background Study
16 min.   color   1951   IJSCA

Prod. and dist: Coronet (sale only). Rental: Indiana (upon request; officially withdrawn), Michigan, Nebraska, Syracuse
His life is set against the times in which he lived.

Abraham Lincoln and the Emancipation Proclamation (The Great
Decisions Series)
25 min.   color   1970   JSC
Dist: American Educational Films. Rental: Nebraska, Syracuse
An open-ended re-enactment of Lincoln's steps toward his
major decision about slavery.

America's Heroes: Abraham Lincoln
11 min.   color   1970   PI
Prod. and dist: Coronet (sale only). Rental: Syracuse
A visit to the places in which Lincoln lived: New Salem,
Springfield, Ill. and Washington, D.C.

Boyhood of Abraham Lincoln
10 1/2 min.   b&w or color   1962   PI
Prod. and dist: Coronet (sale only). Rental: Indiana, Michigan,
Minnesota, Nebraska, Syracuse
Filmed in the reconstructed village of Rockport, Indiana, it
shows how he overcame poverty through the encouragement of his
stepmother.

Carl Sandburg at Gettysburg, Part II, "The Gettysburg Address
and Lincoln the Man"
26 min.   b&w   1961   JSCA
Prod: CBS. Dist: Carousel (sale only). Rental: Association,
Indiana
Sandburg concludes that the Gettysburg address was not
scribbled on an envelope. He also discusses Lincoln's war-time
cabinet. Part I is about the Gettysburg campaign and the Civil
War. Either part can be used alone.

The Emancipation Proclamation (You Are There Series)
26 min.   b&w   1955   JSC
Prod: CBS. Rental: Indiana
An "on the scene" news report dramatization of how and
why Lincoln signed the Proclamation.

The Face of Lincoln
22 min.   b&w   1954   JSCA
Prod: University of Southern California. Dist: Creative Film So-
ciety. Rental: Indiana, Michigan, Minnesota, South Florida,
Syracuse
Professor Marrell Gage describes the life and career of
Lincoln as he sculps him.

Fellow Citizen, A. Lincoln
30 min.   color   1973   IJSCA
Dir: Aram Boyajian. Dist: Southern Baptist Radio-Television
Commission

Lincoln's own descriptions of his early life, education, and politics are the basis of the script. Excerpts from his speeches are used and prints, photographs, paintings from the Library of Congress, the National Archives, and the Smithsonian provide the graphics. Reveals his reliance on God to guide him.

Lincoln in the White House
21 min.   color   1939   IJSCA
Prod: Warner Bros., edited by Teaching Film Custodians.   Dist: Macmillan.   Rental: Minnesota, Nebraska, Syracuse
Shows Lincoln soon after his inaugural address praying for guidance.   Closes with a recitation of his Gettysburg Address.

Lincoln: Trial by Fire
52 min.   color   1974   SC
Prod: Wolper Organization.   Dist: Films Inc.   Rental: Michigan
Filmed on location, it emphasizes his conflict with General McClellan and the effect it had on the War.   Available in two edited parts: The Union Besieged (1861-1862), 22 min. and Emancipation Proclamation (1862-1863), 30 min.

Lincoln's Gettysburg Address
15 min.   color   1973   IJSC
Prod: Art Evans.   Dist: Paramount Oxford
Artwork is utilized to illustrate the events preceding his famous speech, re-enacted by Charlton Heston.

Lincoln's Last Day
27 min.   color   1969   SCA

From Lincoln's Last Day (McGraw-Hill Films)

Prod: ABC. Dist: McGraw-Hill
    Begins with the closing days of the Civil War, which are
re-created. Shot on location at 13 sites, it also utilizes photographs taken by Mathew Brady.

The Lonesome Train
20 1/2 min.   color   1973   IJSCA
Dir: Norman Rose and Barbara Begg. Dist: FilmFair Commu-
    nications
    A tribute to Lincoln in which the camera follows the funeral
train to Springfield, Illinois as the story of his life is told through
anecdotes and legends. Songs sung by Burl Ives.

The Long Shadow: Abraham Lincoln's Early Years
22 min.   color   1968   JSA
Prod: University of Southern California. Rental: Indiana
    From his birth in Kentucky to their move to Indiana, to
their return to Illinois, his paths are traced. Discusses his
mother's death and his father's remarriage. Interviews old timers
who recall stories about the Lincoln family.

Meet Mr. Lincoln
27 min.   b&w   1960   IJSC
Prod: NBC. Dist: Encyclopaedia Britannica (available on video
    by special order). Rental: Indiana, Michigan, Minnesota, Ne-
    braska, Southern California
    Photographs, cartoons and newspaper accounts show how his
contemporaries saw him, beginning in 1860.

Mr. Lincoln's Politics (American Civil War Series)
30 min.   b&w   1958   SC
Prod: Westinghouse Broadcasting. Dist: Association. Rental:
    Syracuse
    Problems and mistakes he made in choosing his Cabinet
and military leaders.

Moonlight Witness: Abe Lincoln, Lawyer
20 min.   b&w   1954   PIJ
Prod: Teaching Film Custodians. Dist: Indiana (lease)
    A dramatization of his defense for the son of a friend
against a murder charge. An excerpt from a Cavalcade of America television picture.

New Salem Story: Lincoln Legend
20 min.   b&w   1964   IJS
Prod: Teaching Film Custodians. Rental: Minnesota
    Based on the stories and legends of people who had known
Lincoln during the New Salem period, though their stories cannot
be verified.

Night of the Assassins (American Civil War Series)
30 min.   b&w   1958   SC
Prod: Westinghouse Broadcasting. Dist: Association
    The day he was shot.

The Nomination of Abraham Lincoln (You Are There Series)
22 min.   color   1972   IJ
Prod: CBS. Dist: BFA. Rental: Syracuse
        The hoopla of the 1860 Republic Party convention and the
ultimate nomination of Lincoln are reported.

The Palmetto Conspiracy: Lincoln, President-Elect
20 min.   b&w   1955   PIJ
Prod: Teaching Film Custodians. Dist: Indiana (lease)
        Allan Pinkerton discovers a plot in Baltimore to assassinate
Lincoln and he convinces the President-elect to change his route.
An excerpt from a Cavalcade of America television movie.

They've Killed President Lincoln!
52 min.   color   1971   JS
Prod: Wolper Organization. Dist: Films Inc. Rental: South
    Florida
        His death and the strange events which surrounded it are
examined. Photographs taken by Mathew Brady are integrated with
the film. Also available in an adapted version called The Assassination of Lincoln (28 min.).

LINDBERGH, CHARLES AUGUSTUS

Charles Lindbergh
24 min.   b&w   1965   IJ
Prod: David L. Wolper. Dist: Sterling (sale only; available on
    8mm). Rental: Mass Media, Southern California, Syracuse
        The shy private figure whose courage made him a very
public person is portrayed.

Charles Lindbergh
21 1/2 min.   b&w   1975   JSCA
Prod: Hearst. Dist: Counselor
        A dramatic biography.

Lindbergh vs. The Atlantic
25 min.   b&w   1964   SCA
Prod: Metromedia Producers. Dist: Films Inc. Rental:
    Southern California
        Authentic shots of his flight across the Atlantic.

LINDSEY, BENJAMIN BARR

Judge Ben B. Lindsey (Profiles in Courage Series)
50 min.   b&w   1955   IJSCA
Prod: Robert Saudek Associates. Dist: IQ Films. Rental:
    Michigan, Syracuse (title: Ben B. Lindsey)
        His initiation of new legislation to deal with juvenile de-
linquency.

LIPCHITZ, JACQUES

The Artist at Work--Jacques Lipchitz, Master Sculptor
12 min.   color or b&w   1968   JSCA
Prod. and dist: Encyclopaedia Britannica (available in Spanish or
    on video by special order.) Rental: Michigan, South California,
    Syracuse
        While he's working, he talks about his methods and subjects.

From The Artist at Work: Jacques Lipchitz, Master Sculptor
(Encyclopaedia Britannica)

Birth of a Bronze (with Jacques Lipchitz)
17 1/2 min.   color   1966   SC
Prod: Walter P. Lewisohn. Dist: Perspective (sale only).
    Rental: Minnesota
        As his show at the Modern Museum is seen, he speaks

about his life and art. He demonstrates the steps which went into
the making of his famous "Madonna."

Jacques Lipchitz (Wisdom Series)
30 min.   b&w   1958   SCA
Prod: NBC.   Dist: Films Inc.   Rental: Minnesota, Southern
   California
      He discusses his career in art.

LISTER, JOSEPH

The Story of Dr. Lister
28 1/2 min.   color   1964   JSCA
Prod: Warner-Lambert Co.   Dist: Association-Sterling (free loan)
      An all-star cast re-enacts his discovery of an antiseptic.

LISZT, FRANZ
   See also   Song Without End (feature)

Liszt and His Music (Famous Composers Series)
13 min.   color or b&w   1957   IJSCA
Prod. and dist: Coronet (special order sale only; no previews).
   Rental: Indiana, Michigan, Syracuse
      Dramatizes his life from boyhood until his last days as a
teacher.   Maps and pictures show where he lived and performed
and who and what influenced his music.

Maestro Franz Liszt at Weimar
10 min.   color   1960   S
Prod: Columbia edited by Teaching Film Custodians.   Dist: Indiana (lease).   Rental: Michigan, Minnesota
      A dramatization of his life and work at Weimar under the
patronage of Duchess Marie Pawlovna.   An excerpt from the feature film Song Without End.

Virtuoso Franz Liszt as Composer
14 min.   color   1960   IJS
Prod: Columbia edited by Teaching Film Custodians.   Dist:
   Indiana (lease).   Rental: Michigan, Minnesota
      On the eve of his wedding to Princess Carolyn Sayn-
Wittgenstein he gives a concert of his work.   Afterwards they discover her annulment of a previous marriage is invalid.   An excerpt from the feature film Song Without End.

LIVINGSTONE, DAVID
   See also   BURTON, SIR RICHARD FRANCIS (The Search for the
   Nile); Stanley and Livingstone (feature)

Livingstone: Clyde to Kalahari
23 min.   color   1973   JSCA

Prod: Hugh Baddeley Productions, England. Dist: Brigham Young
  University
    Follows his greatest journey across the African continent
and presents his life story as well.

Stanley Finds Livingstone (You Are There Series)
28 min.   b&w   1956   JSCA
Prod. and dist: CBS (sale only; no previews).   Rental: Minnesota
    A dramatization of an "on the scene" news report of the
event.

LOMBARDI, VINCE

Lombardi
60 min.
Prod. and dist: National Football League
    A review of his astounding career in football.

LONDON, JACK See Jack London (feature)

LONG, HUEY PIERCE

Huey Long
24 min.   b&w   1965   IJ
Prod: Metromedia Producers. Dist: Sterling (sale only; available on 8mm). Rental: Mass Media, South Florida
    His political career in Louisiana as Governor and as a U.S.
Senator until his assassination in 1935. Utilizes some newsreel
footage.

The Longs of Louisiana
22 min.   b&w   1965   SC
Prod: Metromedia Producers. Dist: Films Inc. Rental: Michigan, Minnesota, Syracuse
    The rise of power of Long, a governor and then Senator,
and his son Russell. Adapted from The Longs: A Louisiana Dy-
nasty.

LONGFELLOW, HENRY WADSWORTH

Henry Wadsworth Longfellow
17 min.   b&w   1949   JS
Prod. and dist: Encyclopaedia Britannica (available on video by
  special order). Rental: Indiana, Minnesota, South Florida,
  Southern California, Syracuse
    Dramatizes his commitment to American poetry and includes
selections from some of his well known poems.

LORENZ, KONRAD

Interview with Dr. Konrad Lorenz (4 pts.)
30 min. each   color   1975   SCA
Prod: Dr. Richard Evans.   Dist: Macmillan
    In Ethology and Imprinting (pt. 1) he discusses animals in
their natural setting; in Motivation (pt. 2) his opinion that human
social motives are instinctive; (pt. 3) the effect of the mass media
on sex and violence; in Reactions and Reflections (pt. 4) the influence Skinner, Fromm, Freud and Jung have had on him and his
book The Naked Ape.   Available separately or together.

LORRAIN, CLAUDE

The Art of Claude Lorrain
25 min.   color   1971   SCA
Prod: Arts Council of Great Britain.   Dist: Films Inc.
    His works.

LOUIS IX (Saint)

La Joie et la Couronne
26 min.   color   1970   SCA
Dir: Edouard Berne.   Prod: Caravelle International Television.
    Rental: FACSEA (available in French dialogue)
    Louis IX as builder, horseman, judge and king.

Saint Louis
25 min.   1950   SCA
Prod: Elizabeth Prévost.   Rental: FACSEA (available in French)
    13th and 14th century miniatures and sculptures tell the
story of his life.

LOUIS XIV
    See also Marie Antoinette (feature); The Rise of Louis XIV
(feature)

The French Revolution: The Bastille (Western Civilization Series)
21 min.   color   1970   JSCA
Prod. and dist: Learning (available in Spanish).   Rental: Michi-
    gan, Minnesota, South Florida
    He and Marie Antoinette's indifference to the hunger of
their people.   A dramatization.

Sun King (Legacy Series)
30 min.   b&w   1965   JSCA
Prod: NET.   Dist: Indiana.   Rental: California, Michigan
    His own writings and speeches are used to reveal his per-
sonality and his exploitation of power.

LOUIS XV See Madame Du Barry (feature)

LOUIS, JOE See The Joe Louis Story (feature)

LOUIS, MORRIS

Artists--The New Abstraction: Morris Louis and Kenneth Noland
30 min.   b&w   1966   SCA
Prod: NET. Dist: Indiana
    Conversations with two color-field painters, art critic
Clement Greenberg, painter Helen Jacobson, and Louis' widow,
Marcella Brenner, about them.

LOWELL, ROBERT

Poetry: Richard Wilbur and Robert Lowell
30 min.   b&w   1966   JSCA
Prod: NET. Dist: Indiana. Rental: California
    Filmed interviews in which Wilbur reads "On the Marginal
Way," "Love Call us to the Things of this World," and "Advice to
a Prophet." Lowell reads his poems "Water," "Soft Wood," "A
Flaw," and "Fall 1961."

LUGOSI, BELA See HARDY, OLIVER (Hardy-Lugosi Interview)

LUMIERE, LOUIS JEAN and AUGUSTE MARIE

Lumière
40 min.   CA
Dir: Ghislain Cloquet. Prod: Nicole-Eva Terquem. Rental:
    FACSEA
    French dialogue only. A history of the Lumière brothers
with film clips from their first pictures. Commentary by Abel
Gance.

LUTHER, MARTIN
    See also Martin Luther (feature)

Martin Luther
29 min.   b&w   1953   JSCA
Prod: Louis de Rochemont Associates. Dist: Indiana (lease),
    Lutheran Film Associates. Rental: California
    A dramatization of his posting of the 95 theses. An ex-
cerpt from a feature with the same title.

Martin Luther and the Protestant Reformation
30 min.   b&w   1969   SCA

Prod: BBC-TV. Dist: Time-Life (available on video). Rental: Minnesota
    The life and convictions of Luther are set against a background of the early 16th century.

The World of Martin Luther
30 min. b&w 1965 IJSCA
Prod. and dist: Lutheran Film Associates. Rental: United Church of Christ
    His life story is told through his own words.

LYON, MATTHEW See ADAMS, JOHN (The Right to Dissent)

MAASS, CLARA

No Greater Love: Nurse Clara Maass
27 min. b&w 1952 PIJ
Prod: Teaching Film Custodians. Dist: Indiana (lease)
    Allows a mosquito to bite her so that Dr. William Gorgas can experiment on yellow fever. An excerpt from a Cavalcade of America movie.

MacARTHUR, DOUGLAS
    See also EISENHOWER, DWIGHT DAVID (Famous Generals)

Douglas MacArthur
23 min. b&w 1975 JSCA
Prod: Hearst. Dist: Counselor
    His life from West point until his famous farewell.

The General
50 min. b&w 1965 SCA
Prod: Metromedia Producers. Dist: Films Inc. Rental: Indiana, Michigan, Minnesota (all have 30-minute versions)
    His life and times. Also available in a 30-minute version.

General Douglas MacArthur
27 min. b&w 1965 IJ
Prod: Metromedia Producers. Dist: Sterling (sale only; available on 8mm). Rental: Mass Media, Southern California, Syracuse
    Newsreel footage traces his military career from his graduation from West Point to World Wars I and II, and its conclusion with his famous "Old Soldiers Never Die" speech.

I Shall Return
15 min. b&w 1952-53 JSCA
Prod: Mike Sklar. Dist: Star Film
    Truman's dismissal. Compiled from the Fox Movietone News Library footage.

The MacArthur Story
20 min.　b&w　1964
Prod: U.S. Dept. of Defense.　Dist: National Audiovisual Center
　　　Highlights his life, his leadership during three wars, and
his other contributions.

MacArthur vs. Truman
25 min.　b&w　1964　SC
Prod: Metromedia Producers.　Dist: Films Inc.　Rental: Minne-
　　sota, Syracuse
　　　The confrontation between the two men, set against the background of the Korean War.　Narrated by Edmond O'Brien.

McCARTHY, JOSEPH

Charge and Counter Charge
43 min.　b&w　1968　SCA
Prod: Prentice Hall.　Dist: Appleton-Century-Crofts.　Rental:
　　California
　　　His political career, with emphasis on the Army-McCarthy
hearings, which are excerpted.

Joseph McCarthy (Biography Series)
26 min.　b&w　1964　SCA
Prod: David Wolper.　Dist: Withdrawn by McGraw-Hill.　Rental:
　　Indiana, Minnesota, Southern California ('59 version), Syracuse
　　　From his childhood through his stormy years as a Senator.
Includes scenes from the famous Army-McCarthy hearings.

McCarthy vs. Welch
25 min.　b&w　1964　SC
Prod: Metromedia Producers.　Dist: Films Inc.　Rental: Syra-
　　cuse
　　　The televised hearings of the conflict between him and the
Army.

McCLELLAN, GEORGE BRINTON　See　LINCOLN, ABRAHAM
　(Lincoln: Trial by Fire)

McCLOSKEY, ROBERT

Robert McCloskey
18 min.　color　1965　IJSCA
Prod. and dist: Weston Woods.　Rental: Syracuse
　　　The people and places of his life which he draws on for his
illustrations.

McCOY, ELIJAH

Black Men and Iron Horses

18 min. color 1969 SA
Prod. and dist: Rediscovery Productions. Rental: Anti-Defamation League
 Briefly lists the contributions to the railroad industry made
by black inventors McCoy, Granville T. Woods, and Charles
Richey. Includes an interview with A. Philip Randolph, who talks
about segregation.

MacDIARMID, HUGH

Hugh MacDiarmid--A Portrait
9 min. b&w 1964
Prod: Ancona Films. Rental: California
 A portrait in which he reads his own poetry.

MacDONALD, ROSS

Ross MacDonald: In the First Person (Writers on Writing Series)
23 min. color 1972 S
Prod: Davidson Films. Dist: General Learning
 The camera follows him in his normal routine as he comments on how he gets ideas, shapes and sharpens them.

McDOWELL, MARY S.

Mary S. McDowell (Profiles in Courage Series)
50 min. b&w 1965 IJSCA
Prod: Robert Saudek Associates. Dist: IQ Films. Rental:
 Michigan, Syracuse
 Fights for freedom of conscience though the U.S. is at war.

MacELHENNY, HUGH

Hugh MacElhenny (Sports Legends Series)
20 min. color 1975 LJ
Prod. and dist: Sports Legends Inc. Rental: Southern California
 Highlights from his years as a player with the Forty-
Niners, Vikings, and Giants.

McGOVERN, GEORGE See NIXON, RICHARD (The Making of the
 President--1972)

MACHIAVELLI, NICCOLO

Man and the State: Machiavelli on Political Power
28 min. color 1972 JSCA
Prod: Bernard Wilets. Dist: BFA. Rental: Michigan, Southern

California, Syracuse
　　Machiavelli's ideas are challenged in this dramatized debate. Open-ended.

MACK, CONNIE

Mr. Baseball
15 min.　b&w　1952-53　JSCA
Prod: Mike Sklar.　Dist: Star Film
　　Compiled from the Fox Movietone News Library footage, this is a look at his baseball career.

MacKENZIE, ALEXANDER

Alexander MacKenzie--Lord of the North
27 min.　color　1966　IJS
Prod: National Film Board of Canada.　Dist: Perennial (sale
　　only; no previews).　Rental: Michigan
　　His 2,000-mile canoe trip on which he discovered the Arctic Ocean is traced.　The narration is based on his own account.

McKINLEY, WILLIAM

William McKinley and American Imperialism (The Great Decisions
　　Series)
25 min.　color　1971　JSA
Prod: Project 7 Productions.　Dist: American Educational Films.
　　Rental: Syracuse
　　An open-ended film about his decision to wage war against Spain in 1898 for the Philippines.

MACKINTOSH, CHARLES RENNIE

Charles Rennie Mackintosh
18 min.　color　1973　SCA
Dir: W. Thomson.　Prod: Louise R. Annand, Scotland.　Dist:
　　Roland Collection
　　The life and work of this art nouveau artist.

Mackintosh
33 min.　color　1970　SC
Prod: Project 7 Films.　Dist: American Educational Films.
　　Rental: Syracuse
　　A look at this little-known Scottish artist of the art nouveau and Bauhaus schools, who influenced modern sculpture, art and architecture.

McLAREN, NORMAN

The Eye Hears, The Ear Sees
59 min.   color   1970   JSCA
Prod: BBC-TV. Dist: International Film Bureau. Rental:
   California, Michigan, Minnesota, Southern California, Syracuse
      Gavin Miller talks with him and Grant Munro, another ani-
mator.   Shows how McLaren creates his style of animation and includes clips from his films.

Window on Canada (An Interview with Norman McLaren)
30 min.   b&w   1954   JSA
Prod: National Film Board of Canada. Dist: International Film
   Bureau. Rental: California, Kit Parker, Minnesota, Syracuse
      Interviewed by Clyde Gilmour, noted critic. McLaren dis-
cusses and demonstrates experimental animation techniques.

McLUHAN, MARSHALL

This Is Marshall McLuhan: The Medium Is the Massage
53 min.   color   1967   CA
Prod: NBC. Dist: McGraw-Hill. Rental: California, Indiana,
   Mass Media, Michigan, Minnesota, Nebraska, South Florida,
   Southern California, Syracuse
      Alternates between him and his supporters and dissenters.
Includes visual interpretations of his views on communication.

MAETERLINCK, COUNT MAURICE

Maurice Maeterlinck
45 min.   CA
Dir: Roland Bernard. Prod: ORTF. Rental: FACSEA
      Portrait of the man and an analysis of the symbolism and
mysticism of his literature.

MAGELLAN, FERDINAND See CABOT, JOHN (Age of Discovery,
   Spanish and Portuguese Explorations)

MAGRITTE, RENE

Magritte
14 min.   color   1963   SCA
Dir: Luc De Heusch. Dist: Films Inc.
      An interview combined with a view of rarely seen modern
works.   English sub-titles.

Magritte: The False Mirror
22 min.   color   1971   SCA
Prod: Arts Council of Great Britain. Dist: Films Inc.

His world as seen through his paintings. Sparse commentary taken from his statements or anecdotes from close friends.

Renée Magritte
20 min.   color   1970   SCA
Prod: BBC-TV. Dist: Time-Life (special orders sale only; no
    previews or rentals)
        The painting "La durée poignardée" is the focal point, but
the film is based on a 1969 retrospective at the Tate Gallery, in
which many private paintings were exhibited.

MAHAN, LARRY

Larry Mahan
22 min.   color   1972   SCA
Prod: Tele-Sports. Dist: Paramount Oxford
        A sports profile.

MAILLOL, ARISTIDE

Maillol
25 min.
Rental: FACSEA (available in French)
        A day in his studio and a retrospective look at his work.

MALCOLM X

Malcolm X
23 min.   color   1971   JSCA
Prod: WCAU-TV. Dist: Carousel (sale only). Rental: Associa-
    tion
        The tenets in which he believed. Spans his life from 8th
grade through his days as a prisoner until his death by assassination.

Malcolm X
92 min.
Prod: Marvin Woth and Arnold Perl. Dist: Warner Bros.

Malcolm X Speaks
44 min.   b&w   1971   IJSCA
Prod: ABC. Dist: Films Inc.
        Covers his early years, his prison term, his conversion to
the Black Muslim faith, and his role as a black leader. Excerpts
from his speeches and interviews with family and friends are included.

Malcolm X--Struggle for Freedom
22 min.   b&w   1967
Dir: Lebert Bethune and Don Taylor. Dist: Films Inc. (available

on EVR on double tape with The Game). Rental: California
    A portrait filmed during his trip to Europe and Africa, which
he took three months before his assassination. He freely discusses
racial problems.

Tribute to Malcolm X
15 min.   b&w   1969   SCA
Prod: NET. Dist: Indiana. Rental: California, Impact, Michigan
    His widow recalls his life.

MALRAUX, ANDRE

André Malraux
24 min.   1957   CA
Dir: L. Keigel. Prod: C. Art, P. A. C. Rental: FACSEA
    French dialogue only. He comments on his own works.
The years between World War I and II, his participation in the
Chinese Revolution and the Spanish War are highlighted.

MANESSIER, ALFRED

Manessier
15 min.   color   1967   CA
Dir: Robert Hessens. Prod: Les Films K. Rental: FACSEA
    (available in French)
    Talks about his concept of creativity.

MANET, EDOUARD

Edouard Manet
15 min.   b&w   1952   SCA
Prod. and dist: Pictura
    When he offered a painting of a nude to the famed Salon, he
shocked France. The story of his gradual acceptance is told.

Edouard Manet (Pioneers of Modern Painting Series)
40 min.   color   1971   SCA
Prod. and dist: Independent Television Corp. Rental: California
    His relationship with Monet, Morisot and other impression-
ists of his time, his life and style of painting, the reactions of the
critics. Narrated and written by Sir Kenneth Clark.

MANN, HORACE

Horace Mann
19 min.   b&w   1951   JSA
Prod: Encyclopaedia Britannica. Dist: Withdrawn by EB.
    Rental: Michigan, Minnesota, Nebraska, Southern California,

Syracuse
Focuses on his careers as teacher, lawyer, state senator, and college president.   States the reforms he sought in education.

MANOLETE (MANUEL RODRIGUEZ)

The Day Manolete Was Killed
19 min.   b&w   1957   SCA
Dist: Films Inc.   Rental: California, Michigan, South Florida,
    Southern California, Viewfinders
The day he came out of retirement to answer the challenge of matador Luis Dominguín.

MANTLE, MICKEY

Mickey Mantle (Sports Legends Series)
20 min.   color   1975   ISCA
Prod. and dist: Sports Legends Inc.   Dist: Counselor Films.
    Rental: Southern California
His life and highlights from his baseball career including newsreel footage from some of his games.

MAO TSE-TUNG

Mao Tse-Tung (Biography Series)
26 min.   b&w   1964   JSCA
Prod: David Wolper.   Dist: Withdrawn by McGraw-Hill.   Rental:
    Michigan, Minnesota, South Florida, Southern California, Syra-
    cuse
Traces his life from his birth in 1893 through the major events of his political career including the Long March, his victory over Chiang, and his years as China's leader.

Mao vs. Chiang (Men in Crisis Series)
25 min.   b&w   1964   SCA
Prod: Metromedia Producers.   Dist: Films Inc.
Mao's victory, the growth of his Army and Chiang's retreat to Formosa are covered.

Maoism and Titoism (Communism--Myth vs. Reality Series)
29 min.   b&w   1962   SCA
Prod: KNXT.   Dist: Southern California
Describes each man, each political philosophy and the relationship of each to Russia.

MARC, FRANZ

Franz Marc
23 min.   color   1972   JSCA

Dir: Gotz van Helmholt.   Prod: Karl F. de Vogt.   Dist: Roland
   Collection
       Founder of modern art; his life and work and association
with avant-garde painters such as Picasso are revealed.

MARCEAU, MARCEL

Marcel Marceau ou l'Art du Mime
17 min.   SCA
Dir: Bernard Bertrand.   Prod: Eidos.   Rental: FACSEA (available in French)
       At home, where he talks about the history of pantomime,
and on stage as Bip and Don Juan.

Marceau on Mime
20 min.   color   1974   IJSCA
Prod: John Gould.   Dist: ACI.   Rental: Syracuse
       An interview with him about the art and history of mime.

The Mime of Marcel Marceau (An Introduction to the Performing
   Arts Series)
22 min.   color   1972   JSCA
Dir: Daniel Camus.   Prod: Paris Match TV.   Dist: Learning.
   Rental: Minnesota, Nebraska, Southern California
       A performance, a rehearsal, and an interview.

MARIE ANTOINETTE
   See also LOUIS XIV (The French Revolution: The Bastille);
   Marie Antoinette (feature)

Marie-Antoinette
54 min.   SCA
Dir: Roland Darbois.   Prod: ORTF.   Rental: FACSEA
       The adventurous but frivolous life of the queen of Louis XIV.

MARK ANTONY (or ANTHONY)

Marc Anthony of Rome
23 min.   b&w   1934   SA
Prod: Paramount, edited by Teaching Film Custodians.   Dist:
   Indiana (lease).   Rental: Michigan, Minnesota, Syracuse
       Includes a brief history of the Roman Empire, Caesar's re-
turn home and his assassination and the formation of the Second
Triumvirate.   An excerpt from the feature of the same title.

MARIN, JOHN

John Marin
20 1/2 min.   color   1968   SCA

Prod: Radio-TV Bureau, University of Arizona. Dist: International Film Bureau
A close look at his paintings and an examination of the influences on his art, his years in Paris, and his impressions of the U. S.

MARQUET, ALBERT

Marquet
16 min.   color
Dir: Arcady and Megret.   Rental: FACSEA (available in French)
Life and works.

MARQUETTE, JACQUES
See also CARTIER, JACQUES (French Explorations in the New World)

Marquette and Jolliet: Voyage of Discovery
14 min.   color   1975   IJ
Prod. and dist: Coronet (sale only).   Rental: Syracuse
Recreates their voyage down the Mississippi from Lake Michigan and their return.

MARSHALL, GEORGE CATLETT
See also EISENHOWER, DWIGHT DAVID (Famous Generals)

General George Marshall
26 min.   b&w   1961   SCA
Prod: CBS.   Rental: Association, Michigan, Southern California
An account of his war victories and his role as "father" of the Marshall Plan.

George Marshall
25 min.   b&w   1965   IJ
Prod: Metromedia Producers.   Dist: Sterling (sale only; available on 8mm)
His military career during and after World War II and the conflicts and controversies he generated.

Soldier of Peace
15 min.   b&w   1952-53   JSCA
Prod: Mike Sklar.   Dist: Star Film
Compiled from the Fox Movietone News Library footage; his winning of the Nobel Prize and his Marshall Plan are covered.

MARSHALL, JOHN

Decision for Justice: John Marshall
20 min.   b&w   1955   JS

Prod: Teaching Film Custodians. Dist: Indiana (lease)
A dramatization of his first Supreme Court case, in which he established the right of the Court to rule on the constitutionality of Congressional legislation. An excerpt from a Cavalcade of America television movie.

John Marshall
50 min.   b&w   1965   SA
Prod: Robert Saudek Associates. Dist: IQ Films. Rental: Michigan, Minnesota, Syracuse
Presiding over Aaron Burr's treason trial.

John Marshall
18 min.   b&w   1951   JS
Prod: Encyclopaedia Britannica. Dist: Withdrawn by EB.
Rental: Michigan, Minnesota, South Florida, Southern California, Syracuse
Key events of his childhood and of his political career. Outlines significant Supreme Court decisions during his tenure as Chief Justice.

MARX, KARL

Marxism (Communism--Myth vs. Reality Series)
29 min.   b&w   1962   SCA
Prod: KNXT-TV. Dist: Southern California
Stills, drawings, and reprints recall his homeland, his life, and his friendship with Engels. Examines the impact of his "Manifesto" and the aims of Marxism.

Marxism: The Theory that Split a World (Western Civilization Series)
26 min.   color   1970   SCA
Dir: George Kaczender. Dist: Learning (available in Spanish).
Rental: Indiana, Minnesota, Nebraska, Syracuse
The philosophy of Marx, his family and friends, and the historical applications of his beliefs are covered.

MARY, QUEEN OF SCOTS (MARY STUART)
See also ELIZABETH I (Elizabeth R., pt. 4); Mary of Scotland (feature); Mary, Queen of Scots (feature)

Mary, Queen of Scots
30 min.   b&w   1969   SCA
Prod: BBC-TV. Dist: Time-Life (special purchase order only; no previews or rentals)
Her tragic life, which ended when she was beheaded by Elizabeth, is recaptured by prints, engravings, and films of castles and the countryside as it then existed.

MASLOW, ABRAHAM

Being Abraham Maslow
30 min.   b&w   1971   SCA
Prod: Warren Bennis and Leonard Zweig.   Dist: Filmmakers Library.   Rental: Nebraska
An interview in which he recalls his immigrant parents, his childhood, his personal life, his successes and disappointments. Filmed shortly before his death.

Maslow and Self-Actualization (2 films)
30 min. each   color   1968   C
Prod. and dist: Psychological Films
In the first film he discusses honesty and awareness; in the second, freedom and trust and how each affects us.

MASON, GEORGE

George Mason (Profiles in Courage Series)
50 min.   b&w   1965   JSCA
Prod: Robert Saudek Associates.   Dist: IQ Films.   Rental: Michigan, Minnesota, Syracuse
He refuses to sign the Constitution without a Bill of Rights.

MASSON, ANDRE

Masson et les quatre éléments
20 min.   color   SCA
Dir: Jean Grémillon.   Prod: Films Dauphin.   Rental: FACSEA (available in French)
His works and techniques.

MASTERSON, BAT   See   EARP, WYATT (Heroes and Villains)

MATHIAS, ROBERT (BOB)   See   The Bob Mathias Story (feature)

MATISSE, HENRI

Henri Matisse
16 min.   color   1971   JSA
Prod: Les Film du Cyprès.   Dist: International Film Bureau.   Rental: Syracuse
The chronological progression of his paintings and his use of color.   Also analyzes the influence of Cézanne.

Matisse
20 min.   color   1970   SCA
Dir: Pierre Alibert.   Prod: Les Films du Cyprès.   Rental:

FACSEA (available in French)
An exhibition of his pictures at the Grand Palais Museum of Paris.

Matisse
30 min.   SCA
Dir: Lucien Joulin.   Prod: La Compagnie Générale Cinématogra-
phique.   Rental: FACSEA (available in French)
A studio visit and a slow motion sequence of him painting.

Matisse--A Sort of Paradise
30 min.   color   1972   SC
Prod: Arts Council of Great Britain.   Dist: Films Inc.
A close-up look at his paintings with a commentary using his own words.

MATTHEW

The Calling of Matthew
28 min.   b&w   1949
Prod: Cathedral.   Rental: Catholic Film Center
He gives up his job as a ruthless tax collector to follow Jesus.

MAUGHAM, WILLIAM SOMERSET

W. Somerset Maugham (Wisdom Series)
30 min.   b&w   1962   SCA
Prod: NBC.   Dist: Films Inc.   Rental: Minnesota (title: A
Conversation with Somerset Maugham), Syracuse
Comments on his own novels and the works of other writers such as Kipling and Lewis.

MAUPASSANT, GUY DE

Le Dernier Matin de Guy de Maupassant
26 min.   1964   CA
Dir: Maurice Fasquel.   Prod: Paris Cité Productions.   Rental:
FACSEA
French dialogue only.   The tragedy of his mental illness.

MAUROIS, ANDRE

André Maurois
16 min.   color   1970   JSCA
Prod: Landmark Educational Media.   Dist: Texture (available in
French).   Rental: Viewfinders
An autobiography filmed in Normandy at Shelley's home, at the retreat of George Sand and the childhood home of Marcel Proust.

MAX, PETER

The Impact of Peter Max
26 min.   color   1973   SCA
Prod: Koplin and Grinker.   Dist: Pictura
        An interview in his studio and on the streets of New York,
where he discusses his past, present, and future.

MAY, ROLLO

Rollo May and Human Encounter (2 films)
30 min. each   color
Prod. and dist: Psychological Films
        The two segments of the first film are "Self-Self Encounter"
and "Self-Other Encounter," in which he describes the elements
man encounters.   The other film deals with "Manipulation and Human Encounter" and "Exploitation of Sex."

MAYAKOVSKY, VLADIMIR

Mayakovsky: The Poetry of Action
22 min.   color   1973   SC
Prod: Harold Mantell.   Dist: Films for the Humanities (avail-
    able on 3/4" videocassette)
        Poet and painter, he became the Russian poet laureate of
the Revolution.   Rare footage shows him giving a speech.   Also
shown in conversation with Boris Pasternak, composer Dimitri
Shostakovitch and other poets.

MAZARIN, JULES

Sur les traces de Mazarin
20 min.   1964   SCA
Dir: Marc de Gastyne.   Prod: Cité Films.   Rental: FACSEA
    (available in French)
        A biography written and narrated by Maurice Schumann.

MEAD, MARGARET

Margaret Mead (Wisdom Series)
30 min.   b&w   1958   SCA
Prod: NBC.   Dist: Films Inc.   Rental: California, Minnesota,
    South Florida
        She discusses her life and work.

Margaret Mead
27 min.   b&w   1969   SCA
Prod: BBC-TV.   Dist: Time-Life (available on video)
        In a warm, relaxed interview she talks about the influence

on the natives in the Pacific Islands that society exerted, racial problems, religion, and her hopes for the future of mankind.

Margaret Mead's New Guinea Journal
90 min.   color or b&w   1968   SCA
Prod: NET. Dist: Indiana. Rental: California, Michigan
 A visit to an island she first studied in 1928.

MEDICI (FAMILY)
 See also Age of the Medici (feature)

Voice Cries Out (Legacy Series)
30 min.   b&w   1965   JSCA
Prod: NET. Dist: Indiana. Rental: California
 A history of the family is visualized by the sculpture and architecture of Florence, created during their rule. The family relationship with Savonarola is described.

MEDVEDKIN, ALEXANDER

The Train Rolls On
33 min.   b&w   1972   SA
Dir: Chris Marker. Dist: New Yorker
 An historical look at the Russian Cine-Trains organized in 1932 by him. He appears on camera to discuss their role in Soviet society.

MEIR, GOLDA

A Conversation with Golda Meir
27 min.   color
Dist: Anti-Defamation League
 An interview conducted by Arnold Forster, General Counsel of the Anti-Defamation League of B'nai B'rith.

Golda Meir
52 min.   color   1972   SCA
Prod: BBC-TV. Rental: Michigan
 An interview in which she talks about the milestones of her life and Israel's struggles.

MELIES, GEORGE

George Méliès
22 min.   1969
Dir: Claude Leroy. Prod: Les Amis de Georges Méliès.
 Rental: FACSEA (available in French)
 Designs, sets, costumes, and photos of his films retrace his life and contributions to motion pictures.

Le Grand Méliès
32 min.   CA
Dir: George Franju.   Prod: Films Dauphin.   Rental: FACSEA
    French dialogue only.   His wife talks about him in this
tribute.

MEMLING (or MEMLINC), HANS

Memlinc: Painter of Bruges
26 1/2 min.   color   1974   SCA
Prod: International Film Bureau and RESOBEL, Brussels.   Dist:
    International Film Bureau.   Rental: Syracuse
    "The Shrine of St. Ursula," "The Mystic Marriage of St.
Catherine," and "The Mystery of the Passion" exemplify the medieval life in Bruges.

MENCKEN, HENRY LOUIS

H. L. Mencken--On Irreverence and Sacred Cows (Touch of Fame
    Series)
29 min.   b&w   1962   SCA
Prod: KNXT-TV.   Dist: Southern California
    Dr. Herman Harvey, using special tape recordings of the
late Mencken, conducts an "interview" of him.   A kinescope.

MENDEL, GREGOR

Gregor Mendel (Great Scientists Speak Again)
24 min.   color   1974   SCA
Prod. and dist: California
    An impersonization of him which gives an account of his
interest in heredity and why he selected the pea for his experiments.   Illustrates his laws on a board.

MENNINGER, KARL

The Age of Anxiety (Twentieth Century Series)
50 min.   b&w   1962   SCA
Prod: CBS.   Dist: Star Film.   Rental: Indiana, Syracuse
    An interview on the subject of mental illness--its causes
and treatments.

Karl Menninger (Wisdom Series)
30 min.   b&w   1960   SCA
Prod: NBC.   Dist: Films Inc.
    An interview in which he discusses the function of psychiatry
and Freud.

MERIAN, MATTHEW

Matthew Merian
14 min.   b&w   1973   JSCA
Dir. and prod: Th. N. Blomberg.   Dist: Roland Collection
    A sketch of his life set against a history of the times,
which he captured in his etchings.

MERIMEE, PROSPER

Les Rencontres de Mérimée
17 min.   color   1971   CA
Dir: Jacques de Casembroot.   Prod: Films J. K. Millet.
    Rental: FACSEA
        French dialogue only.   His stories, his characters Carmen
and Colomba, and his work as a monument inspector are examined.

MICHAUX, HENRI

Michaux ou l'Espace du Dedans
22 min.   color   1964   CA
Dir: Jacques Veinat.   Rental: FACSEA
        French dialogue only.   His ideas as reflected through his
poetry and art.

MICHELANGELO (BUONARROTI)
    See also   The Agony and the Ecstasy (feature)

Michelangelo
30 min.   color or b&w   1965   JSC
Prod. and dist: Encyclopaedia Britannica (available on video by
    special order).   Rental: California, Indiana, Minnesota, Southern
    California, Syracuse
        His development as an artist is shown as the camera re-
veals his masterpieces.   Commentary adapted from his letters and
contemporaneous documents.

Michelangelo
65 min.   color   1972   SCA
Prod: Romor Films.   Dist: Roland Collection
    A biographical sketch interwoven with an intense examina-
tion of the Sistine Chapel, "David," "The Final Judgment," and
other works.   Commentary by Carol L. Ragghianti.   Can be shown
in 2, 3, or 6 parts.

Michelangelo and His Art
16 min.   color   1963   IJSC
Prod. and dist: Coronet (sale only).   Rental: Indiana, Michigan,
    Minnesota, Nebraska, South Florida, Syracuse

His life and career. Among the works photographed are "David," the "Pieta," and "Moses."

Michelangelo: The Last Giant
67 min.   color   1967   SA
Prod: NBC.   Dist: McGraw-Hill.   Rental: Indiana, Minnesota, Southern California, Syracuse
Quotations from biographies about him, his own writings, his paintings, sculpture and architecture tell the story of his life. Shot on location in Europe.   Peter Ustinov portrays him and José Ferrer is narrator.

Michelangelo: The Medici Chapel
22 min.   color   1964   C
Prod: Clifford B. West.   Dist: Film Images
An exploration of the marble figures in the New Sacristy of San Lorenzo in Florence; his sonnets, carved into the stone and sculpture, are read in the original Italian.

The Secret of Michelangelo: Every Man's Dream
51 min.   color   1968   SCA
Dir: Milton Fruchtman.   Prod: Capital Cities Broadcasting.
Dist: Macmillan (sale only).   Rental: Association, South Florida, Syracuse
A close look at the Sistine Chapel; over 100 figures are skillfully photographed.

The Titan, Story of Michelangelo
67 min.   b&w   1940   SCA
Dir: Curt Oertel.   Rental: California, Kit Parker, Michigan, Syracuse
A dramatization of his life and times.   This version was re-edited in 1950 by Robert Flaherty, who added the commentary narrated by Frederic March.   Animated sequences chart the Sistine Chapel.

MIKAN, GEORGE

Mr. Basketball
15 min.   b&w   1952-53   JSCA
Prod: Mike Sklar.   Dist: Star Film
Compiled from the Fox Movietone News Library, this traces his basketball career.

MILLAY, EDNA ST. VINCENT

Edna St. Vincent Millay (Subtitle: Millay at Steepletop)
25 min.   color   1976   JSCA
Dir: Kevin Brownlow.   Prod: Sloan Shelton.   Dist: Films for the Humanities
A combined look at her and her poetry.

MILLER, ALFRED JACOB See CATLIN, GEORGE (George Catlin
and Alfred Jacob Miller)

MILLER, ARTHUR

Psychology and Arthur Miller (2 pts.)
50 min. , 55 min.   b&w   1964   C
Prod: Dr. Richard Evans. Dist: Macmillan (sale only).   Rental:
Association, South Florida, Syracuse
In part 1 he discusses motivation and psychoanalysis of au-
thors through their writing; part 2, art vs. science.

MILLER, HENRY

Henry Miller Asleep and Awake
35 min.   color   1974   SC
Dir: Tom Schiller. Dist: New Yorker
At 81 he presented a cheerful monologue on art, Japanese
writers, sex, women he liked, Zen, his youth and his nightmares.
He even conducts a tour of his bathroom and comments on the
many pictures and photos on the walls.

The Henry Miller Odyssey
110 min.   color and b&w   CA
Dir. and prod: Robert Snyder. Dist: Center for Learning Resources
Culled from more than 15 hours of film and tape, an in-
depth portrait.

MILLET, JEAN-FRANÇOIS

Jean-François Millet (Romantic Versus Classic Art Series)
26 min.   color   1974   JSCA
Prod: Reader's Digest. Dist: Pyramid. Rental: Southern Cali-
fornia (listed under series title)
A study of the artist--his life and works. Narrated by
Kenneth Clark.

MILLETT, KATE See FRIEDAN, BETTY (Woman Talking)

MILNE, ALAN ALEXANDER

Mr. Shepard and Mr. Milne
30 min.   color   SCA
Prod. and dist: Weston Woods. Rental: Indiana, Michigan,
Minnesota
The story of their collaboration on When We Were Young

and <u>Winnie the Pooh</u>. Milne reads the narration and Shepard is interviewed.

MILTON, JOHN

<u>Tragedy of John Milton</u> (You Are There Series)
28 min.   b&w   1962   JSA
Prod. and dist: CBS (sale only; no previews or rentals).   Rental: Indiana, Michigan, Minnesota, Southern California
    A dramatization of an "on the scene" news report of how and why he was forced into hiding when Charles II was restored to the throne of England.

MINGUS, CHARLES

<u>Mingus</u>
60 min.   b&w   1966
Dir. and prod: Thomas Reichman. Dist: Impact, Films Inc.
    A personal portrait of the "hard times" of this musician.

MINOT, GEORGE RICHARDS

<u>Gift of Dr. Minot</u>
20 min.   b&w   1955
Prod: Teaching Film Custodians. Dist: Indiana
    Re-enacts his research for a cure for pernicious anemia despite his own diabetic condition.   An excerpt from the Cavalcade of America television movie.

MITCHELL, WILLIAM

<u>Billy Mitchell</u>
24 min.   b&w   1965   IJ
Prod: Metromedia Producers. Dist: Sterling (sale only; available on 8mm)
    The tragic story of how he tried to convince the Army and the Navy of the importance of an air force.

MODERSOHN-BECKER, PAULA

<u>Paula Modersohn-Becker</u>
15 min.   color   1973   SCA
Dir: Friedhelm Heyde.   Prod: Th. N. Blomberg.   Dist: Roland Collection
    Her life, work, and home as seen through her paintings.

MODIGLIANI, AMADEO

Amadeo Modigliani
12 min.   b&w   1969   SCA
Prod: BBC-TV. Dist: Time-Life (special order purchase only;
    no previews or rentals)
        Through the words of his daughter Jeanne, his short, tragic
life is retold and his paintings and sculptures are analyzed.

MOHAMMED (MAHOMET or MUHAMMAD)

Islam: The Prophet and the People
34 min.   color   1975   SCA
Prod: RAI-Texture Films. Dist: Texture.   Rental: Viewfinders
        A biography of Mohammed the Prophet is combined with a
history of Islam from the 6th century to the present.

MOLIERE (Pseudonym of Jean Baptiste Poquelin)

Portrait de Molière
62 min.   color   CA
Dir: Jean and Louis Barrault. Prod: Eurocitel. Dist: Interna-
    tional Film Bureau (5-year lease)
        In French with English sub-titles. A chronological account
of his life is woven together from scenes from his plays "Le
Tartuffe," "Le Bourgeois Gentilhomme" and "Le Misanthrope."
Commentary by Jean-Louis Barrault.

MONET, CLAUDE

Avec Claude Monet
22 min.   color   SCA
Dir: Dominique Delouche.   Prod: Skira Flag Film Production.
    Rental: FACSEA (available in French)
        Where he lived and worked.

Claude Monet (Pioneers of Modern Painting Series)
40 min.   color   1971   SCA
Prod. and dist: Independent Television Corp.   Rental: California
        Traces the life and artistic development of the founder of
the impressionist movement and shows some of his most famous
work, his rivalry with Manet, and his struggles.   Written and narrated by Sir Kenneth Clark.

MONROE, JAMES

James Monroe--The Man and the Doctrine (Americana Series #8)
30 min.   color   1972   IJSCA
Prod: Leo H. Handel.   Dist: Handel.   Rental: Syracuse

A portrait of the man and the background and meaning of the Monroe Doctrine.

MONROE, MARILYN

Marilyn
26 min.   color   1963
Prod: CBS.   Dist: Cinema 8
Combines newsreel footage and scenes from her earlier films, with commentary by Mike Wallace.

MONTEZUMA See CORTES, HERNANDO (Cortez and Montezuma: Conquest of an Empire)

MONTGOMERY, BERNARD LAW

The Black Beret (Men and Women of Our Times Series)
15 min.   b&w   1952-53   JSCA
Prod: Mike Sklar.   Dist: Star Film
His army's defeat of Rommel.   Compiled from the Fox Movietone News Library footage.

MOORE, HENRY
See also ARMITAGE, KENNETH (Five British Sculptors Work and Talk)

Face to Face: Henry Moore
32 min.   b&w   1970   JSCA
Prod: BBC-TV.   Dist: Time-Life (special order purchase only; no rentals or previews).   Rental: California, Indiana
A visit with him in his studio.

Henry Moore
28 min.   b&w   1952   C
Prod: John Read.   Rental: Indiana
Shown working on a statue.   He talks about his art education, exhibits some of his works and expresses his views on art.

Henry Moore (3 programs)
28-32 min.   b&w and color   1970   SCA
Prod: BBC-TV.   Dist: Time-Life (special order purchase only; no previews or rentals)
I Think in Shapes is a tour of a special exhibition in 1968 at the Tate Gallery.   A Sculptor's Landscape is an interpretation of his work.   Face to Face (above) is a visit with him.

Henry Moore at the Tate Gallery
14 min.   color   1971   SCA
Prod: Arts Council of Great Britain.   Dist: Films Inc.

Henry Moore--The Sculptor (Encyclopaedia Britannica)

An exhibit of his sculptures.

Henry Moore--Man of Form
28 min.   b&w   1966   JSCA
Prod: CBS.   Rental: Indiana, Minnesota, Southern California,
    Syracuse
        An interview, with a narrative about his childhood.   Pre-
sents some of his work.

Henry Moore: Master Sculptor
15 1/2 min.   color   1976   JSCA
Prod. and dist: Centron
        He's seen at work in a studio in England and in Berlin
watching the casting of one of his works in a bronze foundry.   He
also comments on his life and on art.   Henry Moore: Art and the
Art of Living is a companion film which focuses on his sculpture
"Hill Arches. "

Henry Moore--The Sculptor
24 min.   color or b&w   1969   JSC
Prod: Sobany Productions.   Dist: Encyclopaedia Britannica (avail-
    able on video by special order).   Rental: California, Southern
    California, Syracuse
        While in his studio, he talks about and demonstrates his
style of sculpturing.

MOORE, LENNY

Lenny Moore (Sports Legends Series)
20 min.   color   1975   IJSCA
Prod. and dist: Sports Legends Inc.   Rental: Southern California
        His football career; he comments on footage from his games.

MORANDI, GIORGIO

Giorgio Morandi
15 1/2 min.   color   1975   SCA
Prod: Libero Bizzarri (American version by International Film
    Bureau).   Dist: International Film Bureau
        An examination of more than 40 paintings as his develop-
ment is traced; indicates the influence of Cézanne.

MORE, SIR THOMAS See HENRY VIII (Matter of Conscience:
    Henry VIII and Thomas More); A Man for All Seasons (feature)

MOREAU, GUSTAVE

Moreau
20 min.   color   CA

Dir: Nelly Kaplan. Prod: Office de Documentation par le Film. Rental: FACSEA
     French dialogue only. Difficult vocabulary. His paintings in various French museums.

MORRIS, WILLIAM See ROSSETTI, DANTE GABRIEL (Dante's Inferno: The Life of Dante Gabriel Rossetti)

MORSE, SAMUEL FINLEY

Samuel F. B. Morse (Meet the Inventor Series)
9 min.   color   1955   P
Prod: U. P. A. Dist: Macmillan. Rental: Syracuse
     Animated. An "old inventor" tells a small boy about the invention of the telegraph.

What Hath God Wrought: Samuel F. B. Morse
20 min.   b&w   1952   PIJS
Prod: Teaching Film Custodians. Dist: Indiana (lease)
     His development of the Morse Code.

MOSES

Living Personalities of the Old Testament (a series)
30 min. each   b&w   1964
Prod: NBC. Rental: National Council of the Churches of Christ
     Lectures by D. Hagen Staack on the lives and times of Biblical personalities. The 12 films follow: Moses, the Learner; Moses, the Lawgiver; Joshua, the Settler; Samson, the Hero; Ruth, the Foreigner; Samuel, the Kingmaker; Saul, the First King; David, the Apprentice King; David, Israel's Greatest King; Solomon, the Builder King; Josiah, the Reformer King; Ezra, the Teacher.

MOSES, ANNA MARY ROBERTSON (GRANDMA)

Grandma Moses
22 min.   color   1950   JSCA
Prod: Falcon Films. Dist: Film Images. Rental: California, Indiana, Michigan
     At work with examples of her paintings. Archibald MacLeish comments on her earlier life.

MOTHERWELL, ROBERT See DE KOONING, WILLEM (Painters Painting)

MOUNTBATTEN, LOUIS EARL

Mountbatten: Man of Action

26 min.   b&w   1963
Prod: CBS.   Dist: Association
    Traces his military career beginning with his days as a cadet.

MOYNIHAN, PATRICK

Patrick Moynihan
32 min.   b&w   1967   SCA
Prod: BBC-TV.   Dist: Time-Life (special order purchase only; no previews or rentals)
    An interview in which he discusses his childhood in East Harlem, his experiences as a politician and professor, and his controversial ideas.

MOZART, WOLFGANG AMADEUS

Mozart and His Music
12 1/2 min.   color   1954   IJSCA
Prod. and dist: Coronet (sale only).   Rental: Indiana, Michigan, Minnesota, Nebraska, Syracuse
    Selections from his music underscore his background.

The Rise and Fall of Wolfgang Amadeus Mozart
35 min.   b&w   1970   SCA
Prod: BBC-TV.   Dist: Time-Life (special order purchase only; no previews or rentals)
    Films of Vienna, Salzburg, and Prague combined with documents and pictures unveil the story of his Vienna years and his music.

W. A. Mozart (Great Composers Series)
25 1/2 min.   color   1975   JSCA
Prod: Seabourne Enterprises. Dist: International Film Bureau
    An introduction to his life and music.

MUHAMMAD ALI
    See also A. K. A. Cassius Clay (feature)

Baddest Daddy in the Whole World
52 min.   color   1972   JSCA
Dir: Fred Haines. Dist: New Yorker
    A cinéma vérité portrait filmed in Switzerland (1971) before his fight with Jürgin Blin, it shows his practice sessions, the fight, and his family.

Muhammad Ali--Skill, Brains and Guts!
90 min.   color   1976
Prod: Big Fights Inc. Dist: Macmillan

Follows him from his teen-age years until the present, with excerpts from his matches.

MUIR, JOHN

John Muir--Father of our National Parks (They Made a Difference Series)
15 min.   color   1974
Prod. and dist: Walt Disney (long-term license)
Begins with his farm years when he learned to love nature and shows how he later decided to dedicate his life to preserving nature through national parks.

John Muir's High Sierra
27 min.   color   1973   IJSCA
Dir: Dewitt Jones.   Dist: Pyramid
As his writings are read, the camera follows the paths he took.

MUNAKATA, SHIKO

Woodblock Mandala: The World of Shiko Munakata
30 min.   color   1973   SC
Prod: NHK International.   Dist: Films Inc.
The personality and cultural background of this famous Japanese woodblock printer.

MUNCH, EDVARD

Edvard Munch (Pioneers in Modern Painting Series)
40 min.   color   1971   SCA
Prod. and dist: Independent Television Corp.   Rental: California
The life and work of Norwegian painter Munch, his relationship to Ibsen and Strindberg, and his innovations.   Written and narrated by Sir Kenneth Clark.

Edvard Munch
167 min.   color   1976   SCA
Prod: Norsk Rikskring kasting/Sveriges Radio AB Production.
  Dist: New Yorker
Chronicles his childhood and early years up to 1908 (he was born in 1863, died 1944) and also provides a look at his various environments--Christiana, now Oslo, Paris, Berlin, Copenhagen-- and the affect on his art work.

Edvard Munch: Paintings
39 min.   color   1967   SCA
Prod: Clifford B. West (Oslo, Norway).   Dist: Film Images
Analyzes a series of related pictures called the Frieze of Life; the themes of sickness, suffering, and fear of life are all

drawn from his own life. The commentary is taken from his diary.

Edvard Munch: Prints
27 min.   color   1967   SCA
Prod: Clifford B. West (Oslo, Norway). Dist: Film Images
    Primarily a biographical study which also highlights his most famous graphics and his contributions to the technical aspects of printmaking.

MURILLO, BARTOLOME See VELASQUEZ, DIEGO (Treasures from El Prado)

MURPHY, CALVIN

Calvin Murphy
22 min.   color   1972   SCA
Prod: Tele-Sports. Dist: Paramount Oxford
    A sports profile of the "small" basketball player.

MURROW, EDWARD R.

"This Is Edward R. Murrow"
44 min.   b&w   1976   SCA
Prod: CBS. Dist: Carousel
    His life as a journalist and commentator.

MUSSOLINI, BENITO

Mussolini (Biography Series)
26 min.   b&w   1963   JSCA
Prod: David Wolper. Dist: Withdrawn by McGraw-Hill. Rental: Indiana, Michigan, Syracuse
    Traces his life from youth to his rise to power and his ultimate capture and assassination.

Mussolini (Twentieth Century Series)
26 min.   b&w   1959   SCA
Prod: CBS. Rental: Association, California, Indiana, Michigan, Southern California, Syracuse
    His rise during the '20s and '30s, his association with Hitler during World War II, and the last days of the War.

NABOKOV, VLADIMIR

Novel: Vladimir Nabokov
29 min.   b&w   1966   SCA
Prod: NET. Dist: Indiana. Rental: California, Minnesota

"This Is Edward R. Murrow" (Carousel Films, Inc.)

Several interviews in which he talks about American writing, his methodology, Lolita, his home and his hobbies.

NAPOLEON BONAPARTE
See also Bonaparte et la Révolution (feature)

Bonaparte et la naissance de la France moderne
23 min.
Dir: Jean Vidal. Prod: Films Armorial. Rental: FACSEA
    French dialogue only. Easy vocabulary. Engravings are utilized to relate his story.

Conquest
23 min.   b&w   1948
Rental: California
    Excerpted from a feature film, this is primarily a character study; Napoleon is seen at a court reception, in a Polish home, at his marriage, and on Elba.

The Hundred Days: Napoléon--From Elba to Waterloo
40 min.   color   1969   SCA
Prod: BBC-TV. Dist: Time-Life (available on video)
    Shot on location, the three months between his escape from Elba and his final defeat at Waterloo are recounted.

Images d'Epinal
15 min.   color   1964   SCA
Dir. and prod: Jean Image. Rental: FACSEA (available in
    French)
    The most heroic episodes of his career come to life as a hawker in Epinal unwraps a famous picture by Georgin, showing a glorious battle.

La Malmaison
13 min.   color   1964   SCA
Dir: Jacques de Casembroot. Rental: FACSEA (available in
    French)
    At Malmaison, after his abdication but before his exile.

Napoléon
60 min.   1951   SCA
Rental: FACSEA (available in French)
    Engravings and documents are used to tell his story.

Napoléon raconté par un vieux soldat
15 min.   color   1955   CA
Dir: J. Jabely. Prod: Armorial. Rental: FACSEA
    French dialogue only. A knowledge of Napoleonic history is necessary to understand Balzac's parody of a popular view of Napoleon. The "Prints of Epinal" are utilized.

Napoleon: The End of a Dictator (Western Civilization Series)

26 min.   color   1970   JSCA
Prod. and dist: Learning (available in Spanish).   Rental: Michigan,
    Minnesota, Nebraska, South Florida, Southern California, Syra-
    cuse
        A dramatization of the last 100 days of his life, beginning
with his escape from Elba and ending with Waterloo.

Napoleon: The Making of a Dictator (Western Civilization Series)
27 min.   color   1970   JSCA
Prod. and dist: Learning (available in Spanish).   Rental: Indiana,
    Michigan, Nebraska, Minnesota, South Florida, Southern Cali-
    fornia
        A dramatization of his rise to power.

Napoleon's Return from Elba (You Are There Series)
27 min.   b&w   1955
Prod: CBS.   Dist: Withdrawn by McGraw-Hill.   Rental: Indiana,
    Michigan, Minnesota
        His exile and action at the Congress of Vienna.

A Time to Grow: The Louisiana Territory
20 min.   b&w   1953   JS
Prod: Teaching Film Custodians.   Dist: Indiana (lease)
        Napoleon orders Talleyrand to sell the entire Louisiana
Territory.   Talleyrand sets a high price, but Livingston and Mon-
roe agree to it.   A dramatization excerpted from a Cavalcade of
America television movie.

NAPOLEON III, LOUIS

Napoléon III
20 min.   SCA
Dir: Jean Vigne, Edouard Bruley.   Prod: Sofac.   Rental:
    FACSEA (available in French)
        Contemporaneous paintings and photographs trace the growth
of the empire from 1851-1871.

NASH, ODGEN

Ogden Nash (2 pts.; Poets and Poetry Series)
29 min. each   b&w   1959   SC
Prod: NET.   Rental: Indiana
        Reading and commenting on his own verse.

NAST, THOMAS

The Tiger's Tail: Thomas Nast vs. Boss Tweed
20 min.   b&w   1953   SC
Prod: Teaching Film Custodians.   Dist: Indiana (lease)

Focuses on the campaign against Tweed by Nast, a cartoonist for Harper's Weekly.

NEHRU, JAWAHARLAL

Jawaharlal Nehru (Wisdom Series)
30 min.   b&w   1966   SCA
Prod: NBC. Dist: Films Inc. Rental: Michigan, Minnesota, Nebraska
  In an interview with Chester Bowles he talks about his experiences and India's problems.

Nehru
54 min.   b&w   1967   SCA
Prod: Drew Associates. Dist: Time-Life (special order purchase; no previews or rentals)
  Nehru at 73.

Nehru: Man of Two Worlds (Twentieth Century Series)
26 min.   b&w   1966   SA
Prod: CBS. Dist: Association. Rental: Indiana, Michigan, Minnesota, Southern California, Syracuse
  The "father" of democracy in India, from early childhood until his death. His alliance with Gandhi, his imprisonment, and his political role are presented.

Our Prime Minister
21 min.
Dist: Information Service of India (free loan)
  Life of Nehru and how he led India.

NELSON, HORATIO (LORD) See The Nelson Affair (feature)

NERUDA, PABLO

I Am Pablo Neruda
28 1/2 min.   b&w   1968   SC
Prod: Harold Mantell. Dist: Films for the Humanities (available on 3/4" videocassette). Rental: California, Indiana, Southern California
  At home with him in Santiago, Chile as he writes, shops, speaks about poetry, walks among the rocks, visits the zoo, and explores an Inca fortress. Narrated by Anthony Quayle.

Pablo Neruda: Poet
30 min.   b&w   1972   SCA
Prod: Douglas Harris and Dr. Eugenia Neves. Dist: Tricontinental (available in Spanish)
  Filmed at Isla Negra, his seaside home, shortly before his death. He talks about love, hate, life and death, and his work.

A reading of his poems and a narrative about his "black" period and the Spanish Civil War are intercut with the interview.

NEVELSON, LOUISE

Louise Nevelson
25 min.   color   1971   SCA
Prod: Fred Pressburger. Dist: Connecticut. Rental: Michigan, Minnesota
  Made at the Whitney Museum of American Art exhibition, this is an introduction to her and her sculpture.

NEWCOMBE, JOHN

John Newcombe
22 min.   color   1972   SCA
Prod: Tele-Sports. Dist: Paramount Oxford
  A sports profile of the Australian tennis player.

NEWMAN, BARNETT
See also DE KOONING, WILLEM (Painters Painting)

Artist: Barnett Newman
30 min.   b&w   1966   SCA
Prod: NET. Dist: Indiana. Rental: California
  His home, his philosophy, and his art. He explains how he created "The Stations of the Cross."

NEWTON, SIR ISAAC

Isaac Newton (Men of Science Series)
13 1/2 min.   color   1959   JS
Prod. and dist: Coronet (sale only). Rental: Indiana, Minnesota, Nebraska, Syracuse
  Emphasizes his work and research in the binomial theorem, calculus, light and gravity. Stresses his influence on science.

Newton: The Mind that Found the Future (Western Civilization Series)
21 min.   color   1971   JSCA
Dir: George Kaczender. Prod: International Cinemedia Center. Dist: Learning (available in Spanish). Rental: Indiana, Michigan, Minnesota, Nebraska, South Florida, Southern California, Syracuse
  His friend Edmund Halley moves from his time to ours as he talks about Newton's personality and achievements and his link with modern science.

NICHOLAS II (OF RUSSIA)
See also Nicholas and Alexandra (feature)

Nicholas and Alexandra (a series)
26-29 min.   color   1976   SCA
Prod: Columbia Pictures. Dist: Learning
      These three films, which focus on Russia from 1904-1917,
were specially edited from the feature of the same title. Prelude
to Revolution: 1904-1905 is an introduction to Nicholas, his wife,
Lenin, Stalin, and Trotsky. War and the Fall of the Czar: 1914-
17 focuses on Nicholas' role at the front lines and Alexandra's de-
pendency on Rasputin, who is later assassinated. The Bolshevik
Victory: 1917 focuses on Lenin's followers and the execution of
the Romanov family.

NIEPCE, JOSEPH NICEPHORE See DAGUERRE, LOUIS JACQUES
(Daguerre; The Birth of Photography)

NIMITZ, CHESTER WILLIAM

Admiral Chester Nimitz
26 min.   b&w   1965   IJ
Prod: Metromedia Producers. Dist: Sterling (sale only; avail-
    able on 8mm). Rental: Syracuse
      His lifetime career as a naval leader, whose services cul-
minated in his appointment as commander in chief of the U.S.
Pacific fleet in 1942.

Biography of Admiral Nimitz
28 min.   1963
Prod. and dist: Dept. of the Navy (free loan)
      Documents his life with footage from World War II.

Freedom's Admiral
15 min.   b&w   1952-53   JSCA
Prod: Mike Sklar. Dist: Star Film
      Compiled from the Fox Movietone News Library; shows the
U.S. victory in the Pacific.

NIN, ANAIS

Anaïs Observed
68 min.   color   1974   SCA
Prod: Robert Snyder. Dist: Center for Learning Resources
      A candid portrait of her as she talks about her diaries,
her circle of friends, including Henry Miller, and women's libera-
tion.

NIXON, RICHARD MILHOUS
See also EISENHOWER, DWIGHT DAVID (Five Presidents on the Presidency); KENNEDY, JOHN F. (The Making of the President, 1960); HUMPHREY, HUBERT (The Making of the President, 1968)

The Making of the President, 1972
90 min. color 1973 SCA
Prod. and dist: Time-Life (available on video)
Based on Theodore White's book of the same title, this reveals Nixon as a campaigner and loner, and exposes the role of CREP (Committee for Re-Election of the President). Also traces his early political career.

Milhouse: A White Comedy
90 min. b&w SA
Dir: Emile de Antonio. Dist: New Yorker
A critical and satirical view of Nixon's political career -- the Hiss case, the Checkers speech, the '62 farewell to the press, the meeting with Khrushchev, and the '64 and '68 campaigns. Not presented chronologically.

Nixon's Checkers Speech
30 min. b&w 1971 JSA
Dist: New Yorker
A kinescope of his famous speech given in 1952 when he was Eisenhower's running mate in defense of the New York Post's accusation that he used campaign funds unethically.

NIXON: From Checkers to Watergate
26 min. color 1976 JSCA
Dir: Charles Braverman. Dist: Pyramid
Documents his political history.

NOBEL, ALFRED BERNHARD

Story of Alfred Nobel (Passing Parade Series)
11 min. b&w 1939 JSA
Prod: MGM. Rental: Indiana, South Florida
How he accidently discovered dynamite, which is later used for warfare, and how he then strove for ways to achieve peace and established the peace prize.

NOGUCHI, ISAMU

Noguchi: A Sculptor's World
28 min. color 1972 SCA
Prod. and dist: Arnold Eagle. Rental: California
Selecting marble in Italy, discussing his works, working on stone. Ends with footage of his fountains, which were built for the Kyoto World Fair.

NOLAND, KENNETH See LOUIS, MORRIS (Artists--The New Abstraction: Morris Louis and Kenneth Noland); DE KOONING,
   WILLEM (Painters Painting)

NOLDE, EMIL

Emil Noldé
15 min.   color   1972   SCA
Dir: Friedhelm Heyde. Prod: Th. N. Blomberg. Dist: Roland
   Collection
      His paintings and his life in Germany, where the Nazi re-
gime refused to allow him to paint; therefore, he made his water-
color sketches postcard size.

NORRIS, GEORGE W.

Senator George W. Norris (Profiles in Courage Series)
50 min.   b&w   1965   IJSCA
Prod: Robert Saudek Associates. Dist: IQ Films. Rental:
   Syracuse
      Insists on a Congressional discussion about isolation vs.
war (World War I).

NORTH, FREDERICK (LORD)

The American Revolution: 1770-1773--A Conversation with Lord
   North
33 min.   color   1971   JSCA
Prod: CBS. Dist: BFA. Rental: Indiana, South Florida
      Eric Sevareid "interviews" Lord North, played by Peter
Ustinov, about colonial events leading to the Revolution.

NYKVIST, SVEN

Sven Nykvist
26 min.   color   1974   SC
Prod: Visual Programmes Systems Ltd. Dist: Films Inc.
   Rental: Michigan (title: Foto: Sven Nykvist)
      Photographer of "Cries and Whispers." He and his work
are explored with the aid of film clips.

O'CASEY, SEAN
   See also Young Cassidy (feature)

Sean O'Casey (Wisdom Series)
30 min.   b&w   1961   SCA
Prod: NBC. Dist: Films Inc. Rental: Michigan, Minnesota,
   Nebraska, Southern California

An interview at his home in England, where he talks about the poverty he endured and other great playwrights he's known, such as Shaw and Lady Gregory.

O'HARA, FRANK

Poetry: Frank O'Hara and Ed Sanders
30 min.   b&w   1966   JSCA
Prod: NET. Dist: Indiana. Rental: California
In his workshop O'Hara reads his poetry and works on his movie script. Sanders reads an excerpt from his own work while in his bookshop.

OLDENBURG, CLAES

Artists: Claes Oldenburg
30 min.   b&w   1966   SCA
Prod: NET. Dist: Indiana. Rental: California
Shown as he's preparing for an exhibit; he discusses his work and his daily routine.

Claes Oldenburg
52 min.   color   1975   SCA
Prod. and dist: Blackwood Productions
As he works on a sculpture, he talks about art.

OLITSKI, JULES See DE KOONING, WILLEM (Painters Painting)

OTIS, JAMES

A Man's Home: James Otis
20 min.   b&w   1954   JS
Prod: Teaching Film Custodians. Dist: Indiana (lease)
A dramatization of his stand against illegal seizure during the colonial period. An excerpt from the Cavalcade of America television movie.

OUTERBRIDGE, JOHN

John Outerbridge: Black Artist
21 min.   color   1971   JSCA
Prod: Lewis-Wong. Dist: ACI. Rental: Syracuse
As he's creating a sculpture, he talks about his life and work.

OWENS, JESSE

Jesse Owens Returns to Berlin

32 min.   b&w   1965   JSC
Dir. and prod: Bud Breenspan.   Dist: Dept. of the Army
A black athlete, winner of four Olympic medals in 1936,
returns to Berlin, where he recalls the Nazi days.

PAINE, THOMAS See BURKE, EDMUND (Man and the State:
Burke and Paine on Revolution)

PARACELSUS, PHILIPPUS

Paracelsus (Legacy Series)
30 min.   b&w   1965   JSCA
Prod: NET. Dist: Indiana.   Rental: California, Minnesota
The medical theories he presented in the Middle Ages are
remarkably accurate.

PARKS, GORDON

Black Wealth
20 min.   color   1974   JSA
Prod. and dist: Agency for Instructional Television (available on
3/4" videocassette)
Presents the recollections of writer Gordon Parks and
dramatically presents the speech of Sojourner Truth.   Poems by
other black writers are read.

The Weapons of Gordon Parks
28 min.   color   1968   SA
Dir: Warren Forma. Dist: Withdrawn by McGraw-Hill.   Rental:
California, Michigan, Minnesota, Nebraska, Southern California,
Syracuse
How he overcame racism and poverty to become internation-
ally known as a photographer and writer.

PARR, CATHERINE See HENRY VIII (The Six Wives of Henry
VIII); Henry VIII and His Six Wives (feature)

PARRISH, MAXFIELD

Parrish Blue
27 min.   color   1968   SA
Prod: Ronald S. Marquissee. Dist: International Film Bureau.
Rental: Michigan, Syracuse
The life and work of an American artist-illustrator.   Nar-
rated by Norman Rockwell and Maxfield Parrish, Jr.

PARTCH, HARRY

The Dreamer that Remains: A Portrait of Harry Partch
27 min.   color   1973   JSCA
Prod: Tantalus, Inc. Dist: Macmillan. Rental: Syracuse
    A study of this avant-garde composer.

Music Studio: Harry Partch
18 min.   color   1971   SCA
Dist: Grove. Rental: Minnesota
    A study of him at work in his studio. He performs several
of his musical compositions.

PASCAL, BLAISE

Blaise Pascal
22 min.   SCA
Dir: Henri de Hubsch. Prod: Atlantic. Rental: FACSEA (avail-
    able in French)
    How his life and works evolved.

Blaise Pascal
135 min.   color   1972
Dir: Roberto Rossellini. Rental: Macmillan

Blaise Pascal (A Third Testament Series)
55 min.   color   1976   SCA
Prod: BBC-TV. Dist: Time-Life (available on video)
    This 17th-century scientist, mathematician and inventor con-
sidered God the only worthy pursuit for man. His ideas are
summed up in Pensées.

PASOLINI, PIER PAOLO

Pier Paolo Pasolini
30 min.   color   1970   SCA
Dir: Carlo-Heyman-Chaffey. Dist: Macmillan
    Interviews with him and his colleagues reveal the themes in
his works, such as "The Gospel According to St. Matthew." Italian dialogue with English voice-overs.

PASTEUR, LOUIS
    See also The Story of Louis Pasteur (feature)

La Jeunesse de Monsieur Pasteur
16 min.   color   1965   SCA
Dir: Monique and Raymond Millet. Rental: FACSEA (available in
    French)
    From his birth at Dole in 1822 through his studies in Paris
to his first experiment in crystallography.

Louis Pasteur (Great Scientists Speak Again Series)
24 min.   color   1975   SC
Prod. and dist: California
    An impersonation of Pasteur, who "teaches" his scientific
theories.

Louis Pasteur, The Benefactor
16 min.   b&w   n.d.   JS
Prod: Pictorial Films. Rental: Indiana
    His struggle against the prejudices of the French Academy
of Medicine, his famous rabies experiment, and a summary of his
accomplishments.

Louis Pasteur: Man of Science
28 min.   b&w   1955   IJ
Prod: Viking Films. Dist: Sterling (sale only; available on 8mm).
    Rental: Michigan, Syracuse
    A biography from 1857, when he discovered that microbes
cause fermentation, until 1895 when he died. Recounts his contributions to science.

Mr. Pasteur and the Riddle of Life
11 min.   color or b&w   1972   IJ
Prod. and dist: Coronet (sale only). Rental: Michigan, Syracuse
    An animated, humorous look at how he refutes the scientists
of his time.

Pasteur hier et aujourd'hui
13 min.   color   1973   CA
Dir. and prod: Edouard Berne. Rental: FACSEA
    French dialogue only. A tribute to him and his work.
Stresses that his ideas and methods are still in use at the Pasteur
Institute.

The Story of Louis Pasteur--Anthrax Sequence
17 min.   b&w   1936   JS
Prod: Warner Bros., edited by Teaching Film Custodians.
    Rental: Indiana, Minnesota
    A dramatization excerpted from The Story of Louis Pasteur,
which shows his struggle to establish his microbe theory of disease.

The Story of Louis Pasteur--Hydrophobia Sequence
17 min.   b&w   1936   JS
Prod: Warner Bros., edited by Teaching Film Custodians. Dist:
    Indiana. Rental: Minnesota
    A dramatization excerpted from The Story of Louis Pasteur
in which he tries to introduce a serum treatment for hydrophobia.

PATTIE, JAMES OHIO

Mountain Man: James Ohio Pattie
27 min.   b&w   1954

Prod: Teaching Film Custodians.   Dist: Indiana (lease)
His visit to California when it was a Mexican colony is dramatized.   From prison he helps avert a smallpox epidemic by knowledge of the vaccine.   An excerpt from the Cavalcade of America television movie.

PATTON, GEORGE SMITH
See also EISENHOWER, DWIGHT DAVID (Famous Generals); Patton (feature)

Blood and Guts
15 min.   b&w   1952-53   JSCA
Prod: Mike Sklar.   Dist: Star Film
His distinguished military career is recounted; compiled from the Fox Movietone News Library footage.

General George Patton
26 min.   b&w   1965   IJ
Prod: Metromedia Producers.   Dist: Sterling (sale only; available on 8mm).   Rental: Mass Media, Syracuse
His controversial but brilliant military career.

Patton and the Third Army (20th Century Series)
26 min.   b&w   1960   SCA
Prod: CBS.   Dist: Association
A profile and look at his military career, beginning with his landing in North Africa in 1942.

PAUL VI, POPE

The Fourth of October (also known as Pope Paul at the UN)
28 min.   b&w   1965   JSCA
Dir: Ramakantha Sarma.   Dist: United Nations
His speech at the UN.

Pope Paul VI (20th Century Series)
26 min.   b&w   1960   SCA
Prod: CBS.   Dist: Association
How and why he brought innovations to the Church.

The Sixth Paul
58 min.   b&w   1969   SCA
Prod: NET.   Dist: Indiana
The controversial encyclical on birth control is the focal point.

PAUL, SAINT

Life of St. Paul (a series)
30 min. each   b&w   1949-51   JSCA

Prod: Cathedral. Rental: Catholic Film Center, Yale Divinity School
Dramatizations of The Book of Acts. Includes the following: Stephen, First Christian Martyr; The Conversion; Years of Apprenticeship; Return to Jerusalem; Ambassador for Christ: First Missionary Journey; Visit to Corinth: Third Missionary Journey; Trial at Jerusalem; Voyage to Rome; Stoning at Lystra; Second Missionary Journey.

Walk Beside Me
60 min.   1964   SCA
Prod. and dist: Southern Baptist Radio-Television Commission
A documentary of the Apostle Paul which retraces his steps through Israel, Jordan, Greece and Turkey. The narrative is taken from his own writings.

PAVIA, PHILIP See DE KOONING, WILLEM (Painters Painting)

PAVLOV, IVAN PETROVICH

Pavlov: The Conditioned Reflex
25 min.   b&w   1975   SC
Prod: USSR Central Television. English adaptation by Harold Mantell. Dist: Films for the Humanities (available on 3/4" videocassette)
A close-up of the man at work, shown through rare documentary footage and a survey of his career and accomplishments. Narrated by Anthony Quayle.

PAVLOVA, ANNA

Le Cygne Immortal
37 min.   b&w   1965
Prod: Victor Dandre. Dist: Museum of Modern Art
Footage assembled by Pavlova's husband, which shows her dancing and relaxing at home.

PEARY, ROBERT EDWIN
See also HENSON, MATTHEW (Peary and Henson: North to the Pole)

Peary's Race for the North Pole
52 min.   color   1973   JS
Prod: Wolper Organization. Dist: Films Inc. Rental: Michigan
The 64-year controversy between Peary and Dr. Frederick A. Cook over who discovered the North Pole. Diaries, newspapers and re-enacted testimonies tell the story. Lorne Greene is the narrator.

PENN, ARTHUR

Arthur Penn: Themes and Variants
86 min.   color   1970   JSCA
Prod: Robert P. S. B. Hughes.   Dist: Macmillan (lease).
   Rental: California, Syracuse
        At home and directing Dustin Hoffman on location with
"Little Big Man." Colleagues and friends comment on him and his
work, which is represented by scenes from "The Chase," "The
Left Handed Gun," "Alice's Restaurant" and others.

PENN, SIR WILLIAM

The Splendid Dream: William Penn
19 min.   b&w   1954   JS
Prod: Teaching Film Custodians.   Dist: Indiana
        Penn's quarrel with his father over his religious beliefs,
their reconciliation and his founding of a new colony.   An excerpt
from the Cavalcade of America television movie.

William Penn and the Quakers
10 1/2 min.   color   1959   IJ
Prod. and dist: Coronet (sale only).   Rental: Indiana, Michigan,
   Minnesota, Nebraska, Syracuse
        Built around the story of the Quakers' struggle for religious
freedom and Penn's role in founding Pennsylvania.

PERELMAN, SIDNEY JOSEPH

Writers: S. J. Perelman
30 min.   b&w   1966   SCA
Prod: NET.   Dist: Indiana
        At home in Pennsylvania he talks about authors such as F.
Scott Fitzgerald and Nathanael West, reading and travel.

PERLS, FREDERICK
   See also ELLIS, ALBERT (Three Approaches to Psychotherapy)

Frederick Perls and Gestalt Therapy (2 films)
36-39 min.   b&w   CA
Prod. and dist: Psychological Films
        The first film presents the key theories of Gestalt therapy;
the second presents an actual demonstration.

PERON, EVITA

Eva Peron (History Makers of the 20th Century Series)
24 min.   b&w   1965   IJ
Prod: David Wolper.   Dist: Sterling (sale only; available on 8mm)

A portrait of a woman who became a political power in Argentina.

Peron and Evita
26 min.   b&w   1958
Prod: CBS.   Dist: Association
    A contemporaneous view of Peron and his wife.

PERON, JUAN See PERON, EVITA (Peron and Evita)

PERSHING, JOHN JOSEPH
   See also EISENHOWER, DWIGHT DAVID (Famous Generals)

General Pershing
25 min.   b&w   1965   IJ
Prod: Metromedia Producers.   Dist: Sterling (sale only; available on 8mm)
    His leadership role in the military during World War I.
Utilizes newsreel footage.

The Iron Commander
15 min.   b&w   1952-53   JSCA
Prod: Mike Sklar.   Dist: Star Film
    How he inspired his men.   Compiled from the Fox Movietone News Library footage.

PETAIN, HENRI PHILIPPE See DE GAULLE, CHARLES ANDRE
   (De Gaulle vs. Petain: Struggle for France)

PETER, LAURENCE J.

The Peter Principle
25 min.   color   1975   CA
Prod: BBC-TV.   Dist: Time-Life (available on video)
    Dr. Peter, author of the book of the same title, examines
the implications of his assertion that "... an employee tends to
rise to his level of incompetence and that's where he stays."

PETIT, ROBERT (BOB)

Bob Petit (Sports Legends Series)
20 min.   color   1975   JSCA
Prod. and dist: Sports Legends Inc.   Rental: Southern California
    The NBA's most valuable player talks about his career.

PIAGET, JEAN

Evans' Dialogue with Piaget and Inhelder (2 pts.)

40 min. each   color   1972   C
Prod: Dr. Richard Evans.   Dist: Macmillan (sale only).   Rental: Association
    In part 1 he lists the cognitive development steps and in part 2 he discusses his relationship with Freud.

PICASSO, PABLO RUIZ Y

Guernica
12 min.   1952   CA
Dir: Alain Resnais.   Dist: Pictura.   Rental: FACSEA (French dialogue only)
    An exploration of this masterpiece, narrated by Eva La-Galliene.

Chicago Picasso
60 min.   color   1968
Rental: California
    Picasso's largest and most controversial sculpture is discussed by Sir Roland Penrose, his friend and biographer.   The work is seen from the original model until the finished sculpture emerges.

Picasso
50 min.   color   1968   SA
Dir: Luciano Emmer.   Dist: McGraw-Hill.   Rental: Michigan, Southern California
    Uses 477 of his paintings as it traces his life and career.

Picasso
51 min.   color   1972   SCA
Prod: BBC-TV.   Dist: Time-Life (available on video)
    A biography tracing from his early life in Spain to the present.   Shows his circle of friends in Paris during the '20s and his art.

Picasso: Artist of the Century
53 min.   color   1976   SCA
Prod: Film Sonor Marceau.   Dist: Macmillan
    Covers the full range of his work, where he painted them, and the artist at work and at play.   Also available in three parts: Picasso: From 1900 through Cubism (12 min.) covers the Blue and Rose Periods begun in Paris and represented by the paintings the "Three Musicians," "Three Dancers," and "The Studio." Picasso: The Volcanic 30's (17 min.) covers the period after his departure from Paris when he painted "Girl Before a Mirror" and "Guernica." Picasso: The 1940's and After (25 min.) covers his paintings of the sun and the sea, the group of "Classical Fantasies," sculpture, and a return to his harlequin themes.

Picasso Is 90
51 min.   color   1973   JSCA

Picasso (McGraw-Hill Films)

Prod: CBS News. Dist: Carousel (sale only). Rental: Kit
    Parker, Michigan, South Florida.
        Traces his life from early childhood to old age, with com-
ments by his son Claude and his ex-wife Françoise Gilot. A retrospective look at his paintings which are in the Pushkin Museum
in Moscow, the Hermitage in Leningrad, the Museum of Modern
Art and the Metropolitan.

Picasso--Joie de Vivre (History of Art Series)
13 min.   color   1970   JSCA
Dir: Jacques Berthier. Prod: Les Films Michel François.
    Dist: Roland Collection
        In 1946 at the Mediterranean seashore he decorated the
ancient Chateau Antibes with its paintings and drawings. With
commentary.

Picasso: Le Romancero du Picador (History of Art Series)
12 min.   b&w   1970   JSCA
Prod: Time-Life. Dist: New Yorker, Roland Collection

Based on his drawings of a bullfight.

Picasso: Peintre du Siècle
56 min.   color   1973   SCA
Dir: Lauro Venturi.   Prod: Filmsonor Marceau.   Rental:
    FACSEA (available in French)
        Traces the periods of his career from 1900 to 1973.

Picasso, The Sculptor
27 min.   color   1971   SCA
Prod: Arts Council of Great Britain.   Dist: Films Inc.
        His sculpture as he sculpts.

Picasso: War, Peace, Love (Museum Without Walls Series)
51 min.   color   1970   SCA
Dist: Universal Education and Visual Arts.   Rental: Michigan
        A survey of some of his work from "Guernica" to 1970.
He's shown inside his studio near Cannes.

Visit to Picasso
22 min.   b&w   1956   JSA
Prod: Fleetwood.   Dist: Withdrawn by Macmillan.   Rental: Syra-
    cuse
        His development as an artist is shown through examples of
his works at various stages in different mediums.   He paints on a
sheet of plexi-glass placed between him and the audience.

PICCOLO, BRIAN   See   Brian's Song (feature)

PIERCE, DONALD

Donald Pierce
22 min.   color   1973   SCA
Prod: Tele-Sports.   Dist: Paramount Oxford
        Riding in two handicap races and later commenting on them.

PINCAY, LAFFIT, JR.

Laffit Pincay, Jr.
22 min.   color   1972   SCA
Prod: Tele-Sports.   Dist: Paramount Oxford
        A sports profile of a well-known jockey.

PINKERTON, ALLAN   See   LINCOLN, ABRAHAM (The Palmetto
    Conspiracy: Lincoln, President-Elect)

PINTER, HAROLD

Pinter People

58 min.   color   1969   CA
Dir: Gerla Potterton. Dist: Films Inc.
    Interweaves an interview with him at home with five ani-
mated short plays by Pinter--"Trouble in the Works," "Request
Stop," "Applicant," "The Black and White," and "Last to Go."

PIRANESI, GIAN-BATTISTA

Gian-Battista Piranesi (Romantic Versus Classic Art Series)
26 min.   color   1974   JSCA
Prod: Reader's Digest.   Dist: Pyramid.   Rental: Southern California (listed under series title)
    The influences on his life and work are noted.   Illustrations
from his best works are utilized.   Narrated by Kenneth Clark.

PIUS XII, POPE

Pope Pius XII
27 min.   b&w   1965   IJ
Prod: Metromedia Producers.   Dist: Sterling (sale only; available on 8mm)
    Utilizes newsreel footage to help tell the story of his life
from birth until his death in 1876.

PIZARRO, FRANCISCO
   See also CABOT, JOHN (Age of Discovery: Spanish and Portuguese Explorations)

Francisco Pizarro (Age of Exploration Series)
52 min.   color   1976   SCA
Prod: BBC-TV and Time-Life.   Dist: Time-Life (also available
   on video)
    The conflict between him and the Inca man-god Atahualpa.

PLATEAU, JOSEPH ANTOINE

Monsieur Plateau
25 min.   color   1964
Dir: Jean Brismée.   Dist: Macmillan.   Free Loan: Belgian
   Embassy (5 prints)
    His theory of retinal persistance is the basis of motion pic-
tures.   A documentary about his many scientific achievements.

PLATH, SYLVIA

Sylvia Plath
29 min.   color   1977   JSCA
Prod: Harold Mantell.   Dist: Films for the Humanities

A close-up of her and her poetry. Narrated largely by Plath herself.

POE, EDGAR ALLAN

Edgar Allan Poe
29 min.   b&w   1962   SCA
Prod: KNXT-TV.   Dist: Southern California
Dr. Herman Harvey of USC delves into his life and problems and how they affected his work. A kinescope.

Edgar Allan Poe (Poetry by Americans Series)
9 min.   color   1972   JSC
Prod: Art Evans. Dist: Paramount Oxford. Rental: Syracuse
A biographical sketch followed by Lorne Greene's reading and a dramatization of his poem "Annabel Lee."

Edgar Allan Poe: Background for His Works
13 min.   color   1958   JSC
Prod. and dist: Cornet (sale only). Rental: Indiana, Michigan, Minnesota, Nebraska, South Florida, Syracuse
Paintings bring scenes from his work to life as his background is unfolded. Excerpts from "To Helen," "The Fall of the House of Usher," "The Murders in the Rue Morgue," and "The Raven."

POLANSKI, ROMAN

Polanski Meets Macbeth
30 min.   color   1971   SCA
Dir. and prod: Frank Simon. Dist: Macmillan (lease). Rental: Syracuse
A portrait filmed on the set of "Macbeth," the main characters of which comment upon his directing techniques and manner.

POLLOCK, JACKSON
See also DE KOONING, WILLEM (Painters Painting); GUGGEN-HEIM, PEGGY (Peggy Guggenheim: Art in Venice)

Jackson Pollock
10 min.   color   1951   SCA
Dist: Film Images. Rental: California, Minnesota
As he's working, he discusses his unusual and controversial technique of painting. A classic.

POLO, MARCO
See also Adventures of Marco Polo (feature); Marco Polo (feature); Marco the Magnificent (feature)

Marco Polo's Travels
19 min.   b&w   1955   JSCA
Prod. and dist: Encyclopaedia Britannica.   Rental: Michigan,
    Minnesota, Nebraska, South Florida, Southern California
        His 24-year journey from Venice to the court of Kubla Khan
and his return and the impact on the West.

PONCE DE LEON   See   CABOT, JOHN (Age of Discovery)

POONS, LARRY
    See also   DE KOONING, WILLEM (Painters Painting)

Artists--Frank Stella and Larry Poons: The New Abstraction
30 min.   b&w   1966   JSCA
Prod: NET.   Dist: Indiana
        Shown in their studios where they paint and discuss their
abstract works.

PORTER, ELIOT

Eliot Porter (University-at-Large Series)
6 min.   color
Dist: Association
        Based on his photographic essay, "In Wilderness Is the
Preservation of the World."

POSEY, SAM

Sam Posey
22 min.   color   1973   SCA
Prod: Tele-Sports.   Dist: Paramount Oxford
        A sports-file of autoracer Posey.

POUND, EZRA LOOMIS

Ezra Pound
15 min.   b&w   1962   SCA
Dist: Withdrawn by McGraw-Hill.   Rental: California, Michigan
        He talks about his work and quotes extracts from his poems
at his daughter's Castle of Brunnenburg in Merano, Italy.

Ezra Pound: Poet's Poet
28 1/2 min.   b&w   1973   SC
Prod: Harold Mantell.   Dist: Films for the Humanities (avail-
    able on 3/4" videocassette)
        In his 80's he reflects on his past, especially from 1910-
1930.   Talks about his influence on Eliot, Joyce, and Hemingway
and reads excerpts from "Hugh Selwyn Mauberley" and "The Cantos."

POZZATTI, RUDY

Pozzatti (Artists in America Series)
30 min. color 1971 SCA
Prod: Public Television Library. Dist: Indiana. Rental: California
    A major printmaker preparing for a New York show.

PRIESTLEY, JOHN BOYNTON

J. B. Priestley
30 min. b&w 1969 SCA
Prod: BBC-TV. Dist: Time-Life (Special order purchase only; no previews or rentals)
    A humorous, witty conversation with his friend Robert
Robinson.

PROUST, MARCEL

Le Temps d'une vocation, or, Marcel Proust: From a Master-piece to a Master's Work
21 min. color 1961 C
Prod: CAPAC. Rental: California, FACSEA (available in French), Southern California
    His life and times linked to his writing; uses graphics and
paintings. English by Jean-Pierre Aumont.

PUDOVKIN, V. I.

Pudovkin
60 min. b&w 1960 SCA
Dir: Andrei Kustov. Prod: Mosnauchfilm Studios. Dist: Macmillan (5-year lease)
    Working and acting. His life and work are intercut. Clips
of "Mother," "The End of St. Petersburg," "The Return of Vasily
Bortnikov."

RABELAIS, FRANÇOIS

"Jusques au feu exclusivement"
20 min. color 1971 CA
Dir: Marceau Ginesy. Prod: Films Hernes. Rental: FACSEA
    French dialogue only. The events which led to the founding
of the commune Thélème.

RACINE, JEAN BAPTISTE

Racine (Ici La France Series)

20 min.   b&w   1964   SA
Prod: Associated TV Company, France. Rental: Syracuse
    Advanced French only. A professor from Paris discusses
the life and times of poet Racine and Renne Faure and appears in
dramatic excerpts from "Phèdre," "Bernice," and "Andromaque."

RABIN, YITZHAK

Rabin: An Action Biography
52 min.   color   1975   SCA
Prod. and dist: ABC. Dist: Aetna (free loan)
    Focuses on the Israeli Prime Minister's role as statesman
and his predictions for the future of the Middle East.

RALEIGH, SIR WALTER See CABOT, JOHN (Age of Discovery:
  English, French, and Dutch Explorations)

RANDOLPH, A. PHILIP

A. Philip Randolph
11 min.   color   1972   IJS
Prod: Rediscovery Productions. Dist: Rediscovery, Sterling
  (sale only; available in 8mm)
    He talks about his confrontations with Roosevelt and Ken-
nedy and his quest for job equality for blacks.

RAPHAEL

Raphael
20 min.   b&w   1970   SCA
Prod: BBC-TV. Dist: Time-Life (available for special order
  purchase only; no previews or rentals)
    The focal point is "The Miraculous Draught of Fishes," a
tapestry design.

Raphael
28 min.   color
Prod: Scala Art Film. Dist: Macmillan
    Shows the influence of his teachers and other artists such
as Leonardo.

RAUSCHENBERG, ROBERT
  See also DE KOONING, WILLEM (Painters Painting)

Artist: Robert Rauschenberg
30 min.   b&w   1966   SCA
Prod: NET. Dist: Indiana
    Why he stopped painting just as he reached his peak.

RAVEL, MAURICE

Maurice Ravel
51 min.   SCA
Dir: Roland Bernard.   Prod: ORTF.   Rental: FACSEA
    His life and works.

REDDY, HELEN See GIOVANNI, NIKKI (Accomplished Women)

REINIGER, LOTTE

The Art of Lotte Reiniger
16 min.   color   1972   SCA
Prod: Louis Hagen.   Dist: Macmillan
    At work in her studio cutting her well-known cardboard
figures.

REMBRANDT VAN RIJN (or RYN)
    See also Rembrandt (feature)

In Search of Rembrandt
28 min.   color   1972   JS
Prod: NET.   Dist: Films Inc.
    His art.

In Search of Rembrandt
50 min.   color   1969   SCA
Dist: National Gallery of Art (free loan)
    Rembrandt as seen through 600 paintings and drawings.
Narrated by James Mason.

Rembrandt (Human Dimension Series)
30 min.   color   1971   SCA
Prod: Radio-Television Commission.   Dist: Graphic Curriculum
    (available for closed circuit television)
    At the age of 14 he became a painter's apprentice.   His life
and inner thoughts are reflected in his paintings, 76 of which are
included in this film.

Rembrandt and the Bible
30 min.   color   1971   JSCA
Prod: ABC.   Dist: Southern Baptist Radio-Television Commission
    Approximately 100 works located in museums throughout the
world, which reveal his spiritual quest.

Rembrandt: Painter of Man
20 min.   color   1958   IJSCA
Prod: Bert Haanstra.   Dist: Perspective (sale only).   Rental:
    Michigan, Minnesota, Nebraska, Syracuse
    A photographic analysis of over 60 of his paintings.

Rembrandt: Poet of Light
13 min.   b&w   1953   JSA
Prod: International Film Bureau.   Dist: Withdrawn by IFB.
    Rental: Minnesota, Syracuse
        A biographical sketch combined with a discussion of his use
of light, which is explored in several paintings.

Rembrandt Van Rijn: A Self Portrait
27 min.   color   1955   JSC
Prod. and dist: Encyclopaedia Britannica (available on video by
    special order).   Rental: California, Michigan, Minnesota, Ne-
    braska, South Florida, Southern California, Syracuse
        Through his 60-odd self-portraits his life is traced from
his early years as a painter to old age.

REMINGTON, ELIPHALET

The Forge: Remington's Rifle
20 min.   b&w   1954   JS
Prod: Teaching Film Custodians.   Dist: Indiana (lease)
        A drama of his development of his famous rifle.

RENOIR, JEAN

Direction d'Acteur de Jean Renoir
23 min.   color   1971   SCA
Dir: Gisele Braunberger.   Dist: McGraw-Hill.   Rental: Michigan
        Working with actress Gisele Braunberger for her leading
role in "Breakfast with the Nicolaides."

La Direction d'acteurs
22 min.   color   1969   CA
Dir: Gisele Braunberger.   Prod: Films de la Pleiade.   Rental:
    FACSEA
        French dialogue only.   Interpreting a script for an actress.

Voices
55 min.   color   CA
Dir: Richard Mourdant.   Dist: New Line Cinema
        Directing the Rolling Stones in "Sympathy for the Devil,"
plus an interview (in English).

RENOIR, PIERRE AUGUSTE

Renoir
7 min.   color   1975   SCA
Prod. and dist: National Gallery of Art (free loan)
        Uses his own observations about art as the commentary; 15
works are included to show the vibrancy of his art.

Renoir
23 min.   color   1953   SA
Prod: Jerry Winters.   Dist: Withdrawn by McGraw-Hill.   Rental:
      Southern California, Syracuse
          Over 50 of his impressionist works are photographed.

REVERE, PAUL

Midnight Ride of Paul Revere
11 min.   color or b&w   1957   IJS
Prod. and dist: Encyclopaedia Britannica.   Rental: Indiana,
      Michigan, Minnesota, Syracuse
          Points out discrepancies between Longfellow's famous poem
and the actual ride.

Paul Revere's Ride (You Are There Series)
22 min.   color   1972   IJS
Prod: CBS.   Dist: BFA
          A dramatization of an "on the scene" report, which reveals
the conflicts leading to the Revolution and his famous ride.

Paul Revere's Ride
11 min.   b&w   1955   IJ
Prod: Johnson Hunt Productions.   Rental: Minnesota
          Little-known facts about his ride; the narration reflects the
vocabulary and idioms of colonial New England; art work by Bernard Garbutt.

RIBERA, JUSEPE (or JOSE)   See   VELASQUEZ, DIEGO (Treasures
      from El Prado)

RICHARD I (THE LION-HEARTED)

The Crusades
29 min.   b&w   1935   IJS
Prod: Paramount, edited by Teaching Film Custodians.   Dist:
      Indiana (lease)
          An abridged version of a feature film, it pictures the con-
frontation between Richard the Lion-Hearted and Saladin.

RICHELIEU, DUC DE

Richelieu
20 min.   1953   CA
Dir: Jean Vidal.   Prod: Films du Matin.   Rental:
      FACSEA

French dialogue only. His rise to power, his role in French history and his influence on politics and art.

RICHEY, CHARLES See McCOY, ELIJAH (Black Men and Iron Horses)

RICHTER, HANS

Richter on Film
13 min.   color   CA
Dist: Cecile Starr. Rental: Creative Film Society, Minnesota
    Still active at the age of 83, Richter talks to author Cecile Starr about his avant-garde films of the '20s.

RIESSEN, MARTY

Marty Riessen
22 min.   color   1972   SCA
Prod: Tele-Sports. Dist: Paramount Oxford
    A sports profile of the American tennis star.

RINGLING, JOHN

John Ringling--Ca D'Zan (American Life Styles Series)
28 min.   color   1976   IJSCA
Prod: Comco Productions. Dist: Association
    E. G. Marshall conducts a tour of his Florida home, thus revealing the personality of the man who lived there.

ROBERTSON, OSCAR

Oscar Robertson
22 min.   color   1973   SCA
Prod: Tele-Sports. Dist: Paramount Oxford
    A sports profile of one of the greatest basketball players.

ROBINSON, JACKIE
    See also The Jackie Robinson Story (feature)

The Impact of Jackie Robinson
26 min.   color   1973   JSCA
Prod: Koplin and Grinker. Dist: Pictura
    A combination of footage from the '50s, when he broke into the major leagues, and the '70s when he became an active spokesman for the black community.

Jackie Robinson
27 min.   b&w   1965   IJ
Prod: Metromedia Producers. Dist: Sterling (sale only; avail-
    able on 8mm). Rental: Mass Media
        He relates how he paved the way for blacks in the world of
sports, what it was like to live in an all-white neighborhood, and
how he became "Rookie of the Year."

Jackie Robinson
28 min.   b&w   1972   SCA
Prod: CBS. Dist: Anti-Defamation League
        A commemorative documentary about the contributions he
made to the civil rights movement as the first black athlete to
play major-league baseball.

ROCKNE, KNUTE
    See also Knute Rockne, All-American (feature)

Knute Rockne
26 min.   b&w   1965   IJSA
Prod: David Wolper. Dist: Sterling (sale only). Rental:
    Southern California, Syracuse
        A portrait of him which combines newsreel footage with
scenes of him drilling his team.

Knute Rockne
23 1/2 min.   b&w   1975   SCA
Prod: Hearst. Dist: Counselor
        The man who made football history is portrayed. Narrated
by Pat O'Brien.

The Rock of Notre Dame
15 min.   b&w   1952-53   JSCA
Prod: Mike Sklar. Dist: Star Film
        Compiled from the Fox Movietone News Library, his well-
known football career is highlighted.

Rockne of Notre Dame (Twentieth Century Series)
26 min.   b&w   1958   SCA
Prod: CBS. Dist: Films Inc. Rental: South Florida, Southern
    California
        Portrait of the famous coach in action, drilling his team.

ROCKWELL, NORMAN

Norman Rockwell's World ... An American Dream
25 min.   color   1973   JSC
Prod: Concepts Unlimited. Dist: Films Inc. Rental: California,
    Michigan, Nebraska
        Re-enactments, stills, paintings, and old film footage

complement a visit with him as he talks about the America he
knew.   Rockwell also acts as narrator.

RODIN, AUGUSTE

Auguste Rodin (Romantic Versus Classic Art Series)
26 min.   color   1974   JSCA
Prod: Reader's Digest.   Dist: Pyramid.   Rental: Southern
   California (listed under series title)
      The life and works of a great sculptor, last heir of the
Romantics.   Narrated by Kenneth Clark.

L'Enfer de Rodin
16 min.   CA
Dir: Henri Alekan.   Prod: André Costey.   Rental: FACSEA
      The sculptures of Rodin help recreate Dante's descriptions
of life and Hell.   No dialogue.

Homage to Rodin
18 min.   color   1968   JSCA
Dir: Herb Golden.   Dist: Pyramid.   Rental: Southern California
      A tribute to him, which covers many of his sculptures.

Rodin
25 min.   b&w   1943   CA
Dir: Rene Lucot.   Rental: FACSEA
      French dialogue only.   His life and works.

Rodin: The Burghers of Calais
18 min.   SCA
Prod: Fogg Art Museum, Harvard University.   Dist: Film Images
      An examination of his artistic process and philosophy,
which opposed the ideas of his time.   Uses the artist's own writings and contemporaneous sources for the commentary.   Emphasizes his accomplishments.

ROGERS, CARL
   See also ELLIS, ALBERT (Three Approaches to Psychotherapy)

A Conversation with Carl Rogers (2 pts.)
30 min. each   b&w   CA
Prod. and dist: Psychological Films
      Keith Berwick is the moderator of these discussions in
which Rogers comments on his philosophy, practice, and interests.

Dialogue: Dr. Carl Rogers (2 pts.)
50 min. each   color   1971
Prod: Richard I. Evans.   Dist: Macmillan (sale only).   Rental:
   Association, California
      In the first part he discusses motivation, the self, and en-
counter groups; in the second, the educational system.

ROGERS, WILLIAM PENN ADAIR (WILL)
See also The Story of Will Rogers (feature)

The Cowboy Humorist
15 min.   b&w   1952-53   JSCA
Prod: Mike Sklar.   Dist: Star Film
        Compiled from The Fox Movietone News Library, this
describes his benefit performances throughout the Southwest during
the Depression.

Will Rogers
25 min.   b&w   1965   IJ
Prod: David Wolper.   Dist: Sterling (sale only; available on 8mm).
    Rental: Indiana, Mass Media, Nebraska, Syracuse
        The dynamic careers he led as a journalist, actor, poli-
tician, and social commentator.

Will Rogers--California Ranch
28 min.   color   1976   IJSCA
Prod: Comco Productions.   Dist: Association
        E. G. Marshall hosts a tour of his home, a ranch that is
now a state park.

ROLLAND, ROMAIN

Romain Rolland
22 min.   1969   SCA
Dir: Jean Lods.   Prod: Société Nouvelle Armor Films.   Rental:
    FACSEA (available in French)
        His works and friends are used to reveal his life.

ROMBERG, SIGMUND See Deep in My Heart (feature)

ROMMEL, ERWIN

Field Marshal Rommel
25 min.   b&w   1965   IJ
Prod: Metromedia Producers.   Dist: Sterling (sale only; avail-
    able on 8mm).   Rental: Michigan, Syracuse
        A biography emphasizing his military accomplishments and
his growing rejection of Nazism.   Utilizes newsreel footage.

Rommel
26 min.   b&w   1960   JSA
Prod: CBS.   Dist: Association.   Rental: Syracuse
        Why the Desert Fox ultimately failed despite his brilliant
military victories.

RONSARD, PIERRE DE

Pierre de Ronsard: Le Vendômois
15 min.   color   1969   CA
Dir: Georges Rébillard.   Prod: Les Productions de Touraine.
  Rental: FACSEA
    French dialogue only. A look at his native region, Vendô-
mois, and the role it played in his works.

ROOSEVELT, (ANNA) ELEANOR

Eleanor Roosevelt
25 min.   b&w   1965   IJ
Prod: Metromedia Producers.   Dist: Sterling (sale only; available on 8mm).   Rental: Mass Media, Syracuse
    How she grew from a shy insecure child to an active dy-
namic woman.

Eleanor Roosevelt (Wisdom Series)
30 min.   b&w   1956   SCA
Prod: NBC.   Dist: Films Inc.   Rental: Michigan (title: Conversation with Eleanor Roosevelt), Minnesota
    An interview in which she discusses her life in and out of
the White House.

The Eleanor Roosevelt Story
90 min.   b&w   1965
Dir: Richard Kaplan.   Prod: Sidney Glazier.   Dist: Macmillan
  (5-year lease).   Rental: Budget, Twyman
    Scripted by Archibald MacLeish, it tells the story of her
life against the history of our times.

First Lady of the World: Eleanor Roosevelt (The History Makers
  Series)
25 min.   b&w   1974   JSCA
Prod: American School and Library Films.   Dist: ACI.   Rental:
  Syracuse
    Her unhappy childhood and her rediscovery of herself are
told through old photographs and speeches.

ROOSEVELT, FRANKLIN DELANO
  See also HOOVER, HERBERT (Man and the State: Roosevelt
  and Hoover on the Economy); HITLER, ADOLF (Parallels: The
  President and the Dictator); Sunrise at Campobello (feature)

The American Parade: F. D. R. --The Man Who Changed America
29 1/2 min.   color   1976   JSCA
Prod: CBS.   Dist: BFA
    The successes and failures of his domestic programs are
enumerated. Narrated by Henry Fonda.

The Election of 1932
21 min.　b&w　1966　SCA
Prod: ABC.　Dist: Films Inc.　Rental: Indiana, South Florida
　　Hoover's defeat by FDR.

F.D.R.
15 min.　b&w　1952-53　JSCA
Prod: Mike Sklar.　Dist: Star Film
　　Compiled from The Fox Movietone News Library, this
traces his rise in the political field.

F.D.R.
17 min.　b&w　1945
Dist: Select Film Library
　　The highlights of his life and career with excerpts from his
most famous speeches.

F.D.R.: Third Term to Pearl Harbor
26 min.　b&w　1959　JSCA
Prod: CBS.　Dist: McGraw-Hill.　Rental: Association, Michigan,
　　Minnesota, Southern California, Syracuse
　　The controversy of his third term and the Japanese attack.

Franklin D. Roosevelt: The New Deal (The History Makers Series)
22 min.　b&w　1974　JSCA
Prod: American School and Library Films.　Dist: ACI.　Rental:
　　Southern California, Syracuse
　　His early years in politics plus his first election.

Franklin D. Roosevelt, in The History Makers Series (ACI Media, Inc.)

Franklin D. Roosevelt: The War Years (The History Makers
    Series)
20 min.   b&w   1974   JSCA
Prod: American School and Library Films. Dist: ACI. Rental:
    Syracuse
        The events and personalities of 1941-45, including his fourth
victory at the polls.

Franklin D. Roosevelt: War Comes to America (The History
    Makers Series)
24 min.   b&w   1974   JSCA
Prod: American School and Library Films. Dist: ACI. Rental:
    Southern California, Syracuse

Franklin D. Roosevelt's Hyde Park (American Life Styles Series)
23 min.   color   1975   IJSCA
Prod: Comco Productions. Dist: ACI. Rental: Syracuse
        The mementos which reveal the personality of FDR. Hosted
by E. G. Marshall.

Franklin Delano Roosevelt (2 pts.; Biography Series)
26 min. each   b&w   1963   JSCA
Prod: David Wolper. Dist: McGraw-Hill. Rental: Indiana,
    Michigan, Minnesota, Syracuse
        The New Deal emphasizes the years 1933-40. The War
Years begins with his campaign for his third term and ends with
his death in 1945.

The Impact of Franklin Delano Roosevelt
26 min.   color   1973   SCA
Prod: Koplin and Grinker. Dist: Pictura
        Filmed at Hyde Park, this is a look at the man, his family,
and his role in American history.

The Roosevelt Years (a series)
19-21 min.   b&w   1966   SC
Prod: ABC in association with Sextant. Dist: Films Inc.
        Tape recordings, photographs, historical films and materials
help reveal Roosevelt as a politician and a statesman. The titles
are the following: The Election of 1932, Agriculture and the New
Deal, The Hundred Days, and Labor Comes of Age.

United States in the Twentieth Century: 1932-1940
21 min.   b&w   1971   JSC
Prod. and dist: Coronet (sale only)
        The events and people shaping these years, including the
highlights of Roosevelt's administration.

ROOSEVELT, THEODORE

America's Heritage: Theodore Roosevelt
11 min.   b&w

Prod: Warner Pathe News.   Rental: Minnesota
  Retraces his life from Sagamore Hill where he lived.

The Life and Times of Teddy Roosevelt (Twentieth Century Series)
26 min.   b&w   1959   JSA
Prod: CBS.   Rental: Association, California, Minnesota, Southern
  California, Syracuse
  His life and the key events of his administration.

The Panama Canal
22 min.   b&w   1975 (rel.)   SCA
Prod. and dist: Agapé Productions (available on 3/4" videocassette)
  Compiled from newsreel footage, scenes of the early work,
the finished Canal, and Roosevelt on the scene.   Added commentary
by Dr. John Gable.

President Roosevelt
11 min.   b&w   1975 (rel.)   SCA
Prod. and dist: Agapé Productions (available on 3/4" videocassette)
  Compiled from newsreel footage, this lists the activities of
his years as President.   Added commentary.

The River of Doubt
22 min.   b&w   1975 (rel.)   SCA
Prod. and dist: Agapé Productions
  His famous exploration of this river in South America in
1913-14.   Compiled from newsreel footage.   Added commentary.

Roosevelt at Home
11 min.   b&w   1975 (rel.)   SCA
Prod. and dist: Agapé Productions (available on 3/4" videocas-
  sette)
  A personal glimpse of him at his home, Sagamore Hill.
Added commentary.   Newsreel footage.

Roosevelt, Friend of the Birds
11 min.   b&w   1975 (rel.)   SCA
Prod. and dist: Agapé Productions (available on 3/4" videocassette)
  His visit to a bird sanctuary he established on Pelican Island.   Added commentary.

T.R.:   Fighter for Social Justice
10 min.   b&w   1975 (rel.)   SCA
Prod. and dist: Agapé Productions (available on 3/4" videocassette)
  Addressing the nation on the issues of trusts, labor and
housing.   Compiled from early footage prepared for the 1912 campaign.   Added commentary.

T. R. in Africa and Europe
22 min.   b&w   1975 (rel.)   SCA
Prod. and dist: Agapé Productions (available on 3/4" videocassette)
     Early newsreel footage. He's shown on his African expedition, in Berlin with the Kaiser, at the funeral of King Edward VII. Added commentary.

T. R. in World War I
13 min.   b&w   1975 (rel.)   SCA
Prod. and dist: Agapé Productions (available on 3/4" videocassette)
     Compiled from 1920s footage, he's shown touring the country seeking recruits. Added commentary.

Teddy Roosevelt: The Right Man at the Right Time
28 min.   color   1974   JSCA
Dir: William Francisco. Prod: Robert Saudek Associates. Dist: Learning. Rental: Michigan, South Florida, Southern California, Syracuse
     A dramatization of key events of his administration, such as his meeting with J. Pierpont Morgan, Jacob Riis and Upton Sinclair. Shows his "trust busting" activities.

Teddy the Rough Rider
19 min.   color   1940
Prod: Teaching Film Custodians. Dist: Macmillan. Rental: Michigan
     Begins in 1893, when he was President of the New York Police Commission, and shows his subsequent positions up to the climax of his election as President.

The Tenderfoot: Theodore Roosevelt
20 min.   b&w   1953
Prod: Teaching Film Custodians. Dist: Indiana (lease)
     When his wife and mother die, almost simultaneously, he suffers political losses as well and retires from public life in 1886. But he moves into action again when outlaws steal from him. A dramatization excerpted from the Cavalcade of America television movie.

Theodore Roosevelt (Biography Series)
26 min.   b&w   1963   JSCA
Prod: David Wolper. Dist: McGraw-Hill. Rental: Indiana, Michigan, Southern California, Syracuse
     All the aspects of his colorful life are told--rancher, soldier, politician, "trust buster," naturalist and conservationist.

Theodore Roosevelt
20 min.   b&w
Dist: Dept. of the Air Force (free loan)
     Accomplishments and important events of his life.

Theodore Roosevelt, a David Wolper Biography (McGraw-Hill Films)

Theodore Roosevelt--American
20 min.   b&w   1958   JSA
Prod: U.S. Dept. of Defense.   Dist: National Audiovisual Center
     Traces his career from his election to the New York House
of Representatives to the Presidency, his adventures in the West
and in Africa, and his fight against trusts.   Shown through stills,
drawings, and excerpts from motion pictures.

Theodore Roosevelt's Sagamore Hill (American Life Styles Series)
23 min.   color   1975   IJSA
Prod: Comco Productions.   Dist: ACI.   Rental: Syracuse
     E. G. Marshall hosts a tour of the 23-room house he called
home.

ROSENBERG, JULIUS AND ETHEL

The Unquiet Death of Julius and Ethel Rosenberg
90 min.   color   1974   SCA

Prod: N. P. A. C. T.   Dist: Impact
Probes the atmosphere in the U. S. at the time they were convicted of treason and later executed.

ROSENDAHL, CHARLES E.

The Sky Giant
15 min.   b&w   1952-53   JSCA
Prod: Mike Sklar.   Dist: Star Film
Compiled from the Fox Movietone News Library, this shows his command of dirigibles including the Hindenburg.

ROSS, EDMUND

Edmund Ross (Profiles in Courage Series)
50 min.   b&w   1965   IJSA
Prod: Robert Saudek Associates.   Dist: IQ Films.   Rental: Michigan, Syracuse

ROSSETTI, DANTE GABRIEL

Dante's Inferno: The Life of Dante Gabriel Rossetti
90 min.   b&w   1969   SCA
Prod: BBC-TV.   Dist: Time-Life (available on video)
Oliver Reed plays the role of poet-painter Rossetti, whose circle of friends included Swinburne, William Morris and John Ruskin.   Shows his flamboyant life style.

ROSTAND, EDMOND

Edmond Rostand
52 min.   SCA
Dir: Roland Bernard.   Prod: ORTF.   Rental: FACSEA
The life of the playwright as revealed in his plays, which are excerpted.

ROTH, HENRY

Henry Roth
30 min.   b&w   1966   SCA
Prod: NET.   Dist: Indiana
The author of Call It Sleep and novelist John Williams discuss Roth's first novel, its success--30 years later--and his process of writing.

ROUAULT, GEORGES

Artiste Solitaire

15 min.   color   1968   SCA
Prod: Cofilmdoc.   Rental: FACSEA (available in French)
    Life and works from 1912 to 1939.

Georges Rouault
30 min.   color   1973   JSCA
Dir: Isabelle Rouault.   Prod. and dist: Texture.   Rental: View-
    finders
    A complete biography, beginning with childhood and continu-
ing through the Fauve period.   Comments on "Miserere" and "Biblical Landscapes."   Directed by his daughter.

Demain sera beau
14 min.   color   1968   SCA
Prod: Cofilmdoc.   Rental: FACSEA (available in French)
    Life and works from 1940.

Faubourg des longues peines
14 min.   color   1968   SCA
Prod: Cofilmdoc.   Rental: FACSEA (available in French)
    Life and works from 1871 to 1897.

Miserere
18 min.   b&w   1951   CA
Dir: Jacques Lang, Abbe Morel.   Prod: Comptoir des Techniciens
    du Film.   Rental: FACSEA
    French dialogue only.   His thoughts as expressed in the
etchings of his book.

Le Visionnaire
14 min.   color   1968   SCA
Prod: Cofilmdoc.   Rental: FACSEA (available in French)
    Life and works from 1898 to 1911.

ROUSSEAU, HENRI

Henri Rousseau
15 min.   color   1961   C
Prod: Analyze Cinematographique.   Rental: California, Southern
    California
    Photos of Paris during his lifetime and portraits of him and
his friends evoke the work and spirit of his paintings.

Henri Rousseau (Pioneers of Modern Painting Series)
40 min.   color   1971   SCA
Prod. and dist: Independent Television Corp.   Rental: California
    The life and works of this "primitive" painter, with a criti-
cal commentary by Sir Kenneth Clark, who also narrates.

Innocent Eye--Henri Rousseau
25 min.   color   1968   JSCA
Dir: Ralph Luce.   Dist: Pyramid

Sketches, paintings, photographs and his own music tell the story of his life.

ROUSSEAU, JEAN JACQUES

Jean Jacques Rousseau
15 min.   color   1965   CA
Prod: Roger Leenhardt. Dist: Film Images. Rental: Minnesota
A biography of the French philosopher; colored engravings are used for the visuals.

RUBENS, PETER PAUL
See also VELASQUEZ, DIEGO (Treasures from El Prado)

Rubens
45 min.   b&w   1947   CA
Prod: Paul Haesaerts and Henri Storck. Dist: Macmillan.
Rental: Indiana, Kit Parker, Michigan
The paintings in relation to his predecessors, contemporaries, and successors.

Rubens
26 min.   color   1974
Dir: Jean Cleinge. Prod: International Film Bureau and RESO-
BEL, Brussels. Dist: International Film Bureau. Rental:
Syracuse
His release from the Spanish court, his second marriage to Hélène Fourment, who often served as his model, and many of his paintings.

The World of Rubens
20 min.   b&w   1969   SC
Rental: Southern California
Analyzes his life through a close-up look at his paintings.

RUBIN, WILLIAM See DE KOONING, WILLEM (Painters Painting)

RUBINSTEIN, ARTHUR

Love of Life
91 min.   color   SCA
Dir: Francois Reichenbach and S. G. Patris. Prod: François
Reichenbach and Bernard Gavoty. Dist: New Yorker (available
on 35mm)
Follows him on a concert tour of Spain, Persia, Israel and then New York. He also makes a visit to Montmartre in Paris, where he and his wife once lived. Interweaves his music with the story of his life. A personal portrait.

RUDO, FRANÇOIS

François Rudo, Sculpteur
21 min.   1957   CA
Dir: G. Regnier.   Prod: Armor.   Rental: FACSEA
    French dialogue only.   Study of his life and art until he
completed "La Marseillaise" on the Arc de Triomphe.

RUSK, DEAN

Dean Rusk (20th Century Series)
26 min.   SCA
Prod: CBS.   Dist: Association
    A contemporaneous view of Rusk as Secretary of State.

RUSKIN, JOHN See ROSSETTI, DANTE GABRIEL (Dante's Infer-
    no: The Life of Dante Gabriel Rossetti)

RUSSELL, BERTRAND

Bertrand Russell (a series)
13 min. each   b&w   1961   SC
Prod: BBC-TV.   Rental: Indiana, Minnesota, Syracuse
    Conversations with Woodrow Wyatt, BBC commentator.   The
individual titles are: Bertrand Russell Discusses Mankind's Future,
Bertrand Russell Discusses Happiness, Bertrand Russell Discusses
Philosophy, Bertrand Russell Discusses the Role of the Individual.

Bertrand Russell
30 min.   b&w   1958   SCA
Prod: NBC.   Dist: Films Inc.   Rental: California, Michigan
    (title: Conversation with Bertrand Russell), Minnesota
        An interview.

RUTH See MOSES (Living Personalities of the Old Testament);
    Story of Ruth (feature)

RUTH, HERMAN (BABE)

Babe Ruth
25 min.   b&w   1965   IJ
Prod: Metromedia Producers.   Dist: Sterling (sale only; avail-
    able on 8mm).   Rental: Michigan, Southern California
        Stresses his baseball career.   Brief biographical sketch.

Babe Ruth
19 min.   b&w   1975   SCA
Prod: Hearst.   Dist: Counselor

The highlights of his baseball career using newsreel footage. Commentary by Pat O'Brien.

The Fence Buster
15 min.   b&w   1952-53   JSCA
Prod: Mike Sklar.   Dist: Star Film
    Compiled from Fox Movietone News Library footage, this traces his legendary career.

RUTHERFORD, JOHNNY

Eleven-Year Odyssey: Johnny Rutherford (The Winners Series)
48 min.   color   1976   SCA
Prod: Laurel.   Dist: Counselor
    Winner of the 1974 Indianapolis 500 is profiled.

RUTLEDGE, ANN See LINCOLN, ABRAHAM (Abraham Lincoln--
    a series)

RUTSCH, ALEXANDER

The Inner Eye of Alexander Rutsch
14 min.   color   1972   SCA
Prod: IBM.   Dist: Modern Talking Picture Service (free loan)
    The camera follows him as he seeks new inspiration.

SAARINEN, EERO

Eero Saarinen, Architect
29 min.   color   1967
Dir: Stefan Sharff.   Prod: Erik Barnouw and Sumner Glimcher.
    Dist: Center for Mass Communication (sale only).   Rental:
    Michigan
    Concentrates on his most ambitious assignment, the Dulles International Airport.   Commentary by his widow and Prof. Edgar Kaufmann.

SADAT, ANWAR

Sadat: An Action Biography
52 1/2 min.   1975
Prod. and dist: ABC.   Free loan: Aetna
    Begins with his childhood in a tiny, poor Arab village and traces his life until he became President of Egypt.

SAINT-EXUPERY, ANTOINE DE

Plein Ciel

26 min. 1963 SC
Dir: G. Prouteau and J. Lefrançois. Prod: Paris Cité Productions. Rental: FACSEA (available in French)
Retraces the events of the last day of his life.

Saint-Exupéry
20 min. b&w 1964 SC
Dir: Languepin. Prod: Procinex-Cinénim. Rental: FACSEA, Southern California
French dialogue only. Authentic documents, photos, and newsreels tell the story of his life and career. Excerpts from his works. Voices by Michel Auclair and Saint-Exupéry.

SALK, JONAS

The Impact of Jonas Salk
26 min. color 1973 SCA
Prod: Koplin and Grinker. Dist: Pictura
A visit to his lab in California, where he talks about his work and philosophy.

Jonas Salk (Biography Series)
15 min. color 1968 IJSCA
Prod: McGraw-Hill in collaboration with Project 7 Films. Dist: McGraw-Hill
Begins with his early work in a basement lab and traces his career to the present. His discovery of a polio vaccine is depicted against the background of the '50s, when many children were stricken.

Jonas Salk
20 min. color 1971 JSCA
Prod: KPBS. Dist: ACI. Rental: Syracuse
In an interview he describes his cancer research and explains how he views the role of today's scientists.

SALTER, JAMES

James Salter (Artists in America Series)
30 min. color 1971 SCA
Prod: Public Television Library. Dist: Indiana. Rental: California
A portrait of this filmmaker, screenwriter, and novelist at Aspen, Colorado.

SAMMARTINO, BRUNO

Strong Man--Bruno Sammartino (The Winners Series)
48 min. color 1976 SCA
Prod: Laurel. Dist: Counselor

A record-breaking wrestling title-match is portrayed.

SAMPSON, DEBORAH

To a Different Drum
20 min.   1974   IJA
Prod. and dist: Agency for Instructional Television (available on
    3/4" videocassette)
        Focuses on the struggle of two individualists--Henry David
Thoreau and Deborah Sampson, who disguised herself as a male in
order to fight during the Revolutionary War.

SAMSON See MOSES (Living Personalities of the Old Testament)

SAMUEL See MOSES (Living Personalities of the Old Testament)

SAND, GEORGE
    See also Song to Remember (feature)

George Sand
15 min.   1965   SCA
Dir: J. de Casembroot. Prod: Court Film Production. Rental:
    FACSEA
        French dialogue only. Her youth in Nohant, where she lived
and where she returned to write her novels, to live with Chopin
and to entertain. Sand, played by Sylvia Monfort, is "interviewed"
by a young man.

George Sand
51 min.   SCA
Dir: Roland Bernard. Prod: ORTF. Rental: FACSEA
        Life and works.

SANDBURG, CARL

Carl Sandburg (Wisdom Series)
30 min.   b&w   1960   SCA
Prod: NBC. Dist: Films Inc. Rental: Michigan (title: A Visit
    with Carl Sandburg), Minnesota, Nebraska, South Florida,
    Southern California, Syracuse
        Recalls his days as a newspaper reporter and the writing of
Lincoln's biography. He also plays his guitar and sings.

Carl Sandburg at Gettysburg
24-28 min.   b&w   1961   SCA
Prod: CBS. Dist: Carousel. Rental: Indiana, Michigan
        Facts about the Civil War (pt. 1; 28 min.) presents his
observations about slavery and the important people and events of

the Civil War. The Gettysburg Address and Lincoln the Man (pt.
2; 24 min.) is an analysis of the speaker and the speech.

Carl Sandburg Discusses His Work
15 min.   b&w   1961   SCA
Prod: CBS. Dist: Coronet (special order only; no previews).
   Rental: Indiana, Michigan, Minnesota, Syracuse
      Edward R. Murrow interviews him in his home in North
Carolina. He discusses his early life, his struggle to gain recog-
nition as a writer, and his poetry. He reads passages from "The
People, Yes" and "Remembrance Rock. "

Carl Sandburg Discusses Lincoln
12 min.   b&w   1961   SCA
Prod: CBS. Dist: Coronet (sale only; no previews). Rental:
   Indiana, Minnesota, Syracuse
      Discusses with Edward R. Murrow the life of Lincoln, which
he researched for his Pulitzer Prize-winning biography.

The World of Carl Sandburg
59 min.   b&w   1968   JS
Prod: Nathan Kroll. Rental: Southern California
      A tribute which reveals his many accomplishments as
Lincoln's biographer, as a poet, and as a song writer.

SANDERS, ED See O'HARA, FRANK (Poetry: Frank O'Hara and
   Ed Sanders)

SANGER, MARGARET

Margaret Sanger
15 min.   b&w   1972   SCA
Prod: Planned Parenthood World Population. Rental: California,
   Minnesota, Southern California
      Her devotion to women's suffrage and birth control, her
persecution by the law enforcement officials, her exile and return
are all described. Narrated by Katherine Hepburn.

SATYAJIT RAY

Satyajit Ray
28 min.   b&w   1967   SCA
Prod: NET. Dist: Indiana. Rental: California
      The philosophy of his films and his news of Western society.

SAUL See MOSES (Living Personalities of the Old Testament)

<u>Carl Sandburg at Gettysburg</u> (Carousel Films, Inc.)

SAYERS, GALE
   See also Brian's Song (feature)

Gale Sayers (Sports Legends Series)
20 min.   color   1975   IJ
Prod. and dist: Sports Legends Inc. Rental: Southern California
     The exciting moments of his football career and his friend-
ship with Brian Piccolo.

SCHEMBECHLER, BO

Bo Schembechler (Sports Action Pro-file Series)
22 min.   color   1972   SCA
Prod: Tele-Sports. Dist: Paramount Oxford
     His hour-by-hour routine before a game at the University
of Michigan.

SCHUBERT, FRANZ PETER

Schubert (Great Composers Series)
27 min.   color   1975   JSA
Prod: Seabourne Enterprises. Dist: International Film Bureau.
   Rental: Syracuse
     An introduction to his life and his music, emphasizing his
romantic strain.

Schubert and His Music (Famous Composers Series)
13 min.   b&w or color   1954   JS
Prod. and dist: Coronet (special order only; no previews).
   Rental: Indiana, Michigan, Minnesota, Nebraska, Syracuse
     A brief biographical sketch, the influences upon him and his
music are covered. Excerpts from "The Linden Tree," "Serenade," and the "Unfinished Symphony."

SCHUMANN, ROBERT ALEXANDER
   See also Song of Love (feature)

Schumann Story
30 min.   b&w   1950   JS
Prod: Teaching Film Custodians. Rental: Michigan, Minnesota,
   Syracuse
     The works and life of him and his wife Clara, and his as-
sociation with Johannes Brahms. Excerpted from the feature film,
Song of Love.

SCHWEITZER, ALBERT
   See also Albert Schweitzer (feature); Dr. Schweitzer (feature)

SCOTT, ROBERT / 235

Africa and Schweitzer
28 min.   b&w   n.d.   JSCA
Prod: Cathedral.   Rental: Christian Church
    Lowell Thomas, narrator, reveals Schweitzer's accomplish-
ments, including the founding of his mission.   Filmed in Africa.

Albert Schweitzer--The Three Avenues of the Mind
29 min.   b&w   1962   SCA
Prod: KNXT.   Dist: Southern California
    A study of his early life, education and accomplishments
as philosopher, scientist, theologian, and humanitarian are analyzed
by Dr. Herman Harvey, psychology professor at USC.

SCOTT, ROBERT

Robert Scott and the Search for the South Pole
55 min.   color   IJ
Prod: National Film Board of Canada.   Rental: Southern California
    His expedition to the South Pole and the hazards and ob-
stacles it encountered.

Scott's Last Journey
60 min.   b&w   1963   SCA
Prod: BBC-TV.   Rental: Southern California
    A re-creation of the 1910 expedition to the South Pole,
which lasted two years and ended tragically.

SCOTT, SIR WALTER

The Practical Romantic: Sir Walter Scott
24 min.   color   IJ
Dist: Sterling (sale only; available on 8mm)
    Opens at Smailholm where he spent his childhood.   Empha-
sizes the background of his novels, the country he knew and loved.

SCULL, ROBERT C.
    See also   DE KOONING, WILLEM (Painters Painting)

America's Pop Collector
72 min.   color   1974   CA
Prod: E. J. Vaughn.   Dist: Cinema 5
    A record of the auction of 50 of Scull's contemporary art
pieces at the Sotheby-Parke-Bernet Galleries and a portrait of him.

SEALE, BOBBY

Interview with Bobby Seale
15 min.   b&w   1969
Prod: Newsreel.   Dist: Third World Newsreel

An interview with the Chairman of the Black Panther Party while he was in the San Francisco jail (1969).

SEEGER, PETE

Pete Seeger: A Song and a Stone
85 min.   color   1972   SCA
Dir. and prod: Robert Elfstrom.   Dist: Macmillan.   Rental: As-
    sociation
    A documentary of social libertarian and folk-singer Seeger
in concert, on campus, at home, at a peace march, and on television.

Quality of Leadership--III: Pete Seeger
30 min.   b&w   1970
Prod: National Catholic Office for Radio and Television.   Dist:
    Association
    In an interview he expounds his philosophy of life. He sings
well-known folk songs, which represent his feelings towards peace
and poverty.

SEGOVIA, ANDRES

Andrés Segovia (Wisdom Series)
30 min.   b&w   1959   SCA
Prod: NBC.   Dist: Films Inc.   Rental: California, Indiana,
    Minnesota, Southern California
    Famed guitarist is interviewed.   He recalls his childhood
and his decision to play the guitar.

SENDAK, MAURICE

Maurice Sendak
14 min.   color   1966   SCA
Prod. and dist: Weston Woods.   Rental: Syracuse
    An informal visit with him in his studio apartment in New
York.   He talks about the art and music which affected his own
art work.

SENGHOR, LEOPOLD SEDAR

Léopold Sédar Senghor (Creative Person Series)
30 min.   b&w   1967
Rental: California
    Life and work of the first president of Senegal. He talks
about his childhood, his poetry, and his social and political beliefs.

SEQUOYAH

Sequoyah (They Made a Difference Series)
15 min.   color   1971   IJSC
Prod: Anthony Corso. Dist: Walt Disney (license)
     A Cherokee silversmith who created a written Indian lan-
guage.

SERRA, JUNIPERO

The Gentle Conqueror: Junipero Serra
20 min.   b&w   1954   PIJ
Prod: Teaching Film Custodians. Dist: Indiana (lease)
     A dramatization of the story of the founding of the Spanish
missions in California. An excerpt from the Cavalcade of America television picture.

SETON, ELIZABETH

Life of Mother Seton
45 min.   b&w   1959   CA
Prod: Catholic School Board. Dist: Catholic Film Center.
   Rental: Michigan
     The life of the founder of the Sisters of Charity; her own
statements provide much of the narrative.

SEURAT, GEORGES

Georges Seurat (Pioneers of Modern Painting Series)
40 min.   color   1971   SCA
Prod. and dist: Independent Television Corp. Rental: California
     Traces the obscure life of pointillist painter Seurat and
criticizes his works, most of which are shown. Written and narrated by Sir Kenneth Clark.

SEXTON, ANNE

Anne Sexton
30 min.   b&w   1966   SCA
Prod: NET. Dist: Indiana
     Introduces her and her poetry. She reads several poems
including "Her Kind," "Self in 1958," "Ringing the Bells," and
"Those Times. "

SEYMOUR, JANE   See HENRY VIII (The Six Wives of Henry VIII);
   Henry VIII and his Six Wives (feature)

SHAHN, BEN

This Is Ben Shahn
17 min.   color   1968   JSCA
Prod: CBS. Dist: BFA. Rental: Minnesota, Syracuse
    How his philosophy is reflected in his art.

SHAKESPEARE, WILLIAM
    See also ELIZABETH I (Hamlet: The Age of Elizabeth)

The Life of William Shakespeare
28 1/2 min.   b&w   1964   SC
Prod: Westinghouse Broadcasting. Dist: Association. Rental:
    Syracuse
    Dr. Baxter, a professor of English, pieces the Bard's life
together from historical evidence.

Master Will Shakespeare
11 min.   b&w   1936   JSC
Prod: MGM. Dist: Withdrawn by Films Inc. Rental: Minne-
    sota, South Florida, Southern California
    A fictionalized biography. Scenes from "Romeo and Juliet."

The Poet's Eye--A Tribute to Shakespeare
20 min.   color
Dir: Gordon Hales. Dist: Withdrawn by McGraw-Hill. Rental:
    Southern California
    Reveals the times in which he lived, through places where
he lived and worked.

Shakespeare: Soul of an Age
54 min.   color   1963   SA
Prod: NBC. Dist: McGraw-Hill. Rental: Indiana, Michigan,
    Nebraska, Southern California, Syracuse
    Landmarks tell the story of his life and times as Sir
Michael Redgrave recites famous passages from his works.

Shakespeare's Stratford (Fair Adventure Series)
28 1/2 min.   b&w   1969   SCA
Prod: Westinghouse Broadcasting. Dist: Association. Rental:
    Minnesota, South Florida
    Recreates the atmosphere of Stratford-on-Avon and analyzes
how it affected his writing.

Will Shakespeare--Gent
50 min.   b&w   1969   SCA
Prod: Peter Robeck. Dist: Time-Life (special purchase only;
    no previews or rentals)
    A literary detection mystery, which reconstructs his life
and personality through his works and legal documents such as
deeds, money transactions, and his will.

William Shakespeare
25 min.   color or b&w   1955   JSC
Prod. and dist: Encyclopaedia Britannica (available on video by
    special order).   Rental: Indiana, Michigan, Minnesota, Nebras-
    ka, South Florida, Southern California, Syracuse
        Boyhood through death.   Dramatized scenes from "Richard
III," "Hamlet," "Julius Caesar," and "Macbeth."

William Shakespeare: Background for his Works
14 min.   b&w or color   1951   SC
Prod. and dist: Coronet.   Rental: Indiana, Michigan, Minnesota,
    Nebraska
        Visits to historical sites such as Kenilworth Castle and
Stratford-on-Avon reveal his life.   Five very brief episodes from
his well-known plays are presented.

SHANKAR, RAVI

Ravi Shankar
27 min.   b&w
Dist: Information Service of India (free loan)
        A portrait with interviews.

SHAW, GEORGE BERNARD

Best Educated Man in the World
30 min.   color   1973   SCA
Prod: Ontario Education Communication Authority.   Dist: Films
    Inc.
        His schooling, his life, and his writing.

Don Juan in Hell
22 min.   color   1975   SCA
Prod. and dist: North American Films
        A sketch of Shaw, who appears on screen, and an examina-
tion of his unique character Don Juan combined with comments by
original cast members of his plays, Charles Boyer and Charles
Laughton.

George Bernard Shaw (Biography Series)
26 min.   b&w   1964   SCA
Prod: David Wolper.   Dist: Withdrawn by McGraw-Hill.
    Rental: Minnesota, South Florida, Southern California,
    Syracuse
        Film clips help reveal Shaw's major ideas and philosophy.

George Bernard Shaw
16 min.   b&w   1956   SA
Rental: Syracuse
        Made on the 100th anniversary of his birth, this portrait is

supplemented by scenes from some of his plays and the drawings of his friend Topolski.

George Bernard Shaw Speaks for Movietone News
5 min.   b&w   1929
Prod: Fox. Dist: Images. Rental: Images, Creative Film Society, Em Gee, Kit Parker
 An early interview.

Shaw and Women
46 min.   b&w   1969   SCA
Prod: BBC-TV. Dist: Time-Life (special purchase only; no previews or rentals). Rental: Indiana
 His relationships with ten women, how they influenced him and how they were portrayed in his plays. Excerpts from "Candida," "Man and Superman," and "Pygmalion" illustrate his view of women chasing men.

SHAW, WILBUR

Speedway Star
15 min.   b&w   1952-53   JSCA
Prod: Mike Sklar. Dist: Star Film
 The race at Indianapolis Speedway on Memorial Day; compiled from the Fox Movietone News Library footage.

SHEPARD, ERNEST See MILNE, ALAN ALEXANDER (Mr. Shepard and Mr. Milne)

SHERIDAN, RICHARD BRINSLEY

Sheridan's World of Society
17 min.   color   1971   SCA
Prod: ICEM Ltd. and Seabourne Enterprises. Dist: International Film Bureau. Rental: California, Syracuse
 Contemporaneous paintings, cartoons, and portraits set the society in which he lived and trace the events of his life as he changed from a popular playwright to a poor gambling politician.

SIKORSKY, IGOR IVAN

Explorer of the Sky
15 min.   b&w   1952-53   JSCA
Prod: Mike Sklar. Dist: Star Film
 Compiled from the Fox Movietone News Library, shows how he developed the helicopter.

SILVA See VIEIRA DA SILVA, MARIA ELENA

SIMON, MICHEL

Michel Simon
15 min.   b&w   1964   CA
Dir: Ole Roos.   Prod: Laterna Films.   Dist: Images
    An intimate portrait of French actor Simon; he relates the
events of his life and the story of the production of "L'Atlante."

SIMON PETER

Simon Peter, Fisherman
32 min.   b&w   1949
Prod: Cathedral Films.   Rental: Catholic Film Center
    Jesus' call to his disciples Simon Peter, Andrew, James
and John.

SIMPSON, O. J.

Juice on the Loose--O. J. Simpson (The Winners Series)
48 min.   color   1976   SCA
Prod: Laurel.   Dist: Counselor
    A sports perspective with commentary by well-known sports
figures.

SIMPSON, WALLIS WARFIELD   See   EDWARD VIII (For Love of a
    Woman, and The Windsors)

SINCLAIR, UPTON BEALL
    See also ROOSEVELT, THEODORE (Teddy Roosevelt: The
    Right Man at the Right Time)

Upton Sinclair (Sum and Substance Series)
30 min.   b&w   1964   SCA
Prod: Modern Learning Aids.   Dist: Withdrawn by Modern Learn-
    ing Aids.   Rental: Minnesota
    A filmed dialogue in which he talks about his relationship
with industry and his desire for social justice.

SINGER, ISAAC B.

Isaac Singer's Nightmare and Mrs. Pupko's Beard
30 min.   color   1973   JSA
Dir: Bruce Davidson.   Dist: New Yorker
    An unusual film, mixing reality with fiction.   Singer moves
in and out of the dramatization based on his short story, "The
Beard."   He talks about writing, New York and journalists, and
meets with his old friends.

SITTING BULL

Sitting Bull (Profiles in Power Series)
30 min.　color　1976　JSCA
Prod: McConnell Advertising Co. and Ontario Communications Authority. Dist: Learning
　　　Patrick Watson "interviews" Sitting Bull, who is played by August Schellenberg.

SITWELL, SIR OSBERT

Sir Osbert Sitwell (Wisdom Series)
30 min.　b&w　1960　SCA
Prod: NBC. Dist: Films Inc.　Rental: Minnesota
　　　An interview.

SKINNER, BURRHUS FREDERICK
　　See also　THOREAU, HENRY DAVID (Talking with Thoreau)

Interview with Dr. B. F. Skinner (2 pts.)
50 min. each　b&w　1971　C
Prod: Dr. Richard Evans. Dist: Macmillan (sale only). Rental: Association, South Florida, Syracuse
　　　In Part 1 he discusses Freud's and Pavlov's theories and how they affected his work.　In Part II he discusses his book, Walden Two.

SLATER, SAMUEL

Slater's Dream: Slater's Cotton Spinner
20 min.　b&w　1953　PIJ
Prod: Teaching Film Custodians. Dist: Indiana (lease)
　　　A colonial inventor who perfects a cotton spinner.　Dramatized.

SLATON, JOHN M.

Governor John M. Slaton (Profiles in Courage Series)
50 min.　b&w　1965　IJSCA
Prod: Robert Saudek Associates. Dist: IQ Films. Rental: Syracuse
　　　Commutes a murder sentence because he has doubts about the person's guilt.

SMITH, ALFRED EMANUEL

Al Smith
26 min.　b&w　1961　SCA

Prod: CBS. Dist: Association. Rental: Syracuse
His rise from the streets of New York to the threshold of
the White House.

The Happy Warrior
15 min.   b&w   1952-53   JSCA
Prod: Mike Sklar. Dist: Star Film
Compiled from the Fox Movietone News Library; shows him
as governor of New York.

SMITH, JEDEDIAH

Jedediah Smith (Age of Exploration Series)
52 min.   color   1976   SCA
Prod: BBC-TV and Time-Life.   Dist: Time-Life (available on
video)
The relationship between him and General William Henry
Ashley.   Dramatizes the discovery of the Colorado River.

SMITH, CAPTAIN JOHN

Captain John Smith, Founder of Virginia
20 min.   b&w   1955   IJS
Prod. and dist: Encyclopaedia Britannica (Available on video by
special order).   Rental: Indiana, Michigan, Minnesota, Southern
California, Syracuse
Dramatizes his role in holding Jamestown together and how
he was captured and then saved by Pocohontas.

SNEAD, SAM

Sam Snead (Sports Legends Series)
20 min.   color   1975   IJ
Prod. and dist: Sports Legends Inc.   Rental: Southern California
A review of his half-century as a golfer.

SOCRATES

The Death of Socrates (You Are There Series)
27 min.   b&w   1955   SCA
Prod: CBS. Dist: Withdrawn by McGraw-Hill.   Rental: Michigan, Minnesota, Southern California, Syracuse
Refusing to give up his beliefs, he must die.   This is a
dramatized "on the scene" news report.

Man and the State: The Trial of Socrates
28 min.   color   1971   JSA
Prod: Bernard Wilets.   Dist: BFA.   Rental: Michigan, Southern
California, Syracuse

An open-ended drama of Socrates' trial and death.

Plato's Apology: The Life and Teachings of Socrates (Humanities
   Series)
30 min.   color   1962   SC
Prod. and dist: Encyclopaedia Britannica (available on video by
   special order).   Rental: Indiana, Michigan, Minnesota, South
   Florida, Syracuse
      The arresting personality of Socrates as revealed in the
writings of his star pupil.   Dramatized scenes from the dialogue
of Plato.

SOLOMON See MOSES (Living Personalities of the Old Testament)

SOUSA, JOHN PHILIP See   Stars and Stripes Forever (feature)

SOUTINE, CHAIM

Chaim Soutine
28 min.   color   1970   SA
Dir: Jack Lieberman.   Dist: McGraw-Hill
      A psychological portrait of expressionist painter Soutine in
which actors recreate his early life and flight from Nazi Germany.
His friends, in interviews, give their feelings and impressions of
him.

SPEKE, JOHN HANNING See   BURTON, SIR RICHARD FRANCIS
   (The Search for the Nile)

SPOCK, DR. BENJAMIN

Dr. Spock ... and His Babies
27 min.   b&w   1970   JSCA
Dir: Herman J. Engel.   Dist: Texture.   Rental: Viewfinders
      A record of his protest against the Vietnam War.

STALIN, JOSEPH
   See also KHRUSHCHEV, NIKITA (Leninism, Stalinism and
   Khrushchevism)

The Death of Stalin
54 min.   b&w   1963   SCA
Prod: NBC.   Dist: Withdrawn by McGraw-Hill.   Rental: Southern
   California, Syracuse
      His tyranny and his heirs who pledged to work cooperative-
ly while they were trying to eliminate one another.

Stalin (Biography Series)
26 min.   b&w   1963   SCA
Prod: David Wolper.   Dist: McGraw-Hill.   Rental: California,
    Michigan, Minnesota, Southern California, Syracuse
        How he changed Russia through brutality, ruthlessness, and
determination.

The Stalin Era (Red Myth Series)
58 min.   b&w   1960   SCA
Prod: NET.   Rental: Indiana
        Part 1 traces his rise to leadership and his policies, and
the purges of the '30s.   Concludes with the rise of Hitler.   Part
2 outlines the events leading to World War II, the pact between
Russia and Germany, and the eventual inclusion of the Allies.

Stalin vs. Trotsky
25 min.   b&w   1964   SCA
Prod: Metromedia Productions.   Dist: Films Inc.   Rental: South
    Florida, Southern California
        Stalin's victory.

Stalin's Revolution (Revolution in Russia Series)
20 min.   b&w   1970   JSCA
Prod: BBC-TV.   Dist: Time-Life (available in Spanish)
        His five-year plans.

STANISLAVSKY, CONSTANTIN

Stanislavsky
25 min.   b&w   1957   SCA
Dir: Samuel Bubrick.   Prod: Central Documentary Film Studios,
    Moscow.   Dist: Macmillan.   Rental: Syracuse
        Founder of the Moscow Art Theatre.   His career is re-
traced and he is shown with Gorky, Chekhov, Moskvin, his wife
and his students.

Stanislavsky: Maker of the Modern Theatre
28 1/2 min.   b&w   1972   SC
Prod: Harold Mantell.   Dist: Films for the Humanities (available
    on 3/4" videocassette)
        How he developed his theory of "method acting."   Notable
remembrances of the theater such as the opening night of "The
Seagull" are recalled by his widow.

STANLEY, SIR HENRY MORTON
    See also BURTON, SIR RICHARD FRANCIS (The Search for the
    Nile)

Henry Morton Stanley (Age of Exploration Series)
52 min.   color   1976   SCA
Prod: BBC-TV and Time-Life.   Dist: Time-Life

Taken from the journals of Stanley, this dramatization re-traces his steps to find Livingstone and his later exploration of Central Africa.

STARGELL, WILLIE

What If I Didn't Play Baseball--Willie Stargell (The Winners Series)
48 min.   color   1976   SCA
Prod: Laurel. Dist: Counselor
Comments by outstanding baseball players and a look at him at home.

STEFANSSON, VILHJALMUR

Stefansson--The Arctic Prophet
16 min.   b&w   1966   IJSCA
Prod: National Film Board of Canada. Dist: Perennial (special order; no previews)
A biography of his exploration of Victoria Island and his five-year expedition to the Arctic.

STEFFENS, LINCOLN

A Miserable Merry Christmas
15 min.   color   1973   PIJS
Prod: WNET. Dist: Encyclopaedia Britannica (available on video by special order)
Based on the Autobiography of Lincoln Steffens, who wanted nothing for Christmas except a pony--which he received hours after he awoke.

STEICHEN, EDWARD

Edward Steichen (Wisdom Series)
30 min.   b&w   1958   SCA
Prod: NBC. Rental: Minnesota
Looks back at his career and what affected it; describes some of his experiences as a photographer.

This Is Edward Steichen
27 min.   b&w   1965   JSCA
Prod: WCBS. Dist: Carousel (sale only). Rental: Association, Indiana
A portrait of an outstanding photographer, who talks about his philosophy of art and work.

STEIGEL, HENRY W.

Man of Glass

<u>This Is Edward Steichen</u> (Carousel Films, Inc.)

27 min.   b&w   1954   PIJ
Prod: Teaching Film Custodians.   Dist: Indiana (lease)
    The ups and downs of his life and career as an artistic glassmaker.   An excerpt from a Cavalcade of America television movie.

STEIN, GERTRUDE

Gertrude Stein--The Rose That Is a Rose
29 min.   b&w   1962   SCA
Prod: KNXT.   Dist: Southern California
    Dr. Herman Harvey, a USC professor, analyzes her life, work, and motivations from a psychological point of view.   A kinescope.

Gertrude Stein: When This You See, Remember Me
89 min.   color   1971   SA
Dir. and prod: Perry Miller Adato.   Dist: McGraw-Hill.   Rental: Indiana, (3 pts.), Michigan, South Florida
    A portrait of the author's years in Paris, 1905 through the '30s, when Paris was the home of many artists and other creative persons.   Includes home movies of her and Alice B. Toklas and the only radio interview she ever gave.   Virgil Thomson, Jacques Lipchitz and Bennett Cerf share their remembrances of her.

STEINBECK, JOHN

Impression of John Steinbeck
22 min.   color   1969   SCA
Prod: U.S. Information Agency.   Dist: National Audiovisual Center.   Rental: Pyramid
    A series of vignettes about his life.

STEINLEN, THEOPHILE ALEXANDRE

At the Foot of the Tree--A Homage to Steinlen
24 min.   b&w   1972   SCA
Dir: Alain Saury.   Prod: SIPRO.   Dist: Roland Collection
    A sketch of him and his times, which he depicted in his lithographs.

STEINMETZ, CHARLES PROTEUS

Charles Proteus Steinmetz (1865-1923): The Man Who Made
    Lightning
15 min.   b&w   1965   JSC
Prod. and dist: General Electric.   Rental: Nebraska
    The life and work of this electronic master, with emphasis on his theories and inventions.

Gertrude Stein and Thornton Wilder in Gertrude Stein: When This
You See, Remember Me (McGraw-Hill Films)

STELLA, FRANK See POONS, LARRY (Artists--Frank Stella and Larry Poons); DE KOONING, WILLEM (Painters Painting)

STERN, ISAAC

Man with a Violin: Isaac Stern
26 min. b&w 1965 SCA
Prod: CBS. Dist: Macmillan. Rental: Association, Syracuse
   A personal portrait.

STEVENS, THADDEUS See JOHNSON, ANDREW (Impeachment of a President)

STILWELL, JOSEPH WARREN See EISENHOWER, DWIGHT DAVID (Famous Generals)

STONE, ISADOR F.

I. F. Stone's Weekly
62 min. b&w 1974 SCA
Dir. and prod: Jerry Bruck, Jr. Dist: Open Circle
   A portrait of a journalist who stood by his principles despite opposition.

STOUT, RUTH

Ruth Stout's Garden
23 min. color 1975 JSCA
Prod. and dist: Arthur Mokin Productions
   A visit with 90-year old Ms. Stout, who developed a "no dig/no work" method of gardening and who, as a young woman, marched with Carry Nation.

STRAUSS, JOHANN See Eternal Waltz; The Great Waltz; Mister Johann Strauss; and The Waltz King (all features)

STRAVINSKY, IGOR

Igor Stravinsky (Wisdom Series)
30 min. b&w 1958 SCA
Prod: NBC. Rental: Michigan, Minnesota, Nebraska, Southern California
   An interview.

Stravinsky
50 min. b&w 1965 SCA

Dir: Roman Kroiter and Wolf Koenig. Prod: National Film
   Board of Canada. Dist: Macmillan. Rental: Syracuse
   An informal biography showing him at work. His friend
Nicholas Nabokov and his protégé Robert Craft comment on his
early career and artistic development.

Stravinsky
43 min.   b&w   1965   JSCA
Prod: CBS. Dist: Carousel (sale only). Rental: Association,
   Minnesota
   At the age of 83 he talks about his early compositions and
is seen hard at work with George Balanchine. He also visits
Benny Goodman and Alberto Giacometti.

Stravinsky and Benny Goodman--from Stravinsky (Carousel Films, Inc.)

A Stravinsky Portrait
58 min.   b&w   1965   CA
Prod: Richard Leacock and Rolf Liebermann.   Dist: Pennebaker
   A cinema verité portrait of him which reveals his personality, his perceptions and his music.

SULLIVAN, ANNE See KELLER, HELEN (Helen Keller; and Helen
   Keller and Her Teacher); Miracle Worker (feature)

SWINBURNE, ALGERNON C. See ROSSETTI, DANTE GABRIEL
(Dante's Inferno: The Life of Dante Gabriel Rossetti)

TAFT, ROBERT ALPHONSO

Mr. Republican
15 min.   b&w   1952-53   JSCA
Prod: Mike Sklar.   Dist: Star Film
        His political career from the Fox Movietone News Library.

Robert A. Taft (History Makers of the Twentieth Century Series)
27 min.   b&w   1965   IJ
Prod: David Wolper.   Dist: Sterling (sale only; available on 8mm)
        The story of his career in politics as a Senator from Ohio
and as the losing candidate for the Republican Presidential nomination.

Robert A. Taft (Profiles in Courage Series)
50 min.   b&w   1965   IJSCA
Prod: Robert Saudek Associates.   Dist: IQ Films.   Rental:
    Syracuse
        Speaks out against the Nuremberg trials, thereby risking his
career in politics.

TAFT, WILLIAM HOWARD

United States in the Twentieth Century: 1900-1912
11 1/2 min.   b&w   1967   JS
Prod. and dist: Coronet (sale only)
        Newsreel footage tells the story of the Roosevelt and Taft
administrations.

TAGORE, RABINDRANATH

Tagore
54 min.   b&w   1963
Dir: Satyajit Ray.   Dist: Withdrawn by McGraw-Hill.   Rental:
    California
        A biography of this Bengali poet made on the 100th anniver-
sary of his birth.

TANNER, CHUCK

Chuck Tanner
22 min.   color   1973   SCA
Prod: Tele-Sports.   Dist: Paramount Oxford
        A profile of him at work as manager of the White Sox base-
ball team.

TANNER, HENRY O.

Henry O. Tanner--Pioneer Black American Artist (They Made a
  Difference Series)
12 min.   color   1972
Prod: Anthony Corso.   Dist: Walt Disney (long term license).
  Rental: California
     The first important black painter and how his early life in-
fluenced his work.

TAYLOR, PAUL

Paul Taylor and Co.
32 min.   color   1968   SCA
Prod: Harris Communications.   Dist: Pyramid.   Rental: Syracuse
     Taylor and his dance company, on and off the stage.

TCHAIKOVSKY, PETER

The Peter Tchaikovsky Story
30 min.   color   1964   IJS
Prod. and dist: Walt Disney (long term license).   Rental: Association, Michigan, Minnesota, South Florida
     His life--the successes, failures, loves and hates.

TEILHARD DE CHARDIN, PIERRE

The Heart of the Matter: Pierre Teilhard de Chardin (1881-1955)
45 min.   b&w   1969   CA
Prod: BBC-TV.   Dist: Time-Life (available on video)
     Rare films, photos, and interviews with his friends reveal
the important episodes of his life, such as his co-discovery of
Peking man.   His philosophical ideas are analyzed.

TERESA, MOTHER

Mother Teresa of Calcutta
51 min.   color   1971   SCA
Prod: BBC-TV.   Dist: Time-Life (available on video)
     Malcolm Muggeridge conducts an interview of an extraordi-
nary nun who has worked tirelessly in India to help the poor and
the sick.

TERKEL, STUDS

Studs Terkel: At Home on the Air
27 min.   color   1975   SCA

Dir: Nick Egleson and Alan Jacobs. Dist: Odeon
A portrait of America's well-known interviewer on and off the air as he puts his radio program together.

THOMAS, DYLAN

The Days of Dylan Thomas
21 min.   b&w   1965   SA
Dir: Graeme Ferguson. Dist: Withdrawn by McGraw-Hill.
  Rental: Nebraska, South Florida, Southern California
His life and works, including selections read by Thomas himself.

A Dylan Thomas Memoir
28 min.   color   1972   SCA
Dir: Bayley Silleck. Dist: Pyramid. Rental: California, Michigan, Minnesota, Southern California
Recordings of his poetry readings are used for much of the soundtrack while the camera focuses on the people and places he knew.

THOMAS, NORMAN M.

The Dissenter: Norman Thomas
26 min.   1965   SCA
Prod: CBS. Dist: Macmillan. Rental: Association
A close look at this socialist leader.

Norman Thomas
30 min.   b&w   1958   SCA
Prod: NBC. Dist: Films Inc.
An interview.

THOMAS, PIRI

World of Piri Thomas
60 min.   color or b&w   1968   SCA
Prod: NET. Dist: Indiana. Rental: California, Michigan
Author of Down These Mean Streets takes us on a tour of Spanish Harlem.

THOMPSON, BEN See EARP, WYATT (Heroes and Villains)

THOREAU, HENRY DAVID
  See also SAMPSON, DEBORAH (To A Different Drum)

Henry David Thoreau: The Beat of a Different Drummer
20 min.   color   1973   SC

Prod: Canadian Broadcasting Corp. Dist: Films Inc.
　　Two years at Walden Pond, where he stayed in refusal to
pay a poll tax and where he wrote his essay, "Civil Disobedience."

Talking with Thoreau
29 min.　color　1975　S
Prod: Signet Productions. Dist: Encyclopaedia Britannica (avail-
　　able on video by special order). Rental: Syracuse
　　David Brower, conservationist, B. F. Skinner, Rosa Parks,
a black civil rights leader, and Eliot Richardson "visit" him at
Walden Pond.

Walden Pond
15 min.　color　1975　SCA
Prod: BBC-TV. Dist: Time-Life (available on video)
　　His two years at Walden Pond, where he lived alone and
wrote his most famous work.

The Wilderness of Walden
30 min.　b&w　1969　SCA
Prod: ABC in cooperation with the National Council of Churches
　　of Christ. Dist: National Council of Churches
　　A drama of his life at Walden Pond. Stars Biff McGuire,
Marianne Seldes, and Lawrence Keith.

THORPE, JAMES (JIM)　See　Jim Thorpe, All American　(feature)

THORVALDSEN (or THORWALDSEN), BERTEL

Thorvaldsen
9 min.　b&w　1949　JSCA
Dir: Carl Dreyer, Preben Frank. Rental: Kit Parker Films.
　　Free loan: Royal Danish Consulate General
　　A testament to his sculpture.

THURBER, JAMES

James Thurber--Reflections on His Boyhood
21 min.　b&w　n.d.　IJSCA
Prod: Robert Saudek. Dist: IQ Films
　　An interview with Alistair Cook about his daily work.

TILLICH, PAUL J.

Dr. Paul J. Tillich
30 min.　b&w　1959　SCA
Prod: NBC. Dist: Films Inc. Rental: Michigan (title: Con-
　　versation with Dr. Paul J. Tillich), Minnesota, South Florida,
　　Yale Divinity School

An interview in which he talks about leaving Germany.

Paul Tillich (Sum and Substance Series)
30 min.   b&w   1964   SCA
Prod. Modern Learning Aids.   Dist: Withdrawn.   Rental: Minnesota
A filmed dialogue in which he talks about the difference between faith and belief and his other religious ideas.

TINBERGEN, NIKOLAAS

Discussion with Nikolaas Tinbergen (2 pts.)
30 min. each   color   1976   SCA
Prod: Dr. Richard I. Evans.   Dist: Macmillan.   Rental: Association
Nobel winner Tinbergen in Ethology and Genetic Programming vs. Learning (pt. 1) discusses the natural environment's effect on animals; Unique Contributions, Reflections and Reactions (pt. 2) concerns "innate" releasing mechanisms.

TITIAN (TIZIANO VECELLI)   See   VELASQUEZ, DIEGO (Treasures from El Prado)

TITO, MARSHAL (real name: BROZ, JOSIP)   See   MAO TSE-TUNG (Maoism and Titoism)

TOBEY, MARK

Mark Tobey Abroad
30 min.   color   1973   SCA
Prod: Gardner.   Dist: Phoenix.   Rental: Viewfinders
Filmed in and around his home in Switzerland; he discusses his own work and that of other artists such as Picasso.   He also plays the piano, recites poetry and visits Kunstmuseum.

TOLSTOI (or TOLSTOY), LEO

Leo Tolstoy (A Third Testament Series)
55 min.   color   1976   SCA
Prod: BBC-TV.   Dist: Time-Life (available on video)
The spirit and legacy of a man of peace, who gave up his aristocratic standing to become a shoemaker.

Leo Tolstoy
48 min.   b&w   1953   SCA
Prod: Central Documentary Film Studio, Moscow.   Dist: Films for the Humanities
A portrait presented by photos, newsreels, paintings and

engravings. The relationship between his life and novels is noted. Stage scenes from "Anna Karenina," "Resurrection," and "Morning of a Landowner" are included.

TOULOUSE-LAUTREC, HENRI

Henri de Toulouse-Lautrec (1854-1901)
16 min.   b&w   1953   SC
Prod. and dist: Pictura.   Rental: Indiana
    Lilli Palmer narrates the story of his life, illustrated by his sketches and paintings.

Toulouse-Lautrec
15 min.   color   1973   SCA
Dir: Jacques Berthier.   Prod: Les Films Michel François.
  Dist: Roland Collection
    A portrait of the man and the artist, which includes some of his paintings.

Toulouse-Lautrec
22 min.   color   1952   SCA
Dir: Peter Riethof and Carolyn Hector.   Dist: Macmillan.
  Rental: Southern California, Syracuse
    Photographs, paintings, etchings, Parisian street scenes and his own works are used to visually reconstruct his life.

TOWNSEND, PETER

Up the Organization
30 min.   color   1973   CA
Prod: BBC-TV.   Dist: Time-Life (available on video)
    Author of the book of the same title, he gives his views on computers, business ethics, personnel consultants, and public relations.

TOYNBEE, ARNOLD

Arnold Toynbee (Wisdom Series)
30 min.   b&w   1959   SCA
Prod: NBC.   Dist: Films Inc.   Rental: Michigan, Minnesota,
  Nebraska
    An interview in which he talks about his experiences and work.

TRNKA, JIRI

Jiri Trnka
11 min.   color   1968   SA
Dir: Jiri Lehovec.   Prod: Czechoslovak Television.   Dist:

Withdrawn by McGraw-Hill.   Rental: Minnesota
The camera catches him at work on a large scale diorama
for the Montreal "Expo."

TROTSKY (or TROTSKI), LEON   See   Assassination of Trotsky
(feature); LENIN, NIKOLAI (Lenin and Trotsky); STALIN,
JOSEPH (Stalin vs. Trotsky)

TRUMAN, HARRY S
See also EISENHOWER, DWIGHT DAVID (Five Presidents on
the Presidency)

Harry S Truman: Suddenly, Mr. President
20 min.   b&w   1974   JSCA
Prod: American School and Library Films.   Dist: ACI.   Rental:
Syracuse
After the sudden death of FDR, he was responsible for
bringing World War II to a conclusion by use of the atomic bomb.

Harry S Truman: The Challenges of Office
17 min.   b&w   1974   JSCA
Prod: American School and Library Films.   Dist: ACI.   Rental:
Syracuse
The years 1948-52, the start of the McCarthy era.

Harry Truman (2 pts.; Biography Series)
26 min. each   b&w   1964   SCA
Prod: David Wolper.   Dist: Withdrawn by McGraw-Hill.   Rental:
Minnesota, Southern California
The Early Years (pt. 1) begins when he entered politics in
Missouri and ends with his sudden takeover of the Presidency in
1945.   The Presidency (pt. 2) highlights his foreign and domestic
policies.

The Truman Years
19 min.   b&w   1961   SC
Prod: Teaching Film Custodians.   Dist: Indiana (lease).   Rental:
California, Michigan
The significant events of his administration--the end of
World War II, the founding of the United Nations, the "cold war"--
are presented, primarily through newsreels.

The Truman Years (a series)
15-18 min.   b&w   1969   JSCA
Prod. and dist: Learning Corp.   Rental: Indiana (Truman and the
Atomic Bomb only), Southern California, Syracuse
Four films which cover the years 1945-52 and utilize newsreel footage and direct quotes.   Truman and the Atomic Bomb analyzes how he made his decision to bomb Japan.   Truman and the
Cold War indicated his determination to stay in Berlin.   Truman
and the Uses of Power discusses his extension of the executive

powers, and Truman and The Korean War shows the origins of our involvement.

TRUMBO, DALTON

Dalton Trumbo
10 min.   b&w   1971   SCA
Prod: NET. Dist: Indiana. Rental: California, Minnesota
        This once blacklisted author and screenwriter recalls his clash with the House Committee on Un-American Activities.

TRUTH, SOJOURNER See PARKS, GORDON (Black Wealth)

TUBMAN, HARRIET

Harriet Tubman and the Underground Railroad (The Great Adventure
    Series)
54 min.   b&w   1964   SCA
Prod: CBS. Dist: McGraw-Hill. Rental: California, Michigan,
    Syracuse
        A cast including Ethel Waters, Ruby Dee and Ossie Davis portrays the 19 trips she made into slave territory to help free other blacks.

Harriet Tubman and the Underground Railroad (You Are There
    Series)
21 min.   color   1972   IJ
Prod: CBS. Dist: BFA
        A dramatization of a news "report" on her activities.

TURNER, BISHOP

Bishop Turner: Black Nationalist
9 min.   color   1970   JSC
Prod. and dist: Encyclopaedia Britannica (available on video by
    special order). Rental: Indiana, South Florida
        Reveals his influence on the black nationalist movement; he was the first black chaplain in the Union Army.

TURNER, JOSEPH MALLORD WILLIAM

J. M. W. Turner (2 pts.; Romantic Versus Classic Art Series)
26 min. each   color   1974   JSCA
Prod: Reader's Digest. Dist: Pyramid. Rental: Southern
    California (listed under series title)
        The influences in his life and his major works of art are presented. Many consider him to be the first "abstract" painter. Narrated by Kenneth Clark.

Ossie Davis and Ruby Dee in Harriet Tubman and the Underground Railroad (McGraw-Hill Films)

Turner
7 min.   color   1975   SCA
Prod. and dist: National Gallery of Art (free loan)
An exploration of representative English and Venetian land-scapes.

Turner
28 min.   color   1972   SC
Prod: Arts Council of Great Britain.   Dist: Films Inc.
Done in three sections: the first contrasts his paintings of the sea with the English countryside; the second compares his scenes of great cities with catastrophes, and the third surveys the work of his last 20 years.

TUTANKHAMEN

Life and Times of Tutankhamen
20 min.   color   1972
Dist: Time-Life (available for special purchase only; no rentals or previews)

Tutankhamun: The Immortal Pharoah
12 min.   color   1968   IJSA
Prod: University of Houston. Dist: ACI.   Rental: Nebraska, Southern California, Syracuse
Reveals the incredible artifacts found in his Egyptian tomb, which was discovered in 1922.

TWAIN, MARK (pseudonym for Samuel Langhorne Clemens)

The House that Mark Built
26 min.   color   1971   JSCA
Prod: Raphel Associates.   Dist: Fenwick Productions
The years he spent in Hartford, Connecticut, where he had a huge Victorian house built.   During this time he became the most important American writer, his fortune rose and fell, and his daughter Susy died.   Uses excerpts from his autobiography.

Huckleberry Finn (Explorations in the Novel Series)
29 min.   color   1976   JS
Prod: Ontario Education Communication Authority.   Dist: Films Inc.
Juxtaposes his philosophy, habits, and comments with dramatized sequences.

The Legend of Mark Twain
32 min.   color   1968   IJSA
Prod: ABC. Dist: Benchmark.   Rental: Minnesota, Syracuse, Viewfinders
Dramatizes selections from "The Celebrated Jumping Frog of Calaveras County" and the Adventures of Huckleberry Finn in

addition to telling the story of his life and careers. Narrated by
David Wayne.

Mark Twain (Biography Series)
26 min.   b&w   1963   JSCA
Prod: David Wolper. Dist: McGraw-Hill. Rental: Indiana,
  Michigan, Minnesota, Syracuse
      Photographs help tell the story of his experiences as a
steamboat pilot, journalist, writer, and lecturer, which he drew
on for his stories and novels.

Mark Twain and Tom Sawyer
11 min.   color   1950   JSCA
Prod. and dist: International Film Bureau. Rental: Indiana,
  Nebraska, Syracuse
      Shot on location, the film presents the autobiographical ele-
ments of his book The Adventures of Tom Sawyer.

Mark Twain: Background for His Works
13 1/2 min.   color   1957   JSC
Prod. and dist: Coronet (sale only). Rental: Indiana, Michigan,
  Minnesota, Nebraska, South Florida, Syracuse
      His boyhood as reflected in his writing, plus re-enactments
of some of his works.

Mark Twain Gives an Interview
14 min.   color   1961   IJSCA
Prod. and dist: Coronet (sale only). Rental: Indiana, Michigan,
  Minnesota, Nebraska, Syracuse
      Hal Holbrook impersonates Twain in this "interview."

Mark Twain--Hartford Home
28 min.   color   1976   IJSCA
Prod: Comco Productions. Dist: Association
      E. G. Marshall conducts a tour of his Connecticut home,
which reveals much about Twain's personality.

Mark Twain's America
54 min.   b&w   1961   JSCA
Prod: NBC. Dist: McGraw-Hill. Rental: California, Indiana,
  Minnesota, Nebraska, South Florida, Southern California
      One thousand pictures tell the story of his life and the
period in which he lived. A peek at the "Gilded Age."

Mark Twain's Mississippi
10 min.   color   1960   JS
Prod: MGM, edited by Teaching Film Custodians. Rental: Indi-
  ana, Michigan, Minnesota
      Adapted from the feature, The Adventures of Huckleberry
Finn, it focuses on the character of Huck and on the influence the
Mississippi River had on Twain and his writing.

TWEED, WILLIAM MARCY See NAST, THOMAS (The Tiger's
    Tail: Thomas Nast vs. Boss Tweed)

TWORKOV, JACK

Artists: Jack Tworkov
30 min.   b&w   1966
Prod: NET.   Dist: Indiana
        Shown at work on a large painting, he talks about why he
became a painter.

TYLER, JOHN See HARRISON, WILLIAM HENRY (Tippecanoe
    and Tyler Too)

U THANT

Conversation with U Thant
28 min.   b&w   1963
Prod. and dist: United Nations
        A conversation with Alistair Cooke when U Thant was Sec-
retary General of the UN.

ULANOVA, GALINA

Galina Ulanova
37 min.   1965   SCA
Prod: Central Documentary Film Studios, Moscow.   Rental:
    Macmillan, Southern California
        The life and art of this ballerina, who also taught at the
Bolshoi.

UNDERWOOD, OSCAR W.

Senator Oscar W. Underwood (Profiles in Courage Series)
50 min.   b&w   1966   IJSA
Prod: Robert Saudek Associates.   Dist: IQ Films
        Gives up the nomination for the Presidency to fight against
the Ku Klux Klan's efforts to control the election process.

UPDIKE, JOHN

Writers: John Updike
30 min.   b&w   1966   SCA
Prod: NET.   Dist: Indiana.   Rental: California, Minnesota
        The beliefs and attitudes which influenced his writing.   Seen
in and about his Massachusetts home, alone and with his family.
He also reads selections from his short stories.

UTRILLO, MAURICE

L'Univers d'Utrillo
20 min.   color   1954   SCA
Dir: Georges Regnier.   Prod: Francinex S. Gallus Films.
   Rental: FACSEA (available in French)
      His youth, the influence of his mother, Suzanne Valadon, a
painter, his inner thoughts, and his works.

Utrillo
40 min.   1950   CA
Rental: FACSEA
      French dialogue only.   Life and problems until 1950.

VALENTINO, RUDOLPH

Legend of Valentino
55 min.   b&w   1962
Dist: Withdrawn.   Rental: California
      Begins with his arrival in New York in 1913 and traces the
ups and downs of his career including his divorce scandal and remarriage.   Ends with his funeral.   Uses newsreel footage and
film clips.

Rudolph Valentino--Idol of the Jazz Age
10 min.   b&w
Prod: Castle Films.   Dist: Creative Film Society

Valentino Funeral
3/5 min.   b&w   1926
Rental: Kit Parker
      The funeral parlor left in shambles; a few famous clips are
included.   A silent newsreel.

Valentino: Jazz Age Idol
10 min.   1966
Prod: Universal.   Rental: Kit Parker
      A newsreel of his life and films.

VASARELY, VICTOR

Vasarely
22 min.   color   1970   CA
Dir: Robert Hessens.   Prod: Les Films K.   Rental: FACSEA
      French dialogue only.   An interview in which he discusses
pre-kineticism.

Vasarely: Le Précinétisme
23 min.   color   1971   CA
Dir: Robert Hessens.   Prod: Les Films K.   Rental: FACSEA
      French dialogue only.   Discusses his work, especially his

kinetic art.

Who Is: Victor Vasarely
30 min.   color   1968   SCA
Prod: NET. Dist: Indiana. Rental: California
    Hungarian-born founder of "op-art," he discusses his philosophy of geometrical art.

VAUBAN, MARQUIS DE

Vauban
35 min.   SCA
Dir: Roland Bernard. Prod: ORTF. Rental: FACSEA
    Military engineer and marshal of France, his life and accomplishments under Louis XIV are told.

VELAZQUEZ (or VELASQUEZ), DIEGO RODRIGUEZ DE SILVA Y

The Art of Velásquez
25 min.   color   1975   JSCA
Dist: Macmillan
    Surveys his art, though not in chronological order.

Treasures from El Prado (a series)
5-15 min.   color   1970   JSC
Dir: Vincente Lluch. Dist: Macmillan
    Filmed in the El Prado Museum in Madrid, these are close-ups of the work of well-known painters. The series includes the following: Goya Treasures (15 min.); Titian Treasures (6 min.); Bosch Treasures (12 min.); Ribera Treasures (4 min.); Rubens Treasures (8 min.); Murillo Treasures (9 min.); Velázquez Treasures (9 min.); El Greco Treasures (5 min.).

Velázquez
15 min.   color   1955   JSCA
Prod. and dist: International Film Bureau. Rental: Syracuse
    His major works at the Prado Museum are presented within the context of their historical background.

Velásquez
11 min.   color   1952   SCA
Prod: No-Do Productions. Dist: Pictura
    His relationship to the Royal House of Spain and his portraits of the Royal family.

VERMEER, JAN

Vermeer
20 min.   color   1970   SCA
Prod: BBC-TV. Dist: Time-Life (special order purchase only;

no previews or rentals)
The principle painting analyzed is "The Guitar Player" but almost half of the 40 pictures he painted are shown. Liked by contemporaries, he was later forgotten and not rediscovered until the 1900's.

VERDI, GIUSEPPE

Homage to Verdi
52 min.　color　1976
Prod. and dist: Auteur Films.
Sherrill Milnes, a leading baritone of the Metropolitan Opera, takes us to the home of Verdi and to Sant Agata, where he wrote much of his music; he also visits a society of opera lovers in rehearsal and sings two arias.

VERNE, JULES

Jules Verne
24 min.　1970　SCA
Dir: Jean Vidal.　Prod: Eurodis.　Rental: FACSEA (available in French)
Life and works of this science fiction pioneer.

VERRAZANO, GIOVANNI See CABOT, JOHN (Age of Discovery: English, French, and Dutch Explorations); CARTIER, JACQUES (French Explorations in the New World)

VESPUCCI (or VESPUCIUS), AMERICUS See CABOT, JOHN (Age of Discovery: Spanish and Portuguese Explorations)

VICTORIA, QUEEN

Queen Victoria (Profiles in Power Series)
30 min.　color　1976　SCA
Prod: McConnell Advertising Co. and Ontario Communications Authority. Dist: Learning
Kate Reid plays Queen Victoria and is 'interviewed' by Patrick Watson, who acts as a gadfly.

VIDOR, CHARLES KING

Film Makers: King Vidor
28 min.　b&w　1965　SCA
Prod: NET. Dist: Indiana
Talks about the Hollywood of old, and his films, especially "Our Daily Bread," from which a clip is shown.

VIEIRA DA SILVA, MARIA ELENA

Vieira da Silva
17 min.   color   1964   SCA
Dir: Guy Suzuki.   Prod: Telestar.   Rental: FACSEA (available
   in French)
      A survey of life and works and an interview in her studio.

VIGNY, COMTE ALFRED VICTOR DE

Alfred de Vigny: Le Journal d'un Poète
15 min.   1967   CA
Dir: Georges Rebillard.   Prod: Les Productions de Touraine.
   Rental: FACSEA
      French dialogue only.   Set in his castle of Maine Giraud in
Charentes, where he isolated himself when he wrote.

VILLELLA, EDWARD

Ballet with Edward Villella (An Introduction to the Performing
   Arts Series)
27 min.   color   1970   JSCA
Prod: Robert Saudek Associates.   Dist: Learning.   Rental:
   Indiana, Michigan, Minnesota, Nebraska, Southern California,
   South Florida, Syracuse
      Excerpts of his performances in "Apollo," "Jewels," and
"Giselle," as well as a look at a rehearsal.

VINCI, LEONARDO DA

The Drawings of Leonardo da Vinci
28 min.   color   1971   SCA
Prod: Arts Council of Great Britain.   Dist: Films Inc.
      A commentary on his life with emphasis on his drawings.

I, Leonardo da Vinci (Saga of Western Man Series)
54 min.   color   1966   JSCA
Prod: ABC.   Dist: McGraw-Hill.   Rental: Indiana, Southern
   California, Syracuse
      Filmed in Italy and France, it shows two of his greatest
works: "The Battle of Anghiari" and the giant sculptured horse,
the Sforza monument.   His innovations as a painter, sculptor,
architect, engineer and scientist are noted.   Fredric March recites Leonardo's words.

Leonardo da Vinci and His Art
13 1/2 min.   color   1957   JSC
Prod. and dist: Coronet (sale only).   Rental: Indiana, Minnesota,
   Nebraska, Syracuse
      Besides examining his works, his versatility as a scientist,

mathematician, and architect is noted.

Leonardo da Vinci--First Man of the Renaissance (They Made a
    Difference Series)
10 min.   color   1971   IJSC
Prod: Anthony Corso.   Dist: Walt Disney (long term license)
        Begins with his childhood and traces his accomplishments
in many fields.

Leonardo da Vinci--Giant of the Renaissance
25 min.   color or b&w   1957   JSC
Prod. and dist: Encyclopaedia Britannica (available on video by
    special order or in Spanish).   Rental: California, Minnesota,
    Nebraska, South Florida, Southern California, Syracuse
        Presents his life and work as it represented the Renais-
sance spirit.

Leonardo da Vinci: His Inventions
21 min.   b&w   1952   JSCA
Prod. and dist: Pictura
        A comparison of his drawings with the working models of
his inventions.

Leonardo da Vinci: His Life, His Times, His Art
22 min.   color   1952   SCA
Prod. and dist: Pictura
        A biography within the context of his times and supported
by examples of his greatest works.

Leonardo da Vinci: His Notebooks
21 min.   b&w   1952   JSCA
Prod. and dist: Pictura
        A portrait of a man based on his scientific studies, his
drawings, and his manuscripts.

Leonardo da Vinci: Man of Mystery
68 min.   color   1952   JSCA
Dir: Luciano Emmer and Lauro Venturi.   Prod: Leonid Kipnis
    and Herman Starr.   Dist: Pictura
        A biography which shows many of his masterpieces.

Leonardo da Vinci--The Quest for Perfection (Touch of Fame
    Series)
29 min.   b&w   1963   SCA
Prod: KNXT.   Dist: Southern California
        Dr. Herman Harvey, psychology professor, talks about his
childhood, his success as a sculptor, artist, engineer, scientist
and philosopher.

Leonardo: To Know How to See
55 min.   color   1972   SA
Prod: Chandler Cowles and Robert Cosner.   Dist: National Gal-
    lery of Art (free loan)

His greatest works as an artist, scientist, anatomist, within the context of his place and times. Filmed in the U.S. and abroad. Narrated by Sir John Gielgud.

VOLTA, ALESSANDRO

Volta and Electricity
35 min.   color   1976   SCA
Dir. and prod: Samuel Devons.   Dist: Films for the Humanities
        Traces 30 years (1770-1800) of the study of electricity,
primarily by Volta. His experiments are reconstructed.

VOLTAIRE, FRANÇOIS
    See also   Voltaire (feature)

Monsieur de Voltaire
28 min.   1964   CA
Dir: Roger Leenhardt.   Prod: Films Roger Leenhardt.   Rental:
    FACSEA
        French dialogue only.   Life and works.

VONNEGUT, KURT, JR.

Kurt Vonnegut, Jr.: A Self-Portrait
29 min.   color   1975   JSCA
Prod: Harold Mantell.   Dist: Films for the Humanities (available
    on 3/4" videocassette)
        Photographed in his childhood hometown of Indianapolis and
in his present home in New York City, he talks candidly about why
he writes science fiction, the influence of other writers, remembrances of his childhood and family.   Narrated by Vonnegut.

WALKER, JIMMY

Jimmy Walker (20th Century Series)
26 min.   b&w   1964   SCA
Prod: CBS.   Dist: Association
        A portrait of New York's most charismatic mayor.

WALKER, MARY EDWARDS

A Medal for Miss Walker: 1866
20 min.   b&w   1954   PIJ
Prod: Teaching Film Custodians.   Dist: Indiana (lease)
        A dramatization of her role as a civilian surgeon on contract to the Army.   An excerpt from a Cavalcade of America
television movie.

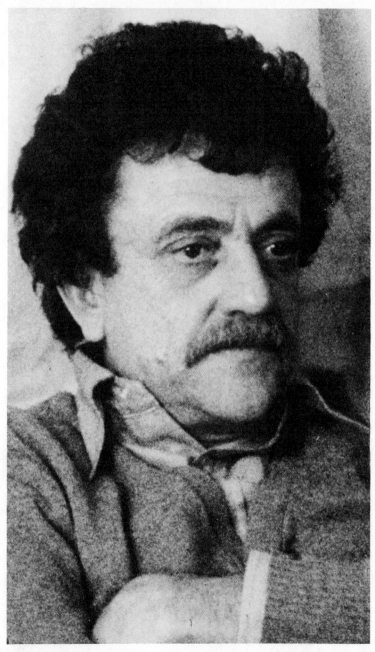

Kurt Vonnegut, Jr.: A Self-Portrait (Films for the Humanities, Inc.)

WARD, ROGER

Roger Ward (Sports Legends Series)
20 min.   color   1975   JSCA
Prod. and dist: Sports Legends Inc.   Rental: Southern California
     He discusses his racing career as film clips from some of
his races are shown.

WARHOL, ANDREW
    See also DE KOONING, WILLEM (Painters Painting)

Andy Warhol
53 min.   color   1975   SCA
Prod. and dist: Blackwood
    A documentary of him and his art.

Super Artist, Andy Warhol
22 min.   color   1967   CA
Dir: Bruce Torbert. Dist: Films Inc.
    A visit to his "Factory," where he is in the process of
making a film.

WARREN, EARL

The Warren Years: Profile Earl Warren (2 pts.)
22-24 min.   b&w   1969   SCA
Prod: NET. Dist: Indiana. Rental: Association, California
    A profile of him and reactions to some of his decisions as
the Supreme Court Chief Justice. The second part (24 min.)
examines the major rulings of the Court while he was on the bench.

WASHINGTON, BOOKER T.

Booker T. Washington
18 min.   b&w   1952   JSA
Prod: Encyclopaedia Britannica. Dist: Withdrawn by EB.
  Rental: Michigan, Minnesota, Nebraska, South Florida, Syracuse
    His childhood, his hardships and struggles to free blacks,
and his founding of Tuskegee Institute.

Booker T. Washington
11 min.   color   1967   IJS
Prod: Vignette Films. Dist: BFA. Rental: Minnesota, Syracuse
    His early years and the founding of Tuskegee Institute.

WASHINGTON, GEORGE
    See also LAFAYETTE, MARQUIS DE (Lafayette and Washington)

American Revolution: The War Years
11 min.   color or b&w   1954   JS
Prod. and dist: Coronet (sale only).   Rental: Indiana
        Traces the growth of the Army under Washington and its
campaigns.

America's Heroes: George Washington
11 min.   color   1970   PI
Prod. and dist: Coronet (sale only).   Rental: Syracuse
        A visit to Mount Vernon, Williamsburg, and Valley Forge
recalls Washington's life.

Boyhood of George Washington
10 min.   b&w or color   1957   PI
Prod. and dist: Coronet (sale only).   Rental: Indiana, Michigan,
    Minnesota, Nebraska
        Show his childhood and young adult years at Ferry Farm
and Mount Vernon.

George Washington
19 min.   b&w   1951   IJS
Prod. and dist: Encyclopaedia Britannica (available on video by
    special order)
        Illustrates the personal qualities which helped him as a mili-
tary leader and later as an organizer of the new country.

George Washington and the Whiskey Rebellion: Testing the Consti-
    tution
27 min.   color   1975   JSCA
Prod: Robert Saudek Associates.   Dist: Learning.   Rental:
    Michigan, South Florida, Syracuse
        A dramatization of Washington's decision to lead troops into
Pennsylvania to quell the farmers' rebellion against the whiskey
tax.

George Washington: The Courage that Made a Nation (Americana
    Series #4)
30 min.   color   1968   IJSCA
Prod: Leo Handel.   Dist: Handel.   Rental: Syracuse
        Begins with his boyhood, his education, his early work as
a surveyor and soldier.   Then it traces his Revolutionary War career as Commander-in-Chief and President.

George Washington: The Making of a Rebel (Decades of Decision:
    The American Revolution Series)
29 min.   color   1975   JSCA
Prod: WQED, Pittsburgh.   Dist: National Geographic Society
    (available on videocassette)
        Col. Washington, an elected burgess, is loyal to England
until the burgesses are dismissed by the Governor; then he sus-
pects compromise with England is impossible.

George Washington's Greatest Victory (Cultural Heritage Series)
17 min.   color   1966   IJSC
Prod: Walter P. Lewisohn. Dist: Coronet (sale only). Rental:
    Indiana, Syracuse
        Through prints and engravings the major events of his boy-
hood and adult years are shown, with stress on how he maintained
morale during the final days of the war.

George Washington's Inauguration (Americana Series #12)
22 min.   color   1972   IJSCA
Prod: Avram Dorion. Dist: Handel. Rental: Syracuse
        Done in a "you-are-there" style, complete with spot cover-
age, songs, and commercials! "Newscasters" give the background
of the events and then interview prominent political figures.

Meet George Washington
54 min.   color   1969   IJSA
Prod: NBC. Dist: Films Inc.
        Uncovers the "real" George Washington and draws heavily
on his own words and contemporaneous accounts of his life and
achievements.

Valley Forge
13 min.   b&w   1955   IJSCA
Prod: McGraw-Hill. Rental: Indiana, Minnesota, Nebraska
        Dramatizes the battle at Valley Forge and Washington's de-
cisions and thoughts regarding the fight.

Washington Crosses the Delaware (You Are There Series)
26 min.   b&w   1956   JSCA
Prod. and dist: CBS (special purchase only; no previews or rent-
    als). Rental: Minnesota
        A dramatization of his surprise attack on the Hessians.

Washington's Farewell
15 min.   color   1973   JSC
Prod: Art Evans. Dist: Paramount Oxford
        The best known portions of his speech are re-enacted by
William Shatner.

Washington's Farewell to His Officers (You Are There Series)
26 min.   b&w   1955   JSCA
Prod. and dist: CBS (special purchase only; no rentals or pre-
    views). Rental: Indiana, Michigan, Minnesota
        A dramatized "on the scene" news report of him saying
good-bye to his officers at Fraunces Tavern.

The World Turned Upside Down
52 min.   color   1974   SC
Prod: Wolper Organization. Dist: Films Inc.
        By stripping away the legends, the complexity and human
qualities are revealed. The first part is about his years as General and the second re-creates some of the battle scenes, his

ultimate victory, and his refusal of the "crown." Shot as though eyewitnesses are giving their accounts. Also available in two edited parts: Washington: Years of Trial (1754-1781), which is 32 min., and Washington: Time of Triumph (1781-1783), 18 min.

WATERHOUSE, BENJAMIN See JEFFERSON, THOMAS (Experiment at Monticello: Thomas Jefferson and Smallpox Vaccination)

WATTS, DANIEL
See also BOND, JULIAN (The Angry Negro)

Daniel Watts (The Dissenters Series)
30 min. b&w 1967 SCA
Prod: NET. Dist: Indiana. Rental: California, Minnesota
Editor of the Liberator, this black spokesman talks about his position on riots, black power, and black religion.

WEBSTER, DANIEL

Daniel Webster
27 min. b&w 1965 JSC
Prod: Encyclopaedia Britannica. Dist: Withdrawn by EB.
Rental: Indiana, Michigan (1951 version), Minnesota, Nebraska, South Florida (1951 version), Southern California, Syracuse
His skills and career as a teacher, a lawyer, a Congressman, orator and Secretary of State are covered.

Daniel Webster (Profiles in Courage Series)
50 min. b&w 1965 IJSCA
Prod: Robert Saudek Associates. Dist: IQ Films. Rental:
Michigan, Minnesota, Syracuse
Defies his abolitionist supporters in an attempt to reach a compromise, which he hopes will save the Union.

The Last Will of Daniel Webster
16 min. b&w 1953 JS
Prod: Teaching Film Custodians. Dist: Indiana (lease)
A dramatization of his political career, which was influenced by the slavery issue. An excerpt from the Cavalcade of America television movie.

Webster's Sacrifice to Save the Union (You Are There Series)
30 min. b&w 1955 JSCA
Prod. and dist: CBS (special sale only; no previews or rentals).
Rental: Minnesota
A dramatization of his final support of Clay's compromise bill to admit California as a free state and allow the territories to choose whether or not they wanted slavery.

WEISKOPF, TOM

On Tour: Tom Weiskopf (The Winners Series)
48 min.   color   1976   SCA
Prod: Laurel. Dist: Counselor
 A sports profile of this champion golfer.

WEST, JESSAMYN

Jessamyn West: My Hand, My Pen (Writers on Writing Series)
17 min.   color   1971   S
Prod: Davidson Films. Dist: General Learning
 At her home she discusses the role of imagination and re-
search in the writing process. She is best known for The Friendly
Persuasion.

WESTON, EDWARD

The Photographer
27 min.   b&w   1947   SCA
Dir: Willard Van Dyke. Rental: Creative Film Society, Kit
 Parker, Minnesota, Museum of Modern Art, Southern California
 At home in California and working with students. Exhibits
of his portraits.

Photography: The Daybooks of Edward Weston--How Young I Was
30 min.   b&w   1965   SCA
Prod: NET. Dist: Indiana. Rental: California, Michigan,
 Minnesota, Museum of Modern Art
 His inner thoughts are reflected in his writings, called his
"Daybooks." Examples of photographs from various periods.
Friends and family members talk about him as an artist.

Photography: The Daybooks of Edward Weston--The Strongest Way
 of Seeing
30 min.   b&w   1965   SCA
Prod: NET. Dist: Indiana. Rental: California, Michigan, Museum of Modern Art
 The simplicity of his photographs represented by many examples of his work.

WESTON, JOAN

Joan Weston
22 min.   color   1973   SCA
Prod: Tele-Sports. Dist: Paramount Oxford
 A sports profile.

WHEATLEY, PHILLIS See BROWN, WILLIAM WELLS (Slavery
 and Slave Resistance)

WHEELOCK, JOHN HALL

John Hall Wheelock (Wisdom Series)
30 min.   b&w   1958   SCA
Prod: NBC.   Dist: Films Inc.   Rental: Michigan, Minnesota
     Former Scribner's editor, he reads two of his poems and talks about important experiences.

WHITMAN, WALT

Walt Whitman (Poetry by Americans)
10 min.   color   1972   JSC
Prod: Art Evans.   Dist: Paramount Oxford (captioned for the
   deaf).   Rental: Syracuse
     A short sketch of his life is followed by Efrem Zimbalist, Jr., reading "O Captain! My Captain!"

Walt Whitman: Background for his Works
12 1/2 min.   color   1957   JSC
Prod. and dist: Coronet (sale only).   Rental: Indiana, Minnesota,
   Nebraska, Syracuse
     The poet's life as reflected by social conditions in America during the 19th century.

Walt Whitman: Poet for a New Age (Humanities Series)
29 min.   color   1972   SC
Prod: Lou Stoument.   Dist: Encyclopaedia Britannica (available
   on video by special order).   Rental: Nebraska, South Florida,
   Southern California, Syracuse
     Emphasizes his beliefs and how they contrasted with the views of his contemporaries.

Walt Whitman's Leaves of Grass
26 min.   color   1965   JSCA
Prod: Francis Raymond Line.   Rental: Minnesota
     His life story and the factors that compelled him to write "Leaves of Grass." Narration is taken from his own words and sections of his poem are read.   Filmed on location.

Walt Whitman's Western Journey
14 min.   color   1965   JSCA
Prod: Francis Raymond Line.   Rental: Minnesota
     Retraces the journey he made across the Rocky Mountains in 1879; the narration is taken from his own words.

Walt Whitman's World (Cultural Heritage Series)
16 min.   color   1966   JSC
Prod: Walter P. Lewisohn.   Dist: Coronet (sale only).   Rental:
   Indiana, Michigan, Minnesota, Nebraska, Syracuse

From the Encyclopaedia Britannica film, Walt Whitman: Poet for a
New Age

Focuses on original manuscripts of his diaries and Civil
War hospital notes.

WHITNEY, ELI

America Becomes an Industrial Nation
25 min.   color   1967
Rental: Indiana

The industrialization of America from 1776-1876, with information about the leading inventors, especially Whitney.

Eli Whitney
18 min.   b&w   1951   IJS
Prod. and dist: Withdrawn by Encyclopaedia Britannica.   Rental:
   Indiana, Michigan, Minnesota, Nebraska, Southern California,
   Syracuse
      Dramatizes his experiments which led to the invention of
the cotton gin and other tools.

Eli Whitney (Meet the Inventors Series)
7 min.   color   1951   P
Prod: U. P. A.   Dist: Macmillan
      Animated.   An "old inventor" tells a small boy about Whitney's cotton gin invention.

Eli Whitney Invents the Cotton Gin (You Are There Series)
26 min.   b&w   1956   JSCA
Prod. and dist: CBS (special sale only; no previews or rentals).
   Rental: Indiana, Minnesota, Southern California, Syracuse
      An "on the scene" news report dramatization of his invention.

Man Who Took a Chance: Eli Whitney
20 min.   b&w   1952   IJS
Prod: Teaching Film Custodians.   Dist: Indiana (lease)
      A dramatization of key events in his life including his
assembly-line theory for the production of muskets.

WHITTIER, JOHN GREENLEAF

John Greenleaf Whittier
18 min.   b&w   1950   JS
Prod. and dist: Withdrawn by Encyclopaedia Britannica.   Rental:
   Indiana, Michigan, Minnesota, Nebraska, South Florida,
   Southern California
      Highlights of his life and poems.

WILBUR, RICHARD   See   LOWELL, ROBERT (Poetry: Richard
   Wilbur and Robert Lowell)

WILDE, OSCAR
   See also   Oscar Wilde (feature)

Oscar Wilde--Whom the Gods Would Destroy (Touch of Fame
   Series)
29 min.   b&w   1962   SCA
Prod: KNXT-TV.   Dist: Southern California
      How his family and the tragedies of his life affected his

writings are analyzed by Dr. Herman Harvey, psychology professor at USC.

WILDER, THORNTON

Thornton Wilder
24 min.   b&w   1966   SC
Prod: Harold Mantel. Dist: Films for the Humanities (available
   on 3/4" videocassette)
        A profile which reveals how his background and tempera-
ment shaped his writing. Rare footage of Wilder with director
Max Reinhardt and Gertrude Stein. He reads excerpts from Our
Town and The Bridge of San Luis Rey.

Thornton Wilder
30 min.   b&w   1967   SCA
Prod: NET. Dist: Indiana
        A biographical sketch based on interviews with his brother
and sister and recorded excerpts from his speeches, writings, and
film clips. Includes an analysis of his writings.

WILHELM (KING OF PRUSSIA) See BISMARCK, PRINCE OTTO
   VON (Bismarck: Germany from Blood and Iron)

WILLIAM I, DUKE OF NORMANDY

The Norman Conquest of England
20 min.   color   1971   SCA
Prod: Roger Leenhardt. Dist: Film Images
        The battles of William I, Duke of Normandy as depicted on
the famous Bayeux tapestry.

WILLIAMS, ROGER

Roger Williams: Founder of Rhode Island
28 min.   b&w   1956   JS
Prod. and dist: Encyclopaedia Britannica (available on video by
   special order). Rental: Indiana, Michigan, Nebraska, Southern
   California, Syracuse
        How and why he founded Rhode Island to establish separa-
tion of church and state.

WILLIAMS, TED

"My Name Is Ted Williams"
28 min.   color
Prod: Sears, Roebuck and Co. Dist: Association-Sterling (free
   loan)

Athlete, sportsman and Marine, he tells his own story.

WILLIAMS, WILLIAM CARLOS

Poetry: William Carlos Williams
30 min.   b&w   1966   JSCA
Prod: NET. Dist: Indiana.   Rental: California
      The life of Williams as revealed through his letters, poems
and autobiography. Like his father, Williams' son is a doctor,
who is shown in practice.

WILLKIE, WENDELL

Of Perfect Loyalty
15 min.   b&w   1952-53   JSCA
Prod: Mike Sklar. Dist: Star Film
      As candidate of the Republican Party for President.   Com-
piled from the Fox Movietone News Library footage.

Wendell Willkie
27 min.   b&w   1965   IJ
Prod: Metromedia Producers. Dist: Sterling (sale only; available on 8mm).   Rental: Syracuse
      Emphasizes his role in international affairs, including
World War II and the Lend-Lease Act.

Willkie
26 min.
Prod: CBS. Dist: Association
      The man who almost defeated FDR is portrayed.

WILLS, HELEN

Miss Poker Face
15 min.   b&w   1952-53   JSCA
Prod: Mike Sklar. Dist: Star Film
      Star of the tennis courts sketched; compiled from the Fox
Movietone News Library footage.

WILSON, WOODROW
      See also EISENHOWER, DWIGHT DAVID (Five Presidents on
the Presidency); COOLIDGE, CALVIN (U.S. in the Twentieth
Century: 1920-1832); Wilson (feature)

Ordeal of Woodrow Wilson
26 min.   b&w   1965   SCA
Prod: NBC. Dist: Films Inc.   Rental: California, Michigan,
   Minnesota, Southern California

The struggle with Congress for U.S. participation in the League of Nations. Commentary by Herbert Hoover.

United States in the Twentieth Century: 1912-1920
12 min.   b&w   1967   JS
Prod. and dist: Coronet (sale only)
    Newsreel footage is used to highlight Wilson's administration.

Wilson vs. the Senate
27 min.   b&w   1964   SC
Prod: Metromedia Producers.   Dist: Films Inc.
    Edmond O'Brien narrates this close-up of Wilson's battle with Congress over the League of Nations.

Wilson's Fight for Peace
30 min.   b&w   1960   SCA
Prod: CBS.   Dist: Films Inc.   Rental: Indiana, Minnesota, Southern California, Syracuse
    His heartbreaking fight with Congress over the League of Nations.

Woodrow Wilson (Biography Series)
26 min.   b&w   1963   JSCA
Prod: David Wolper.   Dist: Withdrawn by McGraw-Hill.   Rental: Indiana, Michigan, Syracuse
    His varied careers as President of Princeton, Governor of New Jersey, and President.

Woodrow Wilson (Profiles in Courage Series)
50 min.   b&w   1965   IJSA
Prod: Robert Saudek Associates.   Dist: IQ Films.   Rental: Michigan, Minnesota, Syracuse
    Supports his nomination of Louis D. Brandeis to the Supreme Court despite religious and political opposition.

Woodrow Wilson--Greek Revival House and Street House (American Life Styles Series)
28 min.   color   1976   IJSCA
Prod: Comco Productions.   Dist: Association
    E. G. Marshall conducts a tour of his home, which sheds light on his personality.

Woodrow Wilson: Spokesman for Tomorrow
27 min.   b&w   1956   JSCA
Prod: Caravel Films.   Dist: Withdrawn.   Rental: Minnesota, South Florida, Southern California
    Actual footage from his speeches and contemporaneous cartoons reveal his concepts of freedom for men and world peace.

Woodrow Wilson: The Fight for a League of Nations (Great Decision Series)
25 min.   color   1971   JSC

Prod: Project 7 Producers. Dist: American Educational Films.
Rental: Syracuse
Presents the factors which led Wilson to his important de-
cison to fight for the League.

Woodrow Wilson: The Fight for Peace (Twentieth Century Series)
26 min. b&w
Prod: CBS. Rental: Association
His conflict with Congress over the League of Nations.

WINDSOR, DUKE OF See EDWARD VIII

WOLFE, THOMAS

Thomas Wolfe--Ghost, Come Back Again (Touch of Fame Series)
29 min. b&w 1962 SCA
Prod: KNXT-TV. Dist: Southern California
Dr. Herman Harvey analyzes the relationship between his
life and his writings; a dramatization from Look Homeward, Angel
reveals the autobiographical nature of the work.

WOOD, GAR

The Silver Fox
15 min. b&w 1952-53 JSCA
Prod: Mike Sklar. Dist: Star Film
His speedboat races compiled from the Fox Movietone News
Library footage.

WOOD, GRANT

Grant Wood
14 min. b&w 1954 SCA
Dist: Pictura. Rental: Michigan
His story plus a view of his best pictures. Commentary
spoken by Henry Fonda.

WOODS, GRANVILLE T. See McCOY, ELIJAH (Black Men and
Iron Horses)

WOOLF, VIRGINIA

Virginia Woolf: The Moment Whole
10 min. color 1972 SCA
Dir: Janet Sternburg. Prod: NET. Dist: ACI. Rental: California, Michigan, Minnesota, Syracuse, Viewfinders

Marian Seldes portrays her in this film essay scripted from her writings--A Room of One's Own and The Waves.

WRIGHT, FRANK LLOYD

Frank Lloyd Wright (Twentieth Century Series)
26 min.   b&w   1958
Prod: CBS. Dist: Macmillan.   Rental: Association, Minnesota,
   South Florida, Syracuse
      The man and his buildings.

Frank Lloyd Wright (Wisdom Series)
30 min.   b&w   1962   SCA
Prod: NBC. Dist: Films Inc.   Rental: California, Michigan,
   Minnesota, Nebraska, Southern California
      An interview in which he discusses his theory of functional
architecture.

Frank Lloyd Wright--Fallingwater (American Life Styles Series)
28 min.   color   1976   IJSCA
Prod: Comco Productions.   Dist: Association
 E. G. Marshall conducts a tour of his Pennsylvania home.

WRIGHT, ORVILLE and WILBUR

First Flight of the Wright Brothers (You Are There Series)
30 min.   b&w   IJSCA
Prod. and dist: CBS (special order sale only; no previews or
 rentals).   Rental: Minnesota
 A dramatized "news report" of their first flight at Kitty
Hawk, North Carolina.

Wings over Kitty Hawk
15 min.   b&w   1952-53   JSCA
Prod: Mike Sklar.   Dist: Star Film
 An account of their first flight; compiled from Fox Movietone News Library footage.

WYETH, ANDREW

The World of Andrew Wyeth
26 min.   color   1968   JSCA
Prod: Al Schwartz and Hal Wallace in cooperation with the Art
 Institute of Chicago and the Whitney Museum of N.Y.   Dist:
 International Film Bureau.   Rental: California, Minnesota
 The important events of his life, the influence of his father,
a well-known illustrator, and 49 of his paintings of people and
places.

The Wyeth Phenomenon
26 min.   color   1968   SCA
Prod: CBS.   Dist: BFA.   Rental: Indiana, Michigan, Southern
 California, Syracuse
 An examination of his life and a detailed analysis of his
work by critic John Canaday.

YEATS, WILLIAM BUTLER

W. B. Yeats: A Tribute
23 min.   b&w   1968   SCA
Dir: George Fleishmann.   Prod: National Film Institute of Ire-
 land.   Dist: Macmillan.   Rental: Nebraska, Syracuse
 His life and work, the poetry is read by Michael Mac-
Liammoir and Siobhan McKenna.

Yeats Country
18 min.   color   1965   SCA
Prod: Aengus Films.   Dist: International Film Bureau.

Rental: California, Minnesota, Syracuse
The setting of his poetry and its effect on his life. Discusses his association with Lady Gregory and the unrest of his middle life.

YEVTUSHENKO, YEVGENY

Yevgeny Yevtushenko: A Poet's Journey
28 1/2 min.   b&w   1969   SCA
Prod: Harold Mantell.   Dist: Films for the Humanities (available on 3/4" videocassette)
Follows this energetic poet at home and in the States, where he gives poetry readings for college students.   He talks candidly about poetic freedom, his enemies in Russia and the barriers of life.

YOUNG, ANDREW

Edge of the Arena
28 min.   color   1972   IJ
Prod. and dist: Rediscovery Productions
His race for Congress in Georgia.   He was the first black candidate since Reconstruction in the South.

YOUNG, BRIGHAM
See also   Brigham Young (feature)

Brigham Young--Beehive House
28 min.   color   1976   IJSCA
Prod: Comco Productions.   Dist: Association
E. G. Marshall conducts a tour of his Greek revival house in Salt Lake City.

Driven Westward
31 min.   b&w   1940   JSCA
Prod: Teaching Film Custodians.   Rental: Indiana
Abridged from the feature, Brigham Young.   He's leading a wagon train to Iowa, where some members of the party remain.

ZEMAN, KAREL

The Magic World of Karel Zeman
16 min.   color   1969   SCA
Prod: Zdenek Rozkopal.   Dist: Withdrawn by McGraw-Hill.
Rental: California
At work on the special effects of "Prehistoric Journey," "The Fabulous World of Jules Verne" and "Baron Münchhausen."

ZENGER, PETER

Mightier than the Sword: Zenger and Freedom of the Press
23 min.　　b&w　　1953　　PIJS
Prod: Teaching Film Custodians.　Dist: Indiana (lease)
　　　The publication of his exposure of the corruption of Royal
Governor William Cosby's administration and his subsequent trial
are dramatized.

ZOLA, EMIL
　　See also　Life of Emil Zola (feature)

The Life of Emil Zola
32 min.　　b&w　　1937　　SC
Prod: Warner Bros. , edited by Teaching Film Custodians.　Dist:
　　Indiana (lease).　Rental: California, Michigan
　　　A dramatization of his trial after the French President
sued him for libel because Zola wrote his famous open letter
"J'Accuse. "　An excerpt from the feature film of the same title.

SELECTED FEATURES

A. K. A. Cassius Clay
79 min.   color   1970
Dir: Jim Jacobs.   Dist: United Artists
    A documentary portrait in which he talks about his fighting
career.   Clips of films of past fights.

Abe Lincoln in Illinois
110 min.   b&w   1940
Dir: John Cromwell.   Prod: RKO.   Dist: Films Inc.
Cast: Raymond Massey, Gene Lockhart, Ruth Gordon.
    Shows his early life, his days as a storekeeper, legislator,
and elected official.

Abraham Lincoln
84 min.   b&w   1930
Dir: D. W. Griffith.   Dist: Images, Kit Parker, Museum of
    Modern Art, National Film Service
Cast: Walter Huston, Una Merkel, Kay Hammond, E. Alyn Warren,
    Hobart Bosworth, Fred Warren, Henry B. Walthall, Frank Campeau.
    A popular version and a rare Griffith sound film.

Adventures of Marco Polo
104 min.   b&w   1938
Prod: Archie Mayo.   Rental: Macmillan.
Cast: Gary Cooper, Basil Rathbone, Sigrid Gurie, Alan Hale,
    Bonnie Barnes, Lana Turner.
    He meets adventure and romance on the way to the court of
Kubla Khan.

Age of the Medici (3 pts.)
84 min. each   color   1973
Dir: Roberto Rossellini.   Rental: Macmillan
Cast: Marcello Di Falco.
    The ascension of Cosimo de Medici.

The Agony and the Ecstasy
123 min.   color   1965
Dir: Carol Reed.   Prod: 20th Century-Fox.   Rental: Films Inc.
Cast: Charlton Heston, Rex Harrison
    The story of how and why the Sistine Chapel was painted.

Al Capone
105 min.   1959
Dir: Richard Wilson.   Rental: Hurlock Cine
Cast: Rod Steiger.

Alexander Hamilton
71 min.   b&w   1931
Dir: John Adolfi.   Rental: United Artists
Cast: George Arliss, Doris Kenyon, Alan Mowbray, Montagu Love.
   A biographical drama with emphasis on his efforts to push through the "Assumption Bill."

Alexander the Great
135 min.   color   1956
Dir: Robert Rossen.   Rental: United Artists
Cast: Richard Burton, Frederic March, Claire Bloom, Danielle Darrieux.
   An epic of him conquering his world.

Anne of a Thousand Days
145 min.   color   1971
Dir: Charles Jarrott.   Prod: Universal.   Rental: Cine Craft, Clem Williams, Swank, Twyman, Universal
Cast: Richard Burton, Genevieve Bujold.
   The epic story of the romance of Henry VIII and Anne Boleyn.

Assassination of Trotsky
105 min.   color   1973
Dir: Joseph Losey.   Prod: Universal.   Rental: Swank
Cast: Richard Burton, Alain Delon
   The suspense and intrigue surrounding Trotsky's assasination.

The Barretts of Wimpole Street
105 min.   color   1957
Dir: Sidney Franklin.   Prod: M-G-M.   Rental: Films Inc.
Cast: Jennifer Jones, John Gielgud, Bill Travers.
   Elizabeth's love for Browning enables her to overcome her ailments.

Becket (Great Britain)
148 min.   1964
Dir: Peter Glenville.   Rental: Films Inc.
Cast: Richard Burton, Peter O'Toole.

Beloved Infidel
123 min.   color   1959
Dir: Henry King.   Prod: Twentieth Century-Fox.   Rental: Films Inc.
Cast: Gregory Peck, Deborah Kerr, Eddie Albert.
   F. Scott Fitzgerald's affair with Sheilah Graham.

The Benny Goodman Story
116 min.   color   1955
Dir: Valentine Davis.   Rental: Universal
Cast: Steve Allen, Donna Reed.

The Bob Mathias Story
80 min.   color   1955
Prod. and dist: Association
    Playing himself winning the Olympic decathlon.

Bonaparte et la Révolution
254 min.   b&w   1927
Dir: Abel Gance.   Rental: Images
Cast: Albert Dieudonne, Koubitzky, Antonin Artaud, Van Daele,
    Abel Gance, Viguier, Phillippe Heriat.
    A drama beginning with the French Revolution and ending
with his campaign through Italy in 1796.   A panorama of French
history with Robespierre, Josephine and others.

Brian's Song
75 min.   color   1971
Prod: Columbia.   Dir: Buzz Kulik.   Rental: Swank, Twyman
Cast: James Caan, Billy Dee Williams, Jack Warden, Shelley
    Fabares.
    A poignant drama of a young man about to die.   Based on
the story of Brian Piccolo and Gale Sayers' friendship.

Brigham Young
115 min.   b&w   1940
Dir: Henry Hathaway.   Prod: 20th Century-Fox.   Rental: Films
    Inc.
Cast: Tyrone Power, Linda Darnell, Jane Darwell, Brian Donlevy,
    Vincent Price.
    Based on the novel by Louis Bromfield.   The problems
created by Young's religious beliefs are the focal point.

Brother Sun, Sister Moon
120 min.   color   1973
Dir: Franco Zeffirelli.   Prod: Paramount.   Rental: Films Inc.
Cast: Graham Faulkner, Judi Bowker, Leigh Lawson, Alec Guinness.
    A quasi-fictional biography of St. Francis of Assisi, found-
er of the Franciscan Order.

Buddha
134 min.   1965
Dir: Kenji Misumi.   Rental: United Artists
Cast: Kojiro Hongo, Charito Solis, Shintaro Katsu.
    His life story is dramatized.

Caesar and Cleopatra (Great Britain)
135 min.   1945
Dir: Gabriel Pascal.   Rental: Janus.
Cast: Vivien Leigh, Claude Rains.

Based on the play by George Bernard Shaw.

Catherine of Russia
105 min.   1965
Rental: Ivy
Cast: Hildegarde Neff.

Catherine the Great (Great Britain)
93 min.   b&w   1934
Rental: Budget, Macmillan
Cast: Elizabeth Bergner, Douglas Fairbanks, Jr.
Her turbulent rise to power.

Catherine the Great
105 min.   1962
Dir: Alexander Korda.   Rental: Classic Film Museum
Cast: Douglas Fairbanks, Jr.

Che!
96 min.   color   1969
Dir: Richard Fleischer.   Prod: 20th Century-Fox.   Rental:
Films Inc.
Cast: Omar Sharif, Jack Palance, Woody Strode, Robert Loggia.
A quasi-documentary style film of Guevara, strategist be-
hind Castro.

Christopher Columbus
103 min.   color   1949
Dir: David McDonald.   Rental: Walter Reade.

Cleopatra (silent)
58 min.   b&w   1912
Dir: Charles L. Gaskill.   Rental: Macmillan
Cast: Helen Gardner.

Cleopatra
102 min.   b&w   1934
Dir: Cecil B. DeMille.   Rental: Cine Craft, Universal

Cleopatra
186 min.   color   1963
Dir: Joseph Mankiewicz.   Rental: Films Inc.   Prod: 20th Cen-
tury-Fox
Cast: Elizabeth Taylor, Richard Burton, Rex Harrison, Pamela
Brown, Roddy McDowall.
A lavish pageant.

Cromwell
139 min.   color   1970
Dir: Ken Hughes.   Prod: Columbia.   Rental: Budget, Cine Hurlock, Institutional Cinema Service, McGraw-Hill
Cast: Alec Guinness, Richard Harris, Robert Morley.

Daniel Boone
80 min. 1936
Dir: David Howard. Rental: Classic Film Museum
Cast: George O'Brien.

The Darwin Adventure
148 min. color 1972
Dir: Jack Couffer. Prod: 20th Century-Fox. Rental: Films Inc.
Cast: Nicholas Clay, Susan Macready.
A quasi-historical film of Darwin as a young man exploring truth through science; traces his life and visits to the Galapagos Islands.

Davy Crockett and the River Pirates
81 min. color 1959
Prod: Walt Disney
Rental: Macmillan, Twyman
Cast: Fess Parker, Buddy Ebsen, Jeff York.
His clash with Mike Fink.

Davy Crockett, Indian Scout
71 min. b&w 1950
Rental: Macmillan
Cast: George Montgomery, Ellen Drew, Phillip Reed.
Leading a wagon train.

Davy Crockett, King of the Wild Frontier
93 min. color 1955
Prod: Walt Disney. Rental: Films Inc., Macmillan, National Film Service, Twyman
Cast: Fess Parker, Buddy Ebsen, Hans Conried.
The legendary story.

Day of Triumph (A Life of Christ)
120 min. 1954
Rental: Cine Craft.
Cast: Lee J. Cobb.

Deep in My Heart
132 min. color 1954
Dir: Stanley Donen. Prod: M.G.M. Rental: Films Inc.
Cast: Jose Ferrer, Helen Trauble, Merle Oberon, Doe Avedon, Walter Pidgeon, Paul Henried.
Sigmund Romberg's rise from a waiter-pianist to a Carnegie Hall conductor.

Diary of Anne Frank
150 min. 1959
Dir: George Stevens. Prod: 20th Century-Fox. Rental: Films Inc.
Cast: Millie Perkins, Joseph Schildkraut, Shelley Winters, Richard Beymer.
A drama based on her diary, written during the two years she hid in an Amsterdam attic.

Disraeli
89 min.   1929
Dir: Alfred E. Green. Rental: United Artists
Cast: George Arliss, Joan Bennett, Florence Arliss.
    Centers on his action to purchase the Suez Canal.

Dr. Schweitzer
92 min.   1955
Rental: Budget, Macmillan
Cast: Pierre Fresnay, Raymond Roleau, Marie Winter.
    Chronicles his trip to reach Africa and then shows his
work there.

The Eddy Duchin Story
123 min.   color 1956
Dir: George Sidney. Rental: Arcus, Institutional Cinema Service,
    Macmillan, Clem Williams
Cast: Tyrone Power, Kim Novak, James Whitmore.
    His heart-warming story, filled with romance and music.

Edison the Man
107 min.   b&w   1940
Dir: Clarence Brown. Prod: M-G-M. Rental: Films Inc.
Cast: Spencer Tracy, Rita Johnson, Charles Coburn, Gene
    Reynolds.
    The events leading to his many inventions.

Edward II
128 min.   color   1976
Prod: BBC-TV. Rental: Time-Life (special order video)
    His downfall, brought about by his relationship with the
scheming homosexual, Graveston.

El Greco
95 min.   color   1966
Dir: Luciano Salce. Prod: 20th Century-Fox. Rental: Films
    Inc.
Cast: Mel Ferrer, Rosanna Schiaffino, Franco Giacobini, Nino
    Crisman.
    His conflicts with the Spanish aristocracy and the Inquisition.

Eternal Waltz
97 min.   color   1959
Cast: Bernhard Wickle. Rental: Macmillan
    A musical about the life and loves of Johann Strauss.

Francis of Assisi
111 min.   color   1961
Dir: Michael Curtiz. Prod: 20th Century-Fox. Rental: Films
    Inc.
Cast: Bradford Dillman, Dolores Hart.
    During battle he hears God calling to him; he rebuilds a
ruined church and founds the Franciscan Order.

Freud
140 min.   1962
Dir: John Huston.   Rental: Cine Craft, Clem Williams, Universal

The Gene Krupa Story
101 min.   1960
Dir: Don Weis.   Rental: Arcus, "The" Film Center, Institutional
  Cinema Service
Cast: Sal Mineo.

Gorky Trilogy (USSR)
100 min.   b&w   1938
Dir: Mark Donskoi.   Rental: Macmillan
Cast: Aloysha Lyarsky, V. O. Massalitinova, M. G. Troyanovsky.
  Based on Maxim Gorky's autobiography.

The Great Caruso
109 min.   color and b&w   1951
Dir: Richard Thorpe.   Prod: M-G-M.   Rental: Films Inc.
Cast: Mario Lanza, Ann Blyth, Dorothy Kirsten.
      His rise to operatic fame, with famous arias from "Aïda,"
"Rigoletto," "La Boheme," "Il Trovatore," "Martha."

The Great Waltz
135 min.   color   1972
Dir: Andrew L. Stone.   Rental: Films Inc.
Cast: Horst Buchholz, Mary Costa, Rossano Brazzi, Nigel
  Patrick.
      A lavish biography of Johann Strauss that begins with his
early years.

Hans Christian Andersen
104 min.   color   1952
Dir: Charles Vidor.   Prod: Sam Goldwyn.   Rental: Budget,
  Macmillan, Twyman
Cast: Danny Kaye, Farley Granger, Jeanmaire.
      A children's film with many songs and beautiful ballet numbers.

Henry V
137 min.   color   1946
Dir: Laurence Olivier.   Rental: Budget, McGraw-Hill, Macmillan,
  Twyman
Cast: Laurence Olivier, Felix Aylmer, Robert Newton.
      Filmed version of Shakespeare's play.

Henry VIII and His Six Wives
125 min.   color   1973
Dir: Waris Hussein.   Prod: Levitt-Pickman.   Rental: Films Inc.
Cast: Keith Michell, Donald Pleasence, Charlotte Rampling, Jane
  Asher.
      Historical drama from a television series.

Hitler: The Last Ten Days
106 min.   color   1973
Dir: Ennio De Concini.   Prod: Paramount.   Rental: Films Inc.
Cast: Alec Guinness, Adolfo Celi, Diane Cilento, Eric Portman.
        Recreation of the bunker where he spent his last days.

Inherit the Wind
127 min.   1960
Dir: Stanley Kramer.   Rental: United Artists.
Cast: Spencer Tracy, Frederic March
        A brilliant drama of the famous monkey trial of Scopes vs.
the State in which Clarence Darrow defended Scopes and William
Jennings Bryan testified for the State.

Ivan the Terrible
186 min.   b&w and color   1946
Dir: Sergei Eisenstein.   Rental: Images, Kit Parker
Cast: Nikolai Cherkassov, Serfina Birman.
        Russian, with English sub-titles.   An epic biography in two parts.

Jack London
90 min.   b&w   1942
Dir: Alfred Santell.   Rental: Budget, Classic Film Museum,
    Films Inc.
Cast: Susan Hayward, Michael O'Shea.
        The drama of his experiences as a journalist and author.

The Jackie Robinson Story
76 min.   1950
Dir: Alfred E. Green.   Rental: Budget, Films Inc., Clem Wil-
    liams Films
Cast: Jackie Robinson, Ruby Dee.
        He plays himself in this "real-life" story.

Jim Thorpe, All-American
107 min.   b&w   1951
Dir: Michael Curtiz.   Prod: Warner Bros.   Rental: Budget,
    Macmillan, Twyman
Cast: Burt Lancaster, Charles Bickford, Steve Cochran.
        A warm biography of a great athlete.

Joan of Arc
100 min.   color   1948
Dir: Victor Fleming.   Rental: Budget, Macmillan
Cast: Ingrid Bergman, Jose Ferrer.
        The battles she fought.

The Joe Louis Story
88 min.   b&w   1953
Dir: Robert Gordon.   Prod: United Artists.   Rental: Macmillan,
    Twyman.
Cast: Coley Wallace, Paul Stewart, Hilda Simms.
        How a back-alley kid became a champion.

John Paul Jones
126 min.   color   1959
Dir: John Farrow. Prod: Warner Bros. Rental: Swank,
   Twyman
Cast: Robert Stack, Marisa Pavan, Charles Coburn, Bette
   Davis.
      His victories at sea and the panorama of American history.

The Jolson Story
128 min.   color   1946
Dir: Alfred E. Green. Rental: Budget, Macmillan, Select
Cast: Larry Parks, Evelyn Keyes, William Demarest, and Bill
   Goodwin as the singing voice of Jolson.
      The times and music of a great entertainer.

Julius Caesar
90 min.   b&w   1950
Dir: David Bradley. Rental: Macmillan, Trans-World
Cast: Charlton Heston.
      First sound version of Shakespeare's play.

Julius Caesar
117 min.   color   1970
Dir: Stuart Burge. Rental: Budget, Ivy, Kit Parker, Macmillan
Cast: Charlton Heston, Jason Robards, John Gielgud, Richard
   Johnson, Robert Vaughn, Richard Chamberlain, Diana Rigg.
      A spectacular film version of Shakespeare's play.

Knute Rockne, All-American
121 min.   1940
Dir: Lloyd Bacon. Rental: Cine Craft, United Artists
Cast: Pat O'Brien, Ronald Reagan, Donald Crisp, Gale Page,
   Albert Basserman, John Litel.
      A biography of Notre Dame's famous coach.

Lady Sings the Blues
144 min.   color   1972
Dir: Sidney J. Furie. Prod: Paramount. Rental: Films Inc.
Cast: Diana Ross, Billy Dee Williams.
      A fictionalized biography of Billie Holiday, blues singer.

Lafayette
99 min.   color   1964
Rental: Macmillan
Cast: Orson Welles, Jack Hawkins, Vittorio De Sica.
      His exciting early years.

Lawrence of Arabia
215 min.   color   1962
Dir: David Lean. Prod: Columbia. Rental: Swank
Cast: Peter O'Toole, Omar Sharif, Anthony Quinn.
      A spectacular.

Life of Emil Zola
110 min.   b&w   1937
Dir: William Dieterle.   Prod: United Artists.   Rental: United
     Artists
Cast: Paul Muni, Gale Sondergaard.
         His defense of Dreyfus and his own trial.

The Lion in Winter
134 min.   color   1968
Dir: Anthony Harvey.   Prod: Joseph E. Levine, Martin Poll
     Production.   Rental: Macmillan
Cast: Katherine Hepburn, Peter O'Toole, Jane Morrow.
         The pageantry and pomp of the reign of Henry II and Elea-
nor of Acquitaine.

Madame Du Barry
77 min.   b&w   1934
Dir: William Dieterle.   Rental: Macmillan.
Cast: Dolores Del Rio, Reginald Owen, Victory Jory.
         The intrigue and love in the court of Louis XV.

The Magnificent Rebel
92 min.   color   1961
Prod: Walt Disney.   Rental: Macmillan.
Cast: Carl Boehm.
         A stirring biography of Beethoven which begins with his ar-
rival in Vienna and ends when the doctor tells him he is going deaf.

The Magnificent Yankee
88 min.   b&w   1951
Dir: John Sturges.   Rental: Films Inc.
Cast: Louis Calhern, Ann Harding.
         A study of jurist Oliver Wendell Holmes.

A Man for All Seasons
120 min.   color   1966
Dir: Fred Zinnemann.   Prod: Columbia.   Rental: Swank
Cast: Paul Scofield, Wendy Hiller, Robert Shaw, Orson Welles.
         A powerful drama of the conflict between Henry VIII and
Thomas More.

Man Named John
94 min.   color   1965
Dir: Ermanno Olmi.   Rental: Macmillan
Cast: Rod Steiger, Adolfo Celi
         A docu-drama based on the diary he kept between the ages
of 14-18; Steiger acts as an "intermediary" between John XXIII and
the audience.

Marco Polo
95 min.   color   1962
Dir: Hugo Fregonese.   Rental: Cine Craft, Clem Williams,
     Macmillan, Twyman.

Cast: Rory Calhoun, Yoko Tani.
His epic journey.

Marco the Magnificent
100 min.   color   1966
Dir: Denys de la Patelliere.   Rental: Cine Craft, Macmillan
Cast: Horst Buchholz, Anthony Quinn, Omar Sharif, Orson Welles,
Elsa Martinelli.
His journey to the court of Kubla Khan.

Marie Antoinette
88 min.   b&w   1938
Dir: W. S. Van Dyke.   Prod: M-G-M.   Rental: Films Inc.
Cast: Norma Shearer, John Barrymore, Tyrone Power, Anita
Louise, Gladys George.
A spectacle of the heroine of the French Revolution.

Martin Luther
103 min.   b&w   1953
Dir: Louis de Rochemont.   Dist: Lutheran Film Associates (orig-
inal version).   Rental: Macmillan (also divided into 3 pts. :
The Ninety-Five Theses, By Faith Alone, Champions of the
Faith.)
Cast: Niall MacGuinnis, John Ruddock.
A study of him and his doctrines.

Mary of Scotland
123 min.   b&w   1936
Dir: John Ford.   Rental: Films Inc.
Cast: Katharine Hepburn, Fredric March, John Carradine,
Florence Eldridge.
Her fight with Elizabeth over the throne of Scotland.

Mary, Queen of Scots
128 min.   color   1972
Dir: Charles Jarrott.   Prod: Universal.   Rental: Swank, Twy-
man, Universal
Cast: Vanessa Redgrave, Glenda Jackson, Patrick McGoohan.
The struggle between her and Elizabeth.

Miracle Worker
107 min.   b&w   1962
Dir: Arthur Penn.   Prod: United Artists.   Rental: United
Artists
Cast: Anne Bancroft, Patty Duke, Victor Jory, Andrew Prine,
Inga Swenson.
Anne Sullivan's breakthrough with Helen Keller.

Mister Johann Strauss
1943
Dir: George Pal.   Rental: Em Gee
Animated.

Murder in the Cathedral
104 min.   b&w   1952
Dir. and prod: George Hoellering.   Rental: Macmillan
Cast: John Groser.
         Based on T. S. Eliot's play.

The Nelson Affair
117 min.   color   1973   PG
Dir: James Cellan Jones.   Prod: Universal.   Rental: Swank,
   Twyman
Cast: Peter Finch, Glenda Jackson, Michael Jayston.
         The infamous romance between Lord Nelson and Lady
Hamilton.

Nicholas and Alexandra
170 min.   color   1971
Dir: Franklin J. Schaffner.   Prod: Columbia.   Rental: Swank
Cast: Michael Jayston, Janet Suzman, Harry Andrews.
         A panorama of Russian history.

Oscar Wilde
1960
Dir: Gregory Ratoff.   Prod. and Rental: Warner Bros.
Cast: Robert Morley, Sir Ralph Richardson, Phyllis Calvert,
   John Neville.

Passion of Joan of Arc
82 min.   b&w   1928
Dir: Carl Theodor Dreyer.   Rental: Images, Kit Parker
Cast: Maria Falconetti, Eugène Sylvanin, Antoine Artaud, André
   Berley, Michel Simon.
         An intense drama.   A silent classic.

Patton: A Salute to a Rebel
169 min.   color   1970
Dir: Franklin Schaffner.   Prod: 20th Century-Fox.   Rental:
   Films Inc.
Cast: George C. Scott, Karl Malden, Edward Binns.
         A bio-epic that highlights his defeat of Rommel.

Pride of the Yankees
128 min.   b&w   1942
Dir: Sam Wood.   Prod: Samuel Goldwyn.   Rental: Macmillan,
   Twyman
Cast: Gary Cooper, Teresa Wright, Babe Ruth, Walter Brennan.
         A humorous and sentimental biography of Lou Gehrig.

Private Life of Henry VIII
97 min.   b&w   1933
Dir: Alexander Korda.   Rental: Images, Kit Parker, Macmillan
Cast: Charles Laughton, Merle Oberon, Elsa Lanchester, Robert
   Donat, Binnie Barnes, Wendy Barrie.
         A chronicle of the King and his times.

Rembrandt
83 min.   1936
Dir: Alexander Korda. Prod: London Films. Rental: Ivy
Cast: Charles Laughton, Elsa Lanchester, Gertrude Lawrence,
    John Bryning.

Rise of Louis XIV
100 min.   1965
Dir: Roberto Rossellini. Rental: Macmillan

St. Louis Blues
93 min.   1958
Dir: Allen Reisner. Prod: Paramount. Rental: Films Inc.
Cast: Nat "King" Cole, Eartha Kitt, Pearl Bailey, Cab Calloway,
    Ella Fitzgerald.
        The life story of W. C. Handy, "father of the blues."

Simon Bolivar
105 min.   color
Rental: Macmillan
Cast: Maxmilian Schell, Rossano Schiaffino.
        A biography of him and his struggle to free South America.

Song of Love
119 min.   1947
Dir: Clarence Brown. Prod: M-G-M. Rental: Films Inc.
Cast: Katharine Hepburn, Paul Henreid, Robert Walker, Henry
    Daniell, Leo G. Carroll.
        The love story of composer Robert Schumann and his wife
Clara.

Song of Norway
110 min.   color   1970
Dir: Andrew L. Stone. Prod: ABC Pictures. Rental: Films Inc.
Cast: Florence Henderson, Toraly Maurstad, Frank Poretta,
    Christina Schollin.
        A musical portraying the life of Edvard Grieg.

Song to Remember
112 min.   color   1944
Dir: Charles Vidor. Rental: Macmillan
Cast: Paul Muni, Merle Oberon, Cornel Wilde.
        The story of Frederic Chopin and his relationship with
George Sand.

Song Without End
130 min.   color   1960
Dir: George Cukor and Charles Vidor. Rental: Macmillan
Cast: Dirk Bogarde, Genevieve Page
        The personal life and crises of Franz Liszt.

Stanley and Livingstone
98 min.   b&w   1939

Dir: Henry King. Rental: Films Inc.
Cast: Spencer Tracy, Nancy Kelly, Walter Brennan, Charles Co-
burn, Cedric Hardwicke.
Stanley's quest to find Livingstone.

Stars and Stripes Forever
89 min.   color   1952
Dir: Henry Koster. Prod: 20th Century-Fox. Rental: Films
Inc.
Cast: Clifton Webb, Debra Paget, Robert Wagner.
John Philip Sousa's life between 1892 and 1900 in service
to the President as leader of the Marine Corps Band.

The Story of Louis Pasteur
87 min.   b&w   1936
Dir: William Dieterle. Rental: United Artists.
Cast: Paul Muni, Anita Louise.
An award-winning biography.

Story of Ruth
132 min.   color   1960
Dir: Henry Koster. Prod: 20th Century-Fox. Rental: Films
Inc.
Cast: Elana Eden, Stuart Whitman, Tom Tryon, Peggy Wood,
Viveca Lindfors.
A warm and moving Biblical story.

The Story of Will Rogers
109 min.   1952
Prod: Warner Bros. Dir: Michael Curtiz. Rental: Warner
Bros.
Cast: Will Rogers, Jr., Jane Wyman, Eddie Cantor, James
Gleason, Noah Beery, Jr.
A biography capturing his versatility and keen wit.

Sunrise at Campobello
143 min.   color   1960
Dir: Vincent Donehue. Rental: Budget, Institutional Cinema
Service, Macmillan, Trans-World
Cast: Ralph Bellamy, Greer Garson, Hume Cronyn.
From the years when he was stricken with polio until his
return to public life.

Tennessee Johnson
100 min.   1942
Dir: William Dieterle. Prod: M-G-M. Rental: Films Inc.
Cast: Van Heflin, Ruth Hussey, Lionel Barrymore.
A depiction of a tactless but sincere politician--Andrew
Johnson.

The Virgin Queen
92 min.   1955
Dir: Henry Koster. Prod: 20th Century-Fox. Dist: Films Inc.

Cast: Bette Davis, Richard Todd, Joan Collins, Herbert Marshall.
Walter Raleigh wins her favor until he falls in love with a
lady-in-waiting.

Voltaire
72 min.   b&w   1933
Dir: John Adolfi.   Rental: United Artists
Cast: George Arliss, Margaret Lindsay.
The dramatic story of his life and his scandals.

The Waltz King
94 min.   color   1964
Prod: Walt Disney.   Rental: Macmillan
Cast: Kerwin Matthews, Senta Berger, Brian Aherne.
A biography of Johann Strauss and a love story.   Sound-
track by the Vienna Symphony Orchestra.

Wilson
119 min.   1945
Dir: Henry King.   Prod: 20th Century-Fox.   Rental: Films Inc.
Cast: Alexander Knox, Charles Coburn, Geraldine Fitzgerald.
A stirring biography of his life at Princeton, as President,
and as supporter of the League of Nations.

Young Bess
112 min.   color   1953
Dir: George Sidney.   Prod: M-G-M.   Rental: Films Inc.
Cast: Jean Simmons, Stewart Granger, Charles Laughton, Deborah
    Kerr.
The story of her childhood until she ascends the throne.

Young Cassidy
110 min.   color   1965
Dir: Jack Cardiff.   Prod: M-G-M.   Rental: Films Inc.
Cast: Rod Taylor, Maggie Smith, Michael Redgrave, Julie Chris-
    tie.
Sean O'Casey's life as a ditchdigger, a member of the
revolutionary army and as a writer.

Young Mr. Lincoln
100 min.   b&w   1939
Dir: John Ford.   Prod: 20th Century-Fox.   Rental: Films Inc.
Cast: Henry Fonda, Ward Bond, Marjorie Weaver, Donald Meek,
    Alice Brady.
His defense of two men accused of murder, his tragic romance with Ann Rutledge, and his meetings with Stephen Douglas
and Mary Todd.

Young Tom Edison
86 min.   1940
Dir: Norman Taurog.   Rental: Films Inc.
Cast: Mickey Rooney.

Young Winston
138 min.   color   1973   PG
Dir: Richard Attenborough.   Prod: Columbia.   Rental: Swank,
    Twyman
Cast: Anne Bancroft, Robert Shaw, Simon Ward.
        Based on Churchill's autobiography.

DISTRIBUTORS/RENTAL SOURCES

ABC Merchandising Inc.
Educational Licensing Div.
1330 Avenue of the Americas
New York, N.Y. 10019

ACI Media, Inc.
35 W. 45th St.
New York, N.Y. 10036

Aetna Life Insurance Co.
151 Farmington Ave.
Hartford, Ct. 06115

Agapé Productions
138 E. 93rd St.
New York, N.Y. 10028

Agency for Instructional Tele-
  vision
Box A
Bloomington, Ind. 47401

Aims Instructional Media
  Services, Inc.
P.O. Box 1010
Hollywood, Calif. 90028

American Educational Films
132 Lasky Dr.
Beverly Hills, Calif. 90212

American Foundation for the
  Blind
15 W. 16th St.
New York, N.Y. 10011

Anti-Defamation League
315 Lexington Ave.
New York, N.Y. 10016

Appleton-Century-Crofts
440 Park Ave.
New York, N.Y. 10016

Arcus Films
1225 Broadway
New York, N.Y. 10001

Arthur Cantor, Inc.
234 W. 44th St.
New York, N.Y. 10036

Arthur Mokin Productions
17 W. 60th St.
New York, N.Y. 10023

Association Films
866 Third Ave.
New York, N.Y. 10022

Association-Sterling
866 Third Ave.
New York, N.Y. 10022

Audley Square, Ltd.
P.O. Box 134
Old Greenwich, Conn. 06870

Auteur Films
1042 Wisconsin Ave. N.W.
Georgetown
Washington, D.C. 20007

Avco Embassy
6601 Romaine St.
Los Angeles, Calif. 90038

BFA Educational Media
2211 Michigan Ave.
P.O. Box 1795
Santa Monica, Calif. 90406

Belgium Embassy
3330 Garfield St. N.W.
Washington, D.C.   20008

Benchmark Films, Inc.
145 Scarborough Rd.
Briarcliff Manor, N.Y. 10510

Blackwood Productions
58 W. 58th St.
New York, N.Y. 10019

Brigham Young University
Dept. of Motion Picture Pro-
   duction
Provo, Utah   84602

Budget Films
4590 Santa Monica Blvd.
Los Angeles, Calif. 90029

CBS/Holt Group
600 Third Ave.
New York, N.Y. 10016

Carousel Films
1501 Broadway
New York, N.Y. 10036

Catholic Film Center
119-20 94 Ave.
Richmond Hill
Queens, N.Y. 11419

Center for Learning Resources
International College
1019 Gayley, Suite 105
Los Angeles, Calif. 90024

Center for Mass Communication of Columbia
University Press
136 S. Broadway
Irvington, N.Y. 10533

Centron Educational Films
1621 W. Ninth St.
Lawrence, Kansas 66044

Christian Church (Disciples of
   Christ)
222 S. Downey Ave.
P.O. Box 1986

Indianapolis, Ind.   46206

Churchill Films
662 N. Robertson Blvd.
Los Angeles, Calif. 90069

Cine Craft
1720 N.W. Marshal
P.O. Box 4126
Portland, Oregon 97209

Cinema Eight
91 Main St.
Chester, Ct. 06412

Cinema 5 - 16mm
595 Madison Ave.
New York, N.Y. 10022

Classic Film Museum
4 Union Sq.
Dover-Foxcroft, Maine 04426

Classroom Film Distributors,
   Inc.
5610 Hollywood Blvd.
Hollywood, Calif. 90028

Clem Williams Films
2240 Noblestown Rd.
Pittsburgh, Pa. 15205

Connecticut Films
6 Cobble Hill Rd.
Westport, Ct. 06880

Coronet Instructional Media
65 E. South Water St.
Chicago, Ill. 60601

Counselor Films
2100 Locust St.
Philadelphia, Pa.   19103

Creative Film Society
7237 Canby Ave.
Reseda, Calif. 91335

Dept. of the Air Force
Air Force Central Audiovisual
   Library
Aerospace Audiovisual Serivce
Norton AFB, Calif. 92409

or
local base

Dept. of the Army
Address to local army installation

Dept. of the Navy
Naval Education and Training
Support Center
Atlantic Commanding Officer
Naval Station
Building Z-86
Norfolk, Va. 23511

Walt Disney Educational Media
Company
500 S. Buena Vista St.
Burbank, Calif. 91521

Doubleday Multimedia
Box 11607
1371 Reynolds Ave.
Santa Ana, Calif. 92705

Arnold Eagle
41 W. 47th St.
New York, N.Y. 10036

Eccentric Circle Cinema Workshop, Inc.
P.O. Box 4085
Greenwich, Ct. 06830

Em Gee Film Library
4931 Gloria Ave.
Encino, Calif. 91316

Embassy of Switzerland
c/o Tribune Films
38 W. 32nd St.
New York, N.Y. 10001

Encyclopaedia Britannica Educational Corp.
425 N. Michigan Ave.
Chicago, Ill. 60611

FACSEA
French American Cultural
Services and Educational Aid
972 Fifth Avenue
New York, N.Y. 10021

Fenwick Productions
Box 277
W. Hartford, Ct. 06107

"The" Film Center
915 12th St. N.W.
Washington, D.C. 20005

Film Images
1034 Lake St.
Oak Park, Ill. 60301

FilmFair Communications
10900 Ventura Blvd.
P.O. Box 1728
Studio City, Calif. 91604

Filmmakers Library
290 West End Ave.
New York, N.Y. 10023

Films for the Humanities
P.O. Box 378
Princeton, N.J. 08540

Films Inc.
1144 Wilmette Ave.
Wilmette, Ill. 60091

Florida Dept. of Commerce
Film Library
Collins Building
107 W. Gaines St.
Tallahassee, Fla. 32304

General Electric
Glenville Film Center
Corporations Park
Bldg. 705
Scotia, N.Y. 12302

General Learning Corp.
250 James St.
Morristown, N.J. 07960

The Graphic Curriculum
P.O. Box 565
Lenox Hill Station
New York, N.Y. 10021

Great Plains National ITV Library
P.O. Box 80669
Lincoln, Neb. 68501

Grove Press (now dist. by
    Films Inc.)
196 W. Houston St.
New York, N.Y. 10014

Handel Film Corp.
8730 Sunset Blvd.
West Hollywood, Calif. 90069

Hurlock Cine World
13 Arcadia Rd.
Old Greenwich, Ct. 06870

I.Q. Films
P.O. Box 326
Wappingers Falls, N.Y. 12590

Images
2 Purdy Ave.
Rye, N.Y. 10580

Impact Films
144 Bleeker St.
New York, N.Y. 10012

Indiana University
A-V Center
Bloomington, Ind. 47401

Independent Television Corp.
555 Madison Ave.
New York, N.Y. 10022

Information Service of India
Film Section
3 E. 64th St.
New York, N.Y. 10021

Insight Exchange
P.O. Box 42584
San Francisco, Calif. 94101

Institutional Cinema Service
915 Broadway
New York, N.Y. 10010

International Film Bureau
332 S. Michigan Ave.
Chicago, Ill. 60604

Ivy Film
165 W. 46th St.
New York, N.Y. 10036

Janus Films
745 Fifth Ave.
New York, N.Y. 10022

Journal Films
930 Pitner Ave.
Evanston, Ill. 60201

Killiam Shows
6 E. 39th St.
New York, N.Y. 10016

Kit Parker Films
Box 227
Carmel Valley, Calif. 93924

Learning Corp. of America
1350 Avenue of the Americas
New York, N.Y. 10019

Lutheran Film Associates
315 Park Ave. S.
New York, N.Y. 10011

McDonnell Douglas Corp.
Santa Monica Library
Film and TV Communications
3000 Ocean Park Blvd.
Santa Monica, Calif. 90406

McGraw-Hill Films
1221 Avenue of the Americas
New York, N.Y. 10020

Macmillan Audio Brandon
34 MacQuesten Parkway S.
Mount Vernon, N.Y. 10550

Mar/Chuck Film Industries
P.O. Box 61
Mt. Prospect, Ill. 60056

Mass Media Associates
2116 N. Charles St.
Baltimore, Md. 21218

Maysles Films
1697 Broadway at 53rd St.
New York, N.Y. 10019

Modern Talking Picture Service
2323 New Hyde Park Rd.
New Hyde Park, N.Y. 11040

or
local office

Museum of Modern Art
11 W. 53rd St.
New York, N.Y. 10019

NASA
Washington, D.C. 20546

National Audiovisual Center
Washington, D.C. 20409

National Council of Churches
    of Christ
475 Riverside Dr.
New York, N.Y. 10027

National Film Board of Canada
16th floor
1251 Avenue of the Americas
New York, N.Y. 10020

National Film Service
14 Glenwood Ave.
Raleigh, N.C. 27602

National Football League
410 Park Ave.
New York, N.Y. 10022

National Gallery of Art
Extension Service
Washington, D.C. 20565

National Geographic Society
Educational Film Division
17th and M St. N.W.
Washington, D.C. 20036

New Line Cinema
853 Broadway, 16th floor
New York, N.Y. 10003

New Yorker Films
43 W. 61st St.
New York, N.Y. 10023

North American Films
Box 919
Tarzana, Calif. 91356

Odeon Films, Inc.
P.O. Box 315
Franklin Lakes, N.J. 07417

Open Circle Cinema, Ltd.
77 Susquehanna St.
Franklin Lakes, N.J. 07417

Paramount Oxford
5451 Marathon St.
Hollywood, Calif. 90038

Pennebaker, Inc.
56 W. 45th St.
New York, N.Y. 10036

Pennsylvania State University
Psychological Cinema Register
6 Willard Bldg.
University Park, Pa. 16802

Perennial Education, Inc.
1825 Willow Rd.
P.O. Box 236
Northfield, Ill. 60093

Perspective Films
369 W. Erie St.
Chicago, Ill. 60610

Phoenix Films
470 Park Ave. S.
New York, N.Y. 10016

Pictura Films
43 W. 16th St.
New York, N.Y. 10011

Portuguese National Tourist
    Office
c/o Modern Talking Picture
    Service
2323 New Hyde Park Rd.
New Hyde Park, N.Y. 11040

Productions Unlimited, Inc.
40 W. 57th St.
New York, N.Y. 10019

Psychological Films, Inc.
110 N. Wheeler St.
Orange, Calif. 92669

Pyramid Films
P. O. Box 1048
Santa Monica, Calif. 90406

rbc films
933 N. La Brea Ave.
Los Angeles, Calif. 90038

Rediscovery Productions
2 Halfmile Common
Westport, Ct. 06880

Roland Collection
1825 Willow Rd.
Northfield, Ill. 60093

Royal Danish Consulate General
Danish Information Office
280 Park Ave.
New York, N.Y. 10017

Sandpiper Productions
409 Walco Building
Atlanta, Ga. 30303

Select Film Library
115 W. 31st St.
New York, N.Y. 10001

Serious Business Co.
1609 Jaynes St.
Berkeley, Calif. 94703

Southern Baptist Radio-Television Commission
P. O. Box 12157
6350 W. Freeway
Fort Worth, Texas 76116

Sports Legends, Inc.
25 City Line Ave.
Bala-Cynwyd, Pa. 19004

Star Film Co.
Div. of Two Star Films
79 Bobolink Lane
Levittown, N.Y. 11756

Cecile Starr
50 W. 96th St.
New York, N.Y. 10025

Sterling Educational Films
241 E. 34th St.
New York, N.Y. 10016

Swank
201 S. Jefferson Ave.
St. Louis, Mo. 63166

Syracuse University
1455 E. Colvin St.
Syracuse, N.Y. 13210

Texture Films
1600 Broadway
New York, N.Y. 10019

Third World Newsreel
16 W. 20th St.
New York, N.Y. 10011

Time-Life
Time-Life Building
Rockefeller Center
New York, N.Y. 10020

Tinc Productions
866 UN Plaza
New York, N.Y. 10017

Trans-World Films
332 S. Michigan Ave.
Chicago, Ill. 60604

The Travelers Film Library
West Glen Films
565 Fifth Ave.
New York, N.Y. 10017

Tricontinental Film Center
244 W. 27th St.
New York, N.Y. 10001

Twyman Films
329 Salem Ave.
Dayton, Ohio 45401

United Artists 16
720 Seventh Ave.
New York, N.Y. 10019

United Church of Christ
Office for Audio-Visuals

1505 Race St.
Philadelphia, Pa. 19102

United Nations
Radio and Visual Services Division
Office of Public Information
New York, N.Y. 10017

Universal Education and Visual Arts
100 Universal City Plaza
Universal City, Calif. 91608

Universal 16
445 Park Ave.
New York, N.Y. 10022

University of California
Extension Media Center
2223 Fulton St.
Berkeley, Calif. 94720

University of Michigan
AV Education Center
416 Fourth St.
Ann Arbor, Mich. 48103

University of Minnesota
Audio-Visual Library Service
3300 University Ave. S.E.
Minneapolis, Minn. 55414

University of Mississippi
University, Miss. 38677

University of Nebraska
IMC
421 Nebraska Hall
Lincoln, Neb. 68588

University of South Florida
Division of Educational Resources/Films
Tampa, Florida 33620

University of Southern California
Film Distribution Center
Division of Cinema
University Park
Los Angeles, Calif. 90007

Viacom International
345 Park Ave.
New York, N.Y. 10022

Viewfinders, Inc.
2550 Green Bay Rd.
Box 1665
Evanston, Ill. 60204

Walt Disney see Disney

Walter Reade 16
241 E. 34th St.
New York, N.Y. 10016

Warner Bros.
Non-Theatrical Division
4000 Warner Blvd.
Burbank, Calif. 91522

Weston Woods Studios, Inc.
Weston, Ct. 06880

Western World Productions
P.O. Box 3594
San Francisco, Calif. 94119

Wombat Productions
Little Lake
Glendale Rd.
Ossining, N.Y. 10562

Yale Divinity School
Visual Education Service
409 Prospect St.
New Haven, Ct. 06511

TITLE INDEX

F

SUBJECT INDEX

DATE DUE —